THE WARSAW GHETTO DIARIES

THE WARSAW GHETTO DIARIES

Dr. Hillel Seidman

Translated by Yosef Israel

TARGUM/FELDHEIM

First published 1997

ISBN 1-56871-133-6

Published by:
Targum Press, Inc.
22700 W. Eleven Mile Rd.
Southfield, MI 48034

in conjuction with:
Mishnas Rishonim

Distributed by:
Feldheim Publishers
200 Airport Executive Park
Nanuet, NY 10954

Distributed in Israel by:
Targum Press Ltd.
POB 43170
Jerusalem 91430

Printed in Israel

מצבת זכרון לזכר עולם

לעילוי נשמת
ר׳ **דוד מאיר** ב״ר ישראל שיפמאן הי״ד מווינא
שנשלח ע״י הרוצחים מדרום צרפת
לגיא ההריגה בסוף שנת תש״ב
ורעיתו **רחל** ב״ר שלמה ווינדהאלץ הי״ד
בנם הבחור היניק **מיכאל** הי״ד
ובתם התינוקת המכונה **טשארלאטע** הי״ד
שנשלחו מאנטווערפען ע״י הטמאים בסוף שנת תש״ב
ידין בגוים לא ישקוט למען הקדושים מושלכים באש
וינקום נקמתם מידי הארורים ששפכו דמם כמים
ותהא נשמותיהם הטהורים צרורים בצרור החיים

לזכר נשמות מרת **מאלע** ב״ר חיים לייב אלטער
ובנותיה הבתולה **באשע** ב״ר משה יהודה האמער
הבתולה **פיניא** ב״ר משה יהודה האמער
והבתולה **מיזה** ב״ר משה יהודה האמער
ילידי נארול שברחו בימי הזעם והחימה
לראוע ראסקא על גבול אוקריינא
ונהרגו בתוך רבבי אחב״י
לא זכו לבוא לקבר ישראל ולא נודע יום מיתתם עק״ש
ארץ אל תכסי דמם ויודע בגוים לעינינו נקמת דמם השפוך
ותהא נשמותיהם צרורים בצרור החיים

Table of Contents

Foreword 11

Translator's Preface 19

Introduction 33

The Warsaw Ghetto Diaries. 41

Reflections after the Revolt 281

The Warsaw Ghetto *Judenrat* 289

Personalities I Knew in the Ghetto 323

FOREWORD

Dr. Hillel Seidman, z"l

On August 28, 1995, the second day in Ellul, our father, Dr. Hillel Seidman, passed away. He is missed by many across the world, including those who have never even met him personally. Some miss his knowledge and keen intelligence, while others miss his insightful newspaper columns and political views. Others miss him as their link to past generations. Many miss him for the favors he was always ready to do. Most of all, our family misses him as a warm, caring, loving, and devoted husband, father, grandfather, and great-grandfather.

Our father lived through some of the most dramatic moments in Jewish history; his life reflected the agonies and triumphs of the Jewish experience. As is true of other Holocaust survivors, there were parts of our father's early life that he never shared with the family or friends he acquired after the War. Most traces of his childhood and youth were lost with the murder of the largest part of his extended family. A few stories, the family names, and a number of photographs sent to relatives in America and Eretz Yisrael before the War are all that remain of those years.

After the War, it was only with great difficulty that our father managed to obtain a few important documents: the certificate of completion of his Ph.D., a number of books he had authored in the 1930s, and of course the diary before you. Although our father wrote voluminously and on an amazing range of topics, this diary is perhaps the most sustained witness of our father's life, covering a crucial, though limited, period in his own experience and in Jewish history.

Of the post-War years, we naturally know more. But a few fascinating documents have survived, including three letters to him from Rabbi Israel Meir Kagan, *zt"l*, the "Chofetz Chaim," that my father kept with him throughout the War years. Two of these ask for his help in obtaining residency permits for a number of Torah scholars escaping from Communist Russia or otherwise stateless, while the third letter thanks our father for expending great efforts to help them obtain residency permits. Our father often said that "it was not he who had saved the letters but rather the letters that saved him!" This correspondence attests to both his ability as a *shtadlan*, an advocate on behalf of the Jewish people, and the measure of respect our father had received at a young age. Other documents, including correspondence with the Gerrer Rebbe, *zt"l*, and Rabbi Chaim Ozer Grodzensky, *zt"l*, confirm these impressions.

The following is a brief biography gleaned either from various documentary sources or — for the later years — from our own knowledge:

Our father was the eldest of eight children, born at the beginning of this century to a learned and well-to-do Husiatiner Chasidic family in Buczacz, Poland (Eastern Galicia). In his youth he studied with Rabbi David Menachem Monish Babad *zt"l*, the rabbi of Tarnopol and one of Galicia's most prominent *rabbanim*. His considerable secular knowledge was acquired less formally, through tutors and by studying as an extern at the Tarnopol Gymnasium. By all accounts, our father was intellectually precocious, conducting while still in his adolescence a learned correspondence on the subject of the Frankist movement in Poland with the Jewish historian Dr. Meir Balaban — later his professor.

After completing his baccalaureate in 1932, our father moved to Warsaw to attend the Joseph Pilsudski University and take classes at the Institute for Jewish Studies. He completed his Ph.D. in History in June of 1939.

During this period, our father occupied various positions: serving as executive secretary of the Agudath Yisrael Youth Movement and the Union of Jewish Parliamentarians of the Sejm (Polish Parliament). A few weeks before the outbreak of the Second World War, he was elected to the Warsaw City Council as its youngest member. His mission in these various settings was one of advocacy for Jews and Jewry. Throughout these years, he also served as correspondent for various Yiddish, Hebrew, and German newspapers.

For him, the 1930s were also a decade of prolific literary activity whose purpose was to defend the rights, honor, and welfare of the Jewish people. One instance occurred when Reverend Stanislaw Trzeciak launched an antisemitic campaign to ban *shechitah* in Poland — which would have deprived Polish Jews of meat and also thousands of Jewish families of their means of support. In response, our father wrote a book entitled *The Truth about Ritual Slaughter* that successfully helped sway the parliamentary vote in favor of the Jewish community. In his book *The Oath According to the Torah* — refuting the antisemitic slur that the *Kol Nidre* prayers absolved Jews from all oaths and thus allow Jews to lie in court — he successfully proved to the Polish public that oaths are taken most seriously in the Torah view. Since his sisters, *Hy"d*, were students of the famed Beth Jacob Seminary in Krakow, he also wrote a treatise entitled *The Religious Revival of Jewish Women: Beth Jacob and Sarah Shenirer,* as well as a book reviewing Talmudic studies in Poland, particularly *Yeshivos Chachmei Lublin*, where his brother, *Hy"d*, studied.

Under German occupation, our father continued his role as Director of the Archives of the Warsaw Jewish community. In this capacity he was able to free a large number of people from forced labor by registering them as employees of the Kehillah. Employment by the Kehillah turned out to be only a temporary reprieve for most, but we know at least two individuals who attribute their survival to it: Rabbi Berish Ehrlich of Brooklyn, N. Y. and Mrs. Guta Sternbuch of Zurich.

Our father worked unceasingly to assist both the great personalities as well as young yeshivah scholars and the small children of the Ghetto. In one instance, our father succeeded in smuggling a young child out of the Ghetto to the Aryan side. This little girl survived the War and came to the United States, where she grew up, married, and raised a beautiful family steeped in Torah learning. Through clear *hashgachah pratis* (Divine Providence), thirty-eight years after our father rescued her from the horrors of the Warsaw Ghetto, his son married her daughter.

Through his connections with Jewish leaders abroad, our father received a Paraguayan passport, which the Germans recognized for a short while. (Apparently they hoped to make use of foreign citizens incarcerated in German prisons in a prisoner exchange for their agents and spies imprisoned abroad.) Shortly before the Warsaw Ghetto uprising, our father was detained in the Pawiak prison in Warsaw, from where he was deported to an internment camp at Vittel, France. While in Vittel, he sent scores of letters through the Red Cross to Switzerland in an attempt to alert Jewish leaders in the United States and Great Britain of the desperate situation.

In April 1944, when the foreign citizen papers of these Jews were officially confirmed as being inauthentic, the Germans began deporting those Jews incarcerated in Vittel to Drancy and from there to Auschwitz. Through the mercy of God, our father, together with ten other Jews (including the aforementioned Guta Sternbuch and her mother), evaded deportation by hiding in a hotel oven. Subsequently our father was hospitalized — thereby his life was spared once again when the Germans deported more Jews a month later. He was finally liberated by General Eisenhower's army on September 1, 1944.

At the conclusion of World War II, our father opened an Agudath Israel Office in Paris to help Jewish refugees streaming there after the war. Despite poor health and the traumatic loss of most of his family, our father turned his attention to helping refugees with their physical and spiritual needs, from assisting them to obtain documents, visas, travel permits, and food rations to opening a kosher kitchen and even taking refugees on a tour of Versailles in order to raise their morale.

In 1946 our father came to the United States where he married the former Sarah Abraham, a Beth Jacob teacher and daughter of Rabbi Zvi Yaakov and Rebbitzen Pearl Abraham, a prominent rabbinical family in Romania.

The *Warsaw Ghetto Diaries* was first published in installments in the Tel Aviv Hebrew daily *Haboker.* As the first printed eyewitness report of the destruction of the great Jewish community of Warsaw, it was eagerly and widely read. Later it was published in book form, first in Hebrew in 1946 and then in Yiddish in 1947.

When Aguda leader Rabbi Yitzchak Meir Lewin was appointed Minister of Social Welfare in the Israeli cabinet, he invited our father to serve as deputy minister for his ministry. Our father accepted the call, and our parents resided in Jerusalem between 1951 and 1952.

In 1952 our parents returned to the United States, where all four children were born. Our father continued to work as a journalist and writer, contributing to Yiddish, Hebrew, and English language newspapers, including *The Morning Journal, Hatzofeh,* and *Der Algemeiner Journal,* on a variety of topics. For more than three decades he worked as public information officer for Israel Bonds. He wrote a weekly column with thoughtful insight on the current Torah portion, faithfully read by thousands, and also a column on the current events affecting the Jewish community.

He was the author of many books, including *Di Sedra fun der Voch* (The Torah Portion of the Week, 1966), *The Glory of the Jewish Holidays* (1968), *Ishim Shehikarti* (Personalities I Knew, 1970), *Rabbi Shraga Feivel Mendelovitz* (1976), and *Menachem Begin, His Life and Legacy* (1990). He was one of the first to expose United Nations Secretary General Kurt Waldheim's Nazi past in his book *United Nations: Perfidy and Perversion* (1982).

Our father served on the boards of various institutions including the Jewish Nazi Victims Organization of America and various Beth Jacob schools and yeshivos. He had a close relationship with many prominent rabbis, political leaders, and literary figures, including Rabbi Menachem Mendel Shneerson (Lubavitcher Rebbe), Rabbi Yosef Kahaneman (Ponevezer Rav), Rabbi J. B. Soleveitchik, and former *Rishon Letzion* Rav Ovadiah Yosef, as well as New York Senator Daniel P. Moynihan, Israeli Prime Minister Menachem Begin, Elie Wiesel, and S. Y. Agnon. Yet at the same time, he loved every Jew and would attempt to assist every individual in need. Our father utilized his keen intelligence and widespread connections, acquired from youth, until the last day of his life, to help any Jewish individual or institution in legal, financial, or other need.

Our father was a warm, devoted, and loving parent, whose children and grandchildren symbolized to him the continuity of the Jewish people and a victory over those who sought to destroy our nation. Together with our mother, *yb"l*, he imbued us with *ahavas Yisrael* and a love of Torah and *Yiddishkeit* and the Land of Israel.

Yehi zichro boruch. May his memory be blessed.

The Seidman Family
Tishrei 5758

TRANSLATOR'S PREFACE

Historical Perspective

The experience of traditional Jewry during the Holocaust has not received the attention it deserves, both by virtue of religious Jewry's sheer weight of numbers and the valiant effort they made to retain some semblance of religious life under unspeakable conditions. Religious Jews, with their distinctive dress, beards, and *peyos,* were an early target, singled out for particular persecution by the Nazis. Yet their unique contribution to spiritual resistance and morale has been largely ignored by secular historians. This English translation, which records the tragedy unfolding in the largest *kehillah* in Europe, in a diary kept from July 1942 to April 1943, hopes to partly remedy this deficiency.

While the short time span covered by this diary encapsulates the peak of Poland's agony, it was but one link in the crushing chain of German tyranny. When the Nazis first swept into power in early 1933 on a rising tide of hyperinflation, catastrophic unemployment, and rabid antisemitism, they set themselves two primary goals: the enlargement of Germany's "natural borders" and the destruction of Europe's Communists/Jews (in Nazi ideology these two appellations were practically interchangeable). As soon as political skullduggery and blatant terror secured their dominance, a torrent of legislation, accompanied with — and sometimes preceded by — mob violence, was unleashed, rapidly reducing the social, legal, and cultural position of German Jews to the Dark Ages.

Even after the annexation of Austria and the subsequent occupation of Czechoslovakia, the Nazi lust for more foreign territory as *lebensraum* remained unsated. In parallel to intensive war preparations, secret plans were drawn up for "the destruction of the Jewish race in Europe," since war offered both the motive and the ideal opportunity to intensify their ruthless campaign against the defenseless populace. The clandestine pact between Communist Russia and Nazi Germany sealed Poland's fate as the Nazis' next victim — notwithstanding solemn guarantees from France and Britain.

Until then, Nazi Germany had captured territories by a mere show of force; now it would involve brutal hostilities. On Friday, September 1, 1939 (17 Elul 5699 — *Erev Shabbos Ki-Savo*), the Germans attacked. Hopelessly outnumbered, outgunned, and outmaneuvered, the Poles struggled desperately on in the vain expectation of outside assistance. But Poland and her approximately 3,300,000 Jews were abandoned to their fate. While the Allies did little concrete to help, Russia waited until most of the fighting was over before marching in and claiming the eastern half of a partitioned Poland. Only Warsaw still held out. On September 23 (*Yom Kippur* 5700) German pilots and gunners mercilessly targeted the Jewish Quarter for ferocious bombing and shelling, finally entering the capital on September 30 (*Chol Hamoed Sukkos*).

Throughout the Thirties, Polish Jews had watched the escalating terror in Germany with growing alarm. Not only were the Nazis uncomfortably close neighbors, Polish Jews had their own enormous sufferings to contend with. Polish communal and religious infrastructure had only slowly recovered from the German invasion of WW1. Furthermore, while Poland had been a relatively peaceful haven during the Middle Ages, two decades of newly won independence between WW1 and WW2 had ushered in periodic pogroms and personal attacks, coupled with harsh economic and educational discrimination.

After 1935, an increasingly fascist government in Poland disenfranchised Jewish citizens outside its borders, planned the "evacuation" of numerous Jews from Poland, and very nearly outlawed *shechitah*. Thus Polish nationalists were consciously aping Nazi oppression and legislation even before the invasion. Yet they still had much to learn about the cold blooded systematization of murder and mayhem.

The massacres and torment began immediately. In the wake of the invasion, six *Einzatzgruppen* extermination squads perpetrated sadistic atrocities with the active compliance of regular *Wehrmacht* soldiers. Prior to the invasion, all army servicemen had been indoctrinated with the principle that the "fight with World Jewry was not a chivalrous argument but a battle against a poisonous parasite, an enemy to all humanity..." (German army indoctrination booklet, pub. 1939), and their troop trains carried the racist slogan "We travel to Poland to smash the Jews!" Within days — occasionally within hours — of a town's capture, its prominent Jews were publicly executed on spurious charges, most synagogues destroyed, businesses looted, confiscated, or burnt, while the general community was exposed to arbitrary humiliations, persecution, and forced labor. The infamous *Kristallnacht* pogrom, which had so shocked the world when it erupted in Germany in November 1938, was re-enacted in most Polish towns and villages captured by German armed forces. This initial reign of terror conditioned both the Poles and Germans for further outrages.

In the depth of that first, icy winter, hundreds of thousands were forced from their homes when central Poland was designated as the *Generalgouvernement,* a general dumping ground for Jews and undesirables. Numerous communities were ruthlessly uprooted from the hastily annexed eastern and northern Poland, while rural Jews were likewise relocated to cities. Overnight, prosperous families were transmuted into penniless refugees frantically searching for shelter. Countless European families were also deported to Poland. Inevitably, many flooded into Warsaw, further straining the city's overstretched resources. These refugees were subsequently selected as the first victims of mass deportations.

These preliminary measures were part of the grand Nazi design that included establishing Councils of Elders (*Judenrate*) to process *Einzatzgruppen* orders, scheduling curfews, mandating identifying *magen David* patches, and setting up ghettos that concentrated Jews near railroad tracks — thus facilitating unspecified and secret measures for the future.

As the unbridled violence settled down to the systematic cruelty of vicious beatings, confiscations, and inhuman toil in slave labor brigades, a chain of ghettos was established in the meanest town quarters all across the *Generalgouvernement.* Warsaw's ghetto was first mooted on Shabbos, November 4, 1939, but only a partial ghettoization resulted. The final decree was sadistically announced on *Yom Kippur,* October 12, 1940. A "closed ghetto," rigidly restricted with high brick walls, became the bitter reality.

Perhaps the Germans had hoped the intolerable, unsanitary, vastly overcrowded conditions prevalent in each ghetto, combined with abject poverty, lack of vital medicines, and artificially induced raging famine would by itself "solve" the Jewish Problem naturally, but Poland's Jews were made of sterner stuff. Although depressed by the string of major allied defeats in Norway, Denmark, Belgium, Holland, France, and the ongoing air blitz against Britain, few succumbed to suicide or despair; their survival instinct remained intact amidst widespread confidence in the ultimate destruction of Nazism.

The crippling cold, hunger, random murders, slave labor, and ill-health had directly accounted for "only" 30,000 deaths, up until the seizure of the rump of Poland, Lithuania, and the Baltic states at the invasion of Russia in June 1941. This was far too slow and inefficient for the impatient Germans. With the outbreak of these renewed hostilities, fresh opportunities for bloodshed became available, and Nazi oppression entered a further stage. Once again, the *Einzatzgruppen* extermination squads fanned out along the new Eastern Front but this time their blood toll was staggering. Across the towns and villages of eastern Poland, Ukraine, and Russia their remorseless tactics were strikingly similar: Jews were rounded up in their thousands, ordered to surrender their valuables and dig large pits, then machine-gunned to death. In an orgy of mass killing, willingly aided by Ukrainian and Lithuanian volunteers, hundreds of thousands were brutally murdered in those first months, with the toll rising eventually to an estimated two million. The Nazi hierarchy spoke openly of *"die endlosung der Judenfrage* — the Final Solution of the Jewish Question."

In central Poland, the mass murderers preferred to use poison gas previously employed in a "Euthanasia Program" to rid

Germany of mental and physical defectives. (Indeed, the cruel hoax of "showers" was first perpetrated for that program.) At first, the Nazis experimented with sealed mobile gas vans with piped-in exhaust fumes, but eventually they decided to replicate their static euthanasia facilities as the most efficient manslaughter system. Accordingly, several death camps were constructed between winter 1941 and spring 1942; the labor camps of Majdanek near Lublin and Treblinka near Warsaw were converted likewise, while Auschwitz near Cracow, on a major railway link, was vastly extended to accept over 100,000 innocent victims at a time. At these camps, most victims were to be murdered on arrival, while a minority were worked to death on starvation rations.

In early 1942, a conference near Berlin cold-bloodedly put in place the state machinery and bureaucratic procedures for the total annihilation of the Jewish race in Europe under the typically deceptive euphemism of "resettlement eastward." This merciless slaughter schedule was to proceed with all speed and take priority even over the crucial battles with Russia on the Eastern Front. Barely two months later, mass deportations began from Lublin and Slovakia, followed by *aktions* in Warsaw. Summer was the turn of Lvov (Lemberg) followed by Jews from Europe, Croatia, and Norway. Deportations began in Bialystok in early 1943 followed by more from Europe and Greece.

In April the final liquidation of Warsaw was ordered. Until then, many Warsaw Jews had relied on their long *galus* experience and had fully expected that the pitiless enemy would eventually tire of killing. As realization now dawned that they would not outlive Nazi brutality, the Uprising broke out. Betrayed by the Polish Resistance, it was quelled after six weeks, when the Ghetto was razed to the ground. The pace of the mass extermination program continued unabated.

During August 1944, as Russian forces recaptured Minsk and Vilna while crushing half the *Wehrmacht* divisions, the Polish Resistance itself rose to retake Warsaw. In turn, they were betrayed by the Russians, who callously halted their advance outside the capital, while obstructing allied assistance. Thus the national revolt was brutally snuffed out within nine weeks and the remainder of Warsaw torched in scenes remarkably reminiscent of the destruction of the Ghetto, fifteen months earlier.

At liberation, at least nine out every ten Polish Jews had been obliterated. From a pre-War Jewish population of 3,300,000, a battered remnant of some 60,000 survived at liberation (and approximately 180,000 in Siberia).

Inevitably, these background details fail to impart the depth of the overwhelming cataclysm and provide scant rational explanation as to why it took place. Periodic torment may not have been unfamiliar in our long history, but it was usually accompanied by religious or territorial motives. Here, for the first time, the options of evading persecution by surrender or baptism were not available; nor did the enemy forbear killing Jews with whom he had no previous contact or quarrel. Irrational hatred reigned supreme.

How did the liberal, law-abiding, intellectual nation of Germans descend so rapidly into the brutish abyss, and how in the so-called civilized 20th century did Jews once again become "an object of scorn and derision among humanity, regarded as sheep for the slaughter: destined to be killed, destroyed, beaten, and humiliated" (*Tachanun*). By what logic were the Jews of northern Africa, similarly under German domination, spared the extermination process when POWs from the desert campaign were shipped off to Auschwitz? Why did the Jews of Sweden, Switzerland, Spain, Portugal, Bulgaria, and deepest Russia merit to escape the worst? The Holocaust generates many questions with few obvious answers.

Perhaps we are too lacking in inspiration and too close to the overwhelming tragedy to fully comprehend the Divine Purpose. However, those who hasten to ask: Where was the Deity at Auschwitz? decline to consider the obverse side to that conundrum: Where was Humanity at the Holocaust? World conscience, like world opinion or the brotherhood of man, proved to be a meaningless concept. Allied intelligence, the Red Cross, the Vatican, and political leaders had all known of the accelerating atrocities from the beginning, yet betrayed their trust by doing next to nothing. And what of the common man who hurried to watch the spectacle of public executions, voluntarily informed on Jews still in hiding, or scurried to loot the dying victims? And what of the killers themselves — family men laughing and joking while callously slaying thousands, who grew so bored of mundane manslaughter that they devised devilish tortures to pique their fancy.

Until the War, most had naively believed that Emancipation and a growing cultural affinity between Jew and Gentile would solve "the Jewish problem." In actuality, successful assimilation only provoked a groundswell of popular resentment and jealousy. Germany had been idolized in eastern Europe as the cultural capital of the world, yet its intelligentsia joined the Jew-baiting and made it respectable. Surprising as it may be to those ignorant of the Torah, the Biblical curses (contained in *Parashas Ki Savo* and subsequent chapters) foreshadowed many salient features of Nazi oppression. Ominously, these *parashios* constituted the designated weekly Torah readings at the 1939 invasion of Poland.

To quote a few scattered examples, these threaten: "a nation of cruel countenance who respects neither the old nor young.... Each morning you will long for evening and each evening you will long for morning, from fear and from the scenes you will witness.... From your previous multitude, you shall be left few in number.... Your suffering shall become an astonishment, a parable, and a byword to the nations...." In a chilling phrase it warns: "Just as Hashem rejoiced to benefit and multiply you, so will Hashem rejoice to destroy you and wipe you out...." Later Hashem predicts that when we "trust and fall prey to the lure of strange nations... I will hide My face from them so they will be consumed amidst enormous evils and suffering...devoured with hunger, burning heat, and bitter destruction.... I shall scatter them to the corners of the earth, contemplate erasing their memory from mankind...could a single foe control a thousand or two chase ten thousand had Hashem not sold and discarded them?"

Many of these dire predictions were reiterated by the prophets. "What you imagine shall not occur, if you hope to imitate the surrounding nations.... As I live, I shall rule over you with a strong hand, an outstretched arm, and an outpouring of fury, says Hashem Elokim" (*Yechezkel* 20). Perhaps the self-styled *Führer* spoke truer words than he realized when he described himself as "a sleepwalker in the hands of providence."

Closer to the catastrophe, some Torah leaders hinted at the approaching calamity. During a bitter polemic with the progressive preacher Zvi Dinov in 1871, the notable Kelmer Maggid, Rabbi Moshe Yitzchak Darshan, delivered a series of memorable speeches in which he declared: "The Germans will not merely persecute the Jews; when they come to power, they will not content themselves with rudimentary oppression. No! They will construct a veritable '*Shulchan Aruch*' of antisemitism, may Heaven protect us! *Morai veRabosai*, heed this well. For the sin of Abraham Geiger amending the *Shulchan Aruch*, there will eventually be a new German Code of Law directed against the Jewish nation! In it will be written 'Kill the best of the Jews! Kill the best of the Jews!' May Hashem protect and deliver us!"

Equally famous words were penned by Rav Meir Simcha Hakohen, the renowned Rabbi of Dvinsk, Latvia, and published in *Meshech Chochmah* (printed posthumously in 1927). In a lengthy and penetrating analysis of the cycle of *galus*, he wrote that "...as Jews grow comfortable in their adopted country, they tend to abandon their Divine mission and assimilate to the alien culture. Modernists may regard Berlin as the new Jerusalem but only a scant remnant will endure when the inevitable storm of destruction radiates from Berlin. Then the survivors will disperse to other states where Judaism will develop fresh roots and young Torah scholars will accomplish unimaginable achievements...."

Shortly before the outbreak of War, some Chasidic leaders recalled a letter of Rebbe Yisrael Baal Shem Tov, the founder of Chasidism, which foretold how the thousand-year-old Polish Judaism would be obliterated in an upsurge of looting and carnage. Less well known then was the testament of the saintly pre-War leader and author of the *Chafetz Chayim*, Rabbi Yisrael Meir Kagan of Radun, who passed away in the early 1930s. Speaking privately to his close disciples in the 1920s, when most thought the Nazis were a spent force, he accurately predicted the year of their rise to power and foresaw that the First World War — despite its vast toll of dead and traumatized — would be considered child's play compared to the next war.

Hinting that the Divine decree was already sealed, he often spoke of the coming conflagration where few places would be safe while Eretz Yisrael would be miraculously spared. Publicly, in his letters and proclamations, he blamed the increasing travail and tribulations on growing negligence of traditional observance within erstwhile religious centers.

His prime disciple and successor, Rav Elchanan Wasserman, claimed in a series of insightful and provoking newspaper articles published before the War (later collated under the title *Kovetz Maamorim*), that the National-Socialist movement posed direct retribution (*middah k'neged middah*) for the prevailing infatuation with nationalism and socialism. Nor was it mere coincidence that the threat originated from Berlin, the fount of Enlightenment.

Rav Wasserman drew an interesting historical analogy with Purim and Chanukah: During the Purim story, on facing an exclusively physical threat, the Jews did not organize a resistance until permitted to do so by the Persian authorities. However, the Chanukah revolt broke out in direct opposition to Greek tyranny since they were threatened then with religious — not physical — oblivion. Because he perceived Nazi oppression as a physical rather than religious persecution, he determined that resistance was both wrong and useless to the Divine Design. Within the religious community, his forthright views colors their response to wartime resistance — including the Warsaw Uprising — to this day.

Rav Wasserman remained true to his strongly held principles. When war appeared imminent he was on a fund-raising mission in America, yet he bravely insisted in boarding the last ship back to Poland. Well-wishers remonstrated with him but he replied that he was returning to his destiny and besides, who knew when the turn of British and American Jewry would come? Later, as he was being marched off to execution in Kovno, Lithuania, he exhorted his followers not to harbor any false notions since by their purity of thought they might yet prove a *kapparah* for Jewry and thus save the Jews of America!

Aside from their anti-*shechitah* legislation, most initial Nazi edicts paradoxically served to reinforce religion and tradition. By being barred from the cultural milieu of cinema and theater, many were forced to rediscover their native roots. Jewish day schools became increasingly popular when Jews were forbidden to either teach or attend German schools and universities. Estranged Jews were now compelled to treat each other medically or conduct business between themselves. Nor could they see it as pure chance that the boycotts against Jewish shops and department stores first began on a Shabbos (April 1, 1933). The hateful Nuremberg race laws rolled back intermarriage and reversed decades of assimilation by searching out Jewish antecedents to the third and fourth generation. Step by painful step, Germany's Jews were driven to renounce their intense patriotism to the Fatherland and recognize their traditional heritage. Judaism flowered during those early years of National Socialism — sparking a religious revival with penitents flocking to overflowing synagogues, including many who had never entered one before.

But this temporary resurgence was cruelly shattered by the *Kristallnacht* pogrom. No longer were synagogues a secure haven of solace and prayer when Jew-baiting acquired an overtly anti-religious slant. Later in Poland, the burning and desecration of synagogues was repeated in every *kehillah* overrun by the Germans. Bearded Jews were singled out for special attention and the devout were often forced to personally defile sacred objects, including Torah scrolls and *tefillin*. Early decrees forbade public gatherings for prayer and outlawed the use of ritual baths. Later, Jewish festivals were routinely selected for macabre torments and tortures in what became infamously known as the "Goebbel's *luach*."

Whether the religious leadership in the Warsaw Ghetto saw their situation in the light of Rav Elchanan Wasserman's analogy as either a "Chanukah" or "Purim" is unclear, but ultimately they lent their authority to the Uprising and encouraged the Resistance. The *rabbanim* (including Rav Menachem Ziemba, Rav Arieh Frumer, R. Dovid Shapira, and R. Shimshon Stockhammer — as detailed in this Diary) publicly advised against volunteering for "labor" at Poniatowa and Trawniki and authorized students at the underground yeshivos to join in the inevitable fighting.

While credit for the Uprising has been almost universally attributed to Mordechai Anielewicz and the *chalutzim* from the Zionist kibbutz at Grochov (with its relative freedom from substantial persecution), many religious Jews did contribute moral and physical support — in addition to their crucial role in maintaining morale and humane standards in face of German bestiality.

This diary chronicles the inexorable course of devastation from the onset of the mass deportations to the final liquidation of the Warsaw Ghetto — home to the largest reservoir of Jewish vitality on European soil. Naturally, it is not the sole surviving war diary extant but it is among the few to record events from a religious background. Its author was uniquely familiar with the Torah leadership and privy to their deliberations. Hopefully, it will somewhat redress the unbalanced perception of religious Jewry, whose fortitude and response was sorely tried and tested under extreme circumstances, and who displayed great heroism and moral fiber.

It remained Dr. Hillel Seidman's wish that his diary appear in English as a *zichron kedoshim,* a memorial to the millions of martyred souls, thousands of precious families, and hundreds of holy communities extinguished without even an individual headstone to mark their grave. Allow not the Earth to conceal their splattered blood. Let Hashem not forget the cries of the humble, and so He shall avenge their blood. May He remember them favorably among the righteous and exact retribution for their spilled blood. May the All-Merciful shelter them under His wing for eternity, binding their souls in the bond of eternal life.

Yosef Israel
12 Sivan 5757/June 17, 1997
London, England

INTRODUCTION

"EVEN a *sefer Torah* resting in the Holy Ark," says the ancient proverb, "depends on *mazal*." Indeed every book needs its luck, too, and never more so than during the precarious period of the World War. So my record of recent history has a little history of its own.

Many Warsaw residents were aware that generally I was not loath to put pen to paper. (Besides countless articles printed in Warsaw's *Togblatt, Moment,* and *Darkenu,* I had also managed to write and publish some ten books in the relatively good years before the war.) Thus they encouraged me to transcribe all Warsaw's travails and tribulations, a written record for future generations, so that the world should eventually learn the truth.

But others were more sceptical. "It's just not worth it," they argued. "Who will want to know? Nobody will want to disturb their sleep or spoil their appetite! No one really wants the truth...." Since this inner conflict also raged within my own soul, at first I decided not to describe everything in graphic detail; merely to collect material and record events as these took place with a few scattered vignettes.

Collecting material was in fact part of my official employment within the Ghetto, where I was chief librarian for the Kehillah's Archives and Record Department, and I was unofficially asked to keep records by Dr. Emanuel Ringelblum (the noted activist and archivist) and Menachem Linder (Library Director of I.K.U.P. — Warsaw's *Yiddishe Kultur Farband*). However, when the Holocaust began in earnest, the greatest tragedy of all time, I began to transcribe episodes more thoroughly and started to systematically keep a daily diary in which I chronicled the continuous events.

This record was written under dire circumstances. When we arose each morning we never knew if we would see nightfall. Never perhaps has the Biblical curse (*Devarim* 28:66), "And your lives shall hang precariously in front of you" seemed so apt as it did then — especially from July 22, 1942 onwards. Little did I then dream that I would personally merit to see my diary published. Nonetheless, I stubbornly continued to write it all down without even taking a day off, and I guarded my precious manuscript with my life. When I was being marched off to Warsaw's *Umschlagplatz* (deportation railway sidings) en route to Treblinka, my manuscript was with me, and all that time I had only one thought: where would I find somebody reliable enough to entrust my diary to?

Finally I gave my diary to a Jewish policeman to pass on to Dr. Tulu Nussblatt, and when I was eventually rescued (due incidentally to the diary being handed over, which alerted the Kehillah to my predicament) I arrived back at my office more dead than alive. Yet when I found that my diary had preceded me, I immediately wrote down all my terrifying experiences.

Again, in early September 1942, I reacted similarly when

the SS with their Latvian and Lithuanian auxiliaries surrounded the block of buildings which included the Kehillah headquarters. All the inhabitants trembled with fear, convinced that their untimely end had arrived. But I continued to chronicle events like one possessed and calmly recorded "SS brigades are now encircling us." Library staff (both the genuine ones who had joined before the war and the fictitious "librarians" who had only joined later to avoid deportation) stared at me in amazement, as if I had become deranged. Dr. Tulu Nussblatt remarked scornfully, "His writings have become a form of madness; just watching him depresses me — to become so stubborn, such an *akshan*...."

But still I did not interrupt my scribbling. Pointing at me, Dr. Schipper described a French Head of Parliament who did not lose his self-control when a bomb explosion rocked the parliament buildings and calmly announced, "The sitting continues!" Dr. Schimkovits, the geographer, recalled how explorers on a doomed expedition to the North Pole, before they succumbed to the cold, recorded their findings with frozen fingers and buried their results to be found in time by their rescuers. Not to be outdone, Dr. Edmund Stein recollected how the radio telegraphist on the Titanic continued to send S.O.S. messages as the ship was going down. But everybody present disagreed with that last analogy since — unlike that S.O.S. — nobody believed that my writings would ever reach the wide world. Certainly my diary would not save us. We were trapped in a large prison while the world as usual reacts far too little and far too late. (That the world would not react at all was not foreseen, even by our bitterest pessimists.)

Yet despite all that, I still felt compelled to write it all down. I was also persuaded by a "simple fellow Jew," not numbered among the "official" activists but an exceptional person nevertheless, blessed with perception, exemplary character, and a *mesiras nefesh* for Jews and Judaism. He was a Warsaw businessman, Reb Berel Gefen of Franciskani Street, a great *lamdan,* with a warm heart whose home and purse were always available to anyone in trouble. He never ceased pressuring me to continue: "*Shreib! Shreib! Kedei es zol bleiben a zecher!* — Write! Just so there should remain a record!" And when I mentioned the doubts as to whether my words would ever see the light of day, Reb Berel paraphrased the *Mishnah* in *Avos* (2:16) "The work is not up to you to complete. Nor are you free to shirk the responsibility...." By my writings, he insisted, the outside world would finally learn what we had to endure. That precious soul (he died in Warsaw on 19 Adar 5703) gave me the encouragement to continue. May his memory be a blessing, for I am deeply grateful.

As well as my writing, I continued to collect incriminating material, and this proved exceedingly difficult. Though the German beasts rained down an unending flood of orders, penalties, and restrictions, they were careful to commit little of this to writing. Since the time the deportations began everything was transmitted verbally. Even the first *Aussiedlung* order (or "resettlement" as the death transports were euphemistically described) of July 22, 1942 was not written down but dictated to the Kehillah President Czerniakow. Afterwards, his successor, Lichtenbaum, would write their orders down himself since the Nazis did not want to leave any written evidence. Apparently, they believed that in this way the outside world would not discover what was really going on. This, too, persuaded me to record everything I could.

I wrote my diary in two separate books. One I used and left

in the office, and the other I used at home. In January 1943, I buried part of my diaries in the cellars of the Kehillah building in Zamenhof 19, while I managed to smuggle the other half to the "Aryan" (i.e., non-Jewish) part of Warsaw and handed this over into the college library's custody, with the help of an old acquaintance from university. But one day this man telephoned me at the Kehillah and asked me to remove these dangerous papers in case of a search.

Reluctantly, I went to the college library and retrieved this part of my diary. On my way back to the Ghetto I was waylaid by a Polish detective who demanded to see my exit permit. Though my permit was perfectly in order (in my capacity as chief librarian I was permitted to leave the Ghetto to consult with the State Library), the detective still confiscated my briefcase and papers, probably believing it contained money.

Understandably, this episode caused me great anguish; not only at the loss of my diary but at the obvious danger if it fell into the hands of the Germans. For a few days I went into hiding and was absent from my office, spending some sleepless nights racked with fear. After a week I began to relax and was persuaded by good friends that the Polish detective was only interested in money and had almost certainly thrown my papers away as worthless. But I still felt the loss of my precious diary most keenly.

In fact, that detective had not thrown my diary away but had handed it over to the Gestapo! And after a week, the Kehillah received the whole bundle of papers with the Gestapo's instructions to have it translated into German. Perhaps you can imagine the fear that gripped us when we discovered this turn of events.

Fortunately, since the Kehillah leaders then were not very

learned, I was able to get involved, and with the help of Nochum Remba (the Zionist leader) and Rabbi Ephraim Zonnenshein, who were meant to carry out the translation, we substituted other papers relating to innocuous tombstone inscriptions without either the Kehillah or the Gestapo realizing. Thus I received my diary safely back.

When I was arrested much later by the Gestapo, I was allowed just fifteen minutes to pack some personal effects. I had already prepared a suitcase with a false bottom, and that was where I hid the pages of my diary. Fortunately, the subsequent search at Pawiak Prison revealed nothing. I shared a cell there with an alumnus of the Lublin Yeshivah, my friend Rabbi Chaim Leibush Berglass, who was a clear thinker as well as a genius, and I confided in him what I had done. He also encouraged me to continue.

"Every Jew always hopes to leave some memory," he insisted, "a son to say *Kaddish,* learn *Mishnayos*, and observe his *yahrzeit.* Others publish *sefarim* or endow a fund for charitable purposes. All leave behind a grave and a *matzeivah*. But now whole families are being wiped out leaving no memory, no *Kaddish,* not even a grave. So we must at least preserve a record for everybody...." Indeed Rabbi Berglass helped me conceal the diary and allowed me to risk my life somewhat recklessly. As soon as we received the order that we were being transferred to France, we realized that we would have to undergo an intensive search. Inside Pawiak, there were some enterprising Jewish tinsmiths who were adept at making tin boxes with false bottoms — usually to conceal gold and diamonds — and I ordered one for my diary. Only a small part of the diary could be hidden this way, and the rest I concealed among my published books, doctoral thesis, and an unpublished manuscript on the history of the Warsaw community.

From Warsaw we were transported as South American citizens to Vittel and then on to Compiegne, so we had to undergo two separate searches. During the second search the German guard noticed my diary, and I went white with fear. But when he saw it carried a Gestapo stamp (from that time it had been confiscated by the Polish detective), he relaxed and remarked, "*Ach,* so they have been passed by the censor!" And so that earlier episode, which could have ended so tragically, turned out for the best.

In the Compiegne camp I was helped by my fellow inmates, particularly Yechiel Schwartzbart (later of Paris) who did much for the public and myself, for which I am heartily grateful. Matters were always arranged to ensure the safety of my diary, but when I was returned to Vittel on July 5, 1943, I was extremely nervous. I had already aroused the suspicions of the Vittel Gestapo after writing from there to Chaim Yisroel Eiss of Zurich and Avraham Zilberstein of Geneva about saving other Polish Jews. Though I had written very guardedly, using only vague hints, both Yechiel Schwartzbart and I were summoned to the camp censor, and it was only with great difficulty that I managed to wriggle out of the situation (mainly due to Mr. Schwartzbart slipping the censor quantities of cigarettes).

So I packed my writings and books separately under the name "Seidman" while I was officially known to the Germans as "Eisenzweig." On reaching Vittel I displayed no interest in that parcel, and the Gestapo duly impounded it in their archives. Both I and family Eisenzweig, under whose name I sheltered, were very fearful that the Gestapo might examine my writings but, fortunately, it later turned out our fears were groundless.

When the Germans vacated Vittel on September 1, 1944, I

immediately began requesting the return of my diaries; but after much searching only a small part was returned to me, since the Gestapo archives had been taken to Frankfurt and Cologne. After much effort and the help of the Internees and Deportees Organization in Paris, I received the remainder that was in their possession.

As for the diaries I had buried in the Ghetto, once I was able to contact Poland after May 1945, I met the Polish minister Dr. Stefan Jandrochovski and Warsaw Mayor Stanislav Tlebinski, who were both in Paris, and with the help of the Polish Jewish Historical Committee made an official request for the buried sections. But without waiting for an official response I organized an unofficial dig there with great difficulty, and a courier brought the rest of my diary to France via Germany. And so was my diary finally saved after risking my life and the lives of others countless times.

Considering the conditions under which I wrote it, I made no effort to achieve any literary excellence, and even when I came to publish it (first in Hebrew and later in Yiddish) I had no inclination to add any flair or flourishes. My sole intention was to report the events as they took place. Some, perhaps, might find my diary dry or bland, but it cost me too much blood and tears to turn it into mere literature. Since the diary contains the whole truth and nothing but the truth, I hope it will prove sufficient.

Obviously the Divine *Hashgachah* willed that these terrifying chapters recording the death throes of the largest *kehillah* in Europe should not be lost forever.

THE WARSAW GHETTO DIARIES

JULY 1942

Friday, July 17

First Rumors of the Terror

All of us within the Ghetto are most uneasy. For days now, there have been frightening rumors racing around the Ghetto about an impending *Aussiedlung* (or "resettlement"). The source for these rumors is the Kohn and Heller factory whose owners are known to have close contacts with the Germans.

But when I asked the *Judenrat* President, Adam Czerniakow, he firmly denied the rumors.

Furthermore, at the beginning of the week, Auerswald, the German *Kommisar* for the Ghetto, relaxed the curfew, allowing Jews to be out on the Ghetto streets until 10 P.M. (instead of 9 P.M. as previously). Since this was apparently a good sign, talk began of a more liberal "new course" for Jews, and the panic started to subside.

Tension was also lessened when the Kehillah (or rather *Judenrat*) offices, which now issue *kenkarten* (Jewish identity cards), published a new schedule detailing when inhabitants of different streets could collect their documents. Since this schedule covers the next six weeks until the end of August and was issued on German instructions, it was also seen as a good sign.

Isolation of Foreign Citizens

This past Wednesday the Gestapo's *Auslandstelle* (foreign affairs section) published an order instructing all Jews with foreign passports to appear before the Jewish Police Station for their "transfer." When everyone asked anxiously, "Transfer to where?" the Gestapo explained, "To be exchanged for German citizens abroad."

When all the foreign Jews assembled this morning at 7 A.M. in the courtyard of the Jewish Police, at 16/17 Krochmalna Street, they were imprisoned in the administrative block of the infamous Pawiak Prison. Bidding farewell to their friends and relatives was a heartbreaking scene. Quite a few voiced the fear, "Who knows if we are not parting forever."

After midday, when those seeing them off returned, everyone began to analyze these latest developments. Why had they separated the foreign Jews and put them in prison? Some speculated they would be sent to America via Portugal. Others felt they would be kept as hostages until the end of the War. But the pessimists insisted that the foreign citizens were being separated only to protect them from the imminent deportations.

Sunday, July 19

Meeting of Activists and Personalities

With rumors of impending mass "resettlement" beginning again (once more the source is Kohn and Heller), a top secret meeting of activists and personalities gathered in the attic of 27 Nowolipki Street.

Those present included the Sochatchover Rebbe (Rabbi Bornstein), the Alexander Rebbe (Rabbi Danziger), and Rabbi Mendel Alter of Kalisch-Pawianitz (the President of Poland's

Agudas Rabbanim). Giterman and Guzik came on behalf of the Joint. Political representatives were present: Dr. Yitzchak Schipper (Labor Zionists), Rabbi Zisha Friedman (Aguda), Mauricy Orzech (Bund), Leib Scharansky (Mizrachi), and Dr. Lipman (Revisionists). On behalf of the now banned Jewish press was the editor Profus, the editor Gavza — and myself.

Also present were Rabbi Yosef Konigsberg (the *menahel* of Lublin Yeshivah) and Zagan (Poalei Zion), while Yehuda Yaffe, Elchanan Zeitlin, and Dr. Tulu Nussblatt (Herzl's biographer) arrived later.

The first item on the agenda was: Were the frightening rumors at all accurate? Inevitably there were both optimists and pessimists. The optimists argued that our strength lies in our sheer numbers. Warsaw itself is a force to be reckoned with. They would not dare destroy half a million people! Besides, many non-Jews have a vested interest in the Ghetto's survival. Even some Germans stand to gain much from our continued existence.

First of all there is the Gestapo's *Transferstelle* (customs post) that takes between 15 and 25 percent of everything passing through the Ghetto; not to mention many "presents" from Warsaw's businessmen. Then there is the *Kommisar* Heinz Auerswald, who personally receives vast bribes from the Kehillah for any relaxation in the Nazi restrictions, plus many "presents."

Even the Gestapo's Jewish section has an interest in the survival of Jews, since we are a useful source for extortion and looting. If we were not around, moreover, these Germans would have to enlist with the SS battalions and be deployed at the dreaded Eastern Front. The Ghetto is extremely productive and an important economic asset which none of the Germans would want to destroy.

The optimists cited all the recent omens: relaxation of the curfew, larger food rations, reopening of Jewish schools and kindergartens — which all point to a more liberal regime in the future. The rumors emanating from Kohn and Heller are definitely untrue, conclude the optimists; perhaps Kohn and Heller have some motive in spreading those false reports.

But the pessimists take the contrary view. Of course the Nazis will dare! They will try anything and cannot be trusted. Why should Warsaw be treated differently to anywhere else? If it could take place in Lublin, Tarnow, and Cracow — why is it not possible in Warsaw? The Germans are not deterred by any obstacles. We are in tremendous danger! It is imperative to consider every option of *hatzalah.* The pessimism grows and the dire situation is reflected on the faces of all present.

How to Avert the Evil Decree?

Various suggestions are put forward: Maybe we should collect huge sums of money or many kilos of gold to bribe the Gestapo. Some point out that the Gestapo also has special extermination squads who need to be neutralized. Others suggest sending a delegation to Hans Frank, the Governor General (of German-occupied Poland, known as *Generalgouvernement*). Perhaps we should consider setting up many factories and workshops to show Jews as a productive element and thus save them from deportation.

Rabbi Yosef Konigsberg, who recently arrived from Lublin (where he escaped the mass deportations by a miracle), described the harrowing scenes of the *churban* which he personally witnessed there. He pleaded with us not to fall prey to any false hopes but to instead explore every possible avenue immediately. He and Rabbi Zisha Friedman propose sending a courier to Switzerland to alert World Opinion. There is an urgent need that England should recognize all Jews — at least until the end of the war — as citizens of Palestine. It is important that America should take us under her protection. The Germans must be warned against any further steps. We must persuade the Pope to publicize a special appeal. We must....We should....

But what can we possibly do when we are all locked into a vast prison? How can we feasibly dispatch couriers to Switzerland when we cannot even cross to the next street without being shot at? And will those living abroad finally comprehend fully the real danger of total annihilation? Will they try — can they indeed manage — to sway World Opinion? World Opinion is such a fickle creature.

The meeting proceeds ponderously, and the day slowly turns to night. As the growing darkness penetrates the narrow attic, black shadows dance across the faces — and within the hearts — of the representatives of the largest *kehillah* in Europe. Slowly but surely realization dawns on the gathering that all our plans are unrealistic, impossible to carry out. The knowledge of our total helplessness grows more tangible by the minute as we realize that we are condemned to our fate.

The secret meeting breaks up slowly; everybody leaves separately so as not to attract unhealthy attention. As I slip out through a roundabout route into Krochmalna Street, the crush is as great as usual. Staring people with sunken faces and hooded eyes push and shove each other in their desperate struggle to earn a crust of bread. All exert themselves to somehow keep their heads above water and not sink into oblivion. Can they survive?

In my imagination I can already see the shadow of the *malach hamaves* hovering over the crowded streets. Can they possibly win; will all of us win? I return home deeply depressed, bereft of all hope.

Monday, July 20

Rumors of the rapidly approaching "resettlement" grow apace. In my office at the Kehillah — now *Judenrat* — Library, my colleague Dr. Schimkovits tells me that all his rich friends have smuggled themselves out through breaches in the Ghetto walls to hide in the Aryan section. Before they left, they told him they have firm evidence that the expulsions will begin on Wednesday, July 22.

Rabbi Yosef Moshe Haber (Kehillah President of Kalisch) and Rabbi Zisha Friedman approach me and ask, "*Nu, vos vet zein?*" So I enter the office of the Kehillah President, the architect Czerniakow, and ask him the same question. He replies, "Officially I have been told nothing."

I can understand the underlying meaning of such a reply — in fact, it was enough to steal a glance at Czerniakow's face to read the whole truth. I return to the library where I meet the famous historian Professor Dr. Meir Balaban. He had always been a pessimist and now he is completely disillusioned. He confides in me the secret that his brother-in-law, Dr. Alter (director of the Tachkemoni Seminary), has fled to the Aryan side with all his children.

Tuesday, July 21

The Gestapo Prepares for Deportations

When I crossed over to the Aryan side this morning (as the records director I had an official pass allowing me to visit the City Library at the Town Hall) I met a non-Jewish acquaintance, Dr. Lagavov, who is now working for a chemical firm, and he also told me that the deportations will begin on Wednesday, July 22. I hurried back to my office. But as I arrive at the Ghetto entrance on Grzybowska Street, I find an increased German security presence in front of the gate and I notice they are cementing that gate closed — in fact, I was the last to pass through that entrance. As I later discovered, the Germans were tightening the noose around us by sealing four out of the seven Ghetto gates leading to the Aryan section.

I entered the Kehillah buildings at 26–28 Grzybowska Street to find a larger crowd than usual. They are waiting for something to happen, without knowing quite what to expect. "Something" does indeed happen. Three cars full of SS arrive and enter the *Judenrat* building. After ten minutes they come out again, bringing with them some Kehillah members: Avraham Gefner, Rabbi Shimshon Stockhammer, the editor A. B. Ackerman, Bulislav Rosenblum, and the engineer Stoltzman (later I heard they also took Dr. Driblinski and Winter from the Ghetto supply office). All those arrested were taken to Pawiak prison to be held as hostages — it was believed against Jewish resistance during the deportations.

The panic in the Ghetto is now very great. What can happen next? Within a few hours Gefner, Stoltzman, and Driblinski were released. No official notice of the deportation has been issued but everyone realizes what is about to take place.

After midday a Gestapo car cruises through the Ghetto streets, firing randomly at passersby. Tens of Jews were killed in Karmelicka Street and Chlodna Street and the panic rises to fever pitch.

Crowds Fight for Labor Cards

The pace on the crowded street quickens extraordinarily. Everybody rushes back and forth seeking employment in the workshops. Above all they seek a position in the German factories set up in the Ghetto — Tobbens, Shultz, Dehring, and Sneh — by using all manner of bribes and *protexia* (influence). Huge sums are paid for any position in one of those factories. Those with energy and enterprise set up workshops of their own, mainly to process German goods — they buy sewing machines and set to work.

I enter the house of my cousin Yaakov Frankel from Bilitz, where he was a well-known textile factory owner. Now he and his whole family (including Shirkel his father-in-law, Rabbi Rabinowitz his brother-in-law, and Perel Kornitzer, the widow of the Cracow Rav) roll up their sleeves and begin working — confident that no one engaged in productive work will be deported.

I pass by Nowolipie Street where the firm of Shultz has been established in the home of the Chasidic industrialist Avraham Hendel. Huge crowds, mainly religious Jews — *yeshivah bachurim, rabbanim,* and Chasidim — gather in front of the two factory gates, since a religious Jew might find a placement here with Avraham Hendel's help; whereas that would be very difficult, if not impossible, anywhere else. But it is very hard to reach Hendel. While thousands line up outside, the factory gates are firmly locked and bolted. Every so often, a small wicket gate is opened, but the Jewish guard allows only one or two to enter.

Huge crowds form outside all the other factories, too, but these are made up of a different kind entirely. In the streets of Leszno and Prosta, where W. B. Tobbens is situated, many Zionists gather since Menachem Kirschenbaum, the Zionist leader, holds great sway here. While in front of Hoffmann in Nowolipki Street are crowds of Bundists hoping for the recommendations of Mauricy Orzech, who personally invested large sums in this business. In short "every tradesman turned to his fellow craftsman"; all help each other as much as possible.

Thousands also line up in front of 80 Leszno Street (the premises of the old "Collegium" Gymnasium-High School), where work cards are now issued confirming the holder as a factory employee — since they believe card-holders will not be deported.

Finally, I arrive at my own office in Grzybowska Street, and again thousands wait outside. Men seek official marriage certificates to protect their wives, since there is also a rumor that those holding marriage certificates will not be deported. Inside the Kehillah, too, depression reigns; everybody believes that workers alone will not be expelled.

Incidentally, in the house of Rabbi Yitzchak Meir Kanal at 6 Twarda Street are also large crowds — busily getting married! Bachelors who have work cards marry women who have no work, to save them from deportation. These mass marriages are conducted in great haste. Zionist *chalutzim* marry *chalutzot; tzukunftisim* (Bundists) marry *tzukunftisiot*. Women still unmarried seek "husbands." The ancient prophesy rings true: "And on that day seven women will clutch at one man saying we will eat our own bread, wear our own clothes — just allow your name to protect us."

Wednesday, July 22

Warsaw's Destruction Begins

The deportation rumors are confirmed; the catastrophe begins. Early this morning, at 6 A.M., my neighbor bangs on my door. "Have you heard? About fifty Jews were dragged from their beds and shot in the street!" Names are mentioned — both known and unknown to me — as we try and discover a common factor, but it is impossible. These were people from all walks of life and every strand of society: rich and poor, young and old, working class, lawyers, and businessmen. The only possible rationale we can fathom is to cause panic. If so, this is the prelude to the bloodbath.

I run to the Kehillah building nearby. Groups of men gather in the courtyard whispering among themselves — what does it all mean and what will it portend? At 11 A.M., three cars arrive with the letters "Pol" on the side (at first we mistook this for "Poland," later we discover it meant "*Politzei*"). A few Gestapo and SS officers emerge, enter the Kehillah President Czerniakow's office, and close the door behind them. After being closeted with him for about half an hour, they leave the premises.

With the speed of lightning the news spreads: "*Aussiedlung*!" This terrible word sows the fear of death. (Strange how the Jews accepted this German euphemism, meaning only "resettlement," instead of using clearer language like pogrom or mass murder.) I enter Czerniakow's board room. One look at him was enough — the chalk white face, shaking hands, and staring eyes that see nothing. Around him sit a few *Judenrat* members. Finally Czerniakow notices me and points to a scrap of paper on his desk. "Is there no official notice?" I ask. "No," comes the reply. "This is all there is."

I recognize Czerniakow's writing and begin to read, the letters dancing before my eyes. Later I made a copy for the archives. (The Germans tried to cover up their war crimes by not issuing written instructions; everything was dictated or given over verbally. The *Aussiedlung-befehl* of July 22, 1942 was dictated to Czerniakow. Later decrees were only transmitted orally.)

The Ghetto Surrounded

I walk out into the street as does everybody else thirsting for news, only to discover that from this morning the Ghetto has been surrounded by Ukrainian militia! These include some Latvians and Lithuanians — *malachei chavalah* (angels of destruction) of every type. Anyone approaching the Ghetto walls is shot on the spot. We are ensnared in a trap secured with seven locks; there is no way out, no escape. And can those who managed to get out possibly hide there?

The Jews who had already gone over to the Aryan side return to the Ghetto. It is impossible to live there among informers and blackmailers. We are all in the Nazis' grasp; we have been abandoned to our most dangerous enemy, who have condemned us all to total destruction.

The Aussiedlung-Befehl

Groups of Jews gather in front of the notice boards pasted with the *Aussiedlung* orders trying to extract some nuggets of hope. It clearly states that the decree does not apply to *Judenrat* or Joint officials, or workers employed by the workshops or German firms, and it further promises that all those capable of work will also be allowed to stay. If so, the decree really only applies to those dependant on welfare (mainly refugees) or those without work or a roof over their heads.

People begin roughly adding all this up. *Judenrat* officials amount to about 10,000, and with their families that comes to about 50,000. Officials and families of the Joint (which under the Germans became known as ZSS — *Zydowska Samopomoc Spoleczna* or Jewish Communal Self-Help) also comes to 50,000. Factory workers and their families totaled 200,000. There were another 10,000 capable of work and if you take into account their families, then the *Aussiedlung* affects "only" about 50,000 Jews. (Officially there were 387,000 Jews registered in the Warsaw Ghetto, but unofficially the numbers were estimated at about 450,000 and later estimates put the number above 500,000. No accurate figures actually existed.)

As a result, the pressure to obtain work at any price and by any means intensifies. Every avenue or influence is pursued to obtain a work-permit — seen rather as a life-permit. People ask, beg, or threaten. A director of a factory suddenly becomes a "*meyuches*," in his hands may depend their fate: for life or death. In front of Tobbens and Shultz thousands line up, desperate to escape the sinking ship, for the ship is surely sinking.

Despite all their exceptions and promises not to harm any workers, disillusion begins to set in — woe to anyone who has to rely on German promises! People still clutch at faint hopes, but fear gnaws at their hearts. Meanwhile, since the Ghetto has been tightly sealed off, smuggling has also become impossible and inflation soars. The price of bread climbs to 35 zlotys a kilo, and difficult to obtain at that. So a new terror looms — starvation.

The first victims of the *Aussiedlung* are already rounded up: refugees from the surrounding townlets who were subsisting on welfare or staying at refugee centers, as well as prisoners from the "Jewish Prison" in Gesia Street (how petty the "crimes" they committed). All are loaded onto horse-drawn wagons.

As I pass the corner of Zamenhof and Muranowska Streets at a late hour, a Ukrainian patrol attempts to drag away a blind man soliciting *tzedakah*. He is an invalid from the First World War and his chest is covered with medals. (One of the Germans' first orders was the payment of Jewish war invalids' and widows' pensions.)

It is a tragic sight; the blind Jew does not understand what they want from him or where they are taking him. He produces documents, points to his medals, but the Ukrainians just guffaw at the spectacle. The small boy who usually guides the blind beggar speaks to the officer in charge of the patrol and asks if he can go with him. In reply the German kicks him viciously and the young child falls weeping onto the sidewalk. The wagon moves off as the blind man is loaded on. Haunted by the heartrending sobs and pleas of the small boy, I flee this terrible scene. "Not far" answers the German when the blind Jew asks him where he is being taken.

"Not far" is Stawki Street and the railway yard where goods were usually loaded or unloaded for the Ghetto. Here the Jews were now loaded into freight wagons and transported "*Nach Osten* — eastward" to quote the German euphemism. Where that really means, no one knows.

The Night of Tears

As night falls I finally reach home, my brain bursting with terrifying images. Crossing our courtyard I notice our small *shtiebl*. (Because of the danger of being caught out on the street, every block organized its own private *minyan.*) About twenty men sit on upturned benches — it's *Tisha B'Av* tonight! Two flickering candles at the temporary *amud* dimly light up the bent heads, with their eyes staring into the far distance, as that heartrending tune wells up: "*Eichah...*"

The tune that was perhaps first composed at the exile from Jerusalem and has since absorbed the tears of generations.

Every age has its particular *Eichah.* But somehow this *Eichah* from our generation has a special ring to it, different to that from any previous calamity. Perhaps it is the very last *Eichah.*

"*How alone it sits, the great city of many inhabitants....*" Indeed how alone, how forlorn we are today.

"*All her pursuers entrapped her in dire straits.... I called to my friends but they betrayed me.*" How true, how real those ancient lamentations read; how accurate they describe our present catastrophe. That was when it all started, when we were driven from our land and lost our sovereignty 1872 years ago. Today is but another link in a long chain.

We Jews of Warsaw, sons of those exiles, sit on the ground to mourn our own personal *churban*, the destruction of a major *kehillah* — the largest and most vigorous in Europe — which resulted from that earlier *Churban.* We weep at our fate, a nation without a land, within the grasp of our fiercest enemy and condemned to death. We grieve both for the loss of the *Beis Hamikdash* and the extinction of our lives. True our lives were full of suffering, yet we always harbored hopes that will now never be realized. Yes, our lives were tough but despite everything they were still rich and purposeful. Now, however, our enemies scheme to wipe us all off the face of the earth.

Thursday, July 23

Thousands Dragged to Umschlagplatz

In the Ghetto there is complete panic laced with utter despair. Ukrainian, Latvian, and Lithuanian militia systematically surround blocks of houses, then one of them enters the courtyard and orders all the inhabitants out to assemble in the courtyard. Then they are lined up in rows and marched off to the *Umschlagplatz* (deportation railway yard).

The Germans force the *Judenrat*'s Jewish policemen to assist in the mass deportations. Generally it is the old or destitute who are expelled. Certificates from the Joint and *Judenrat* are ignored, just as the work cards are. There are heartbreaking scenes as those condemned beg and implore for mercy, but to no avail.

"Exceptional incidents" also occur. One building at 80 Zelazna Street, owned by Eliyahu Mazar (past Kehillah President of Warsaw), was surrounded by SS; they ordered all the inhabitants into the street, where most were shot and the remainder taken to the *Umschlagplatz*. No certificates or documents were of any help here since someone threw a stone from one of the windows at German officers — or so the Gestapo allege.

The widespread fear reaches fever pitch.

Czerniakow Commits Suicide

Though it was getting late, I was still in my office when two SS officers arrive and demand to see Czerniakow. As he was at home, the Kehillah official (and *talmid chacham*) Rabbi Shmuel Harbstein was sent to fetch him. After fifteen minutes, Czerniakow arrived and met with the SS in his boardroom; they left after about ten minutes. Czerniakow then rang his bell and asked his *shammash* to fetch him a glass of water. He was alone for only a few minutes when one of the clerks, Marcel Reich, knocked on his door but received no reply. Eventually he pushed the door open and found Czerniakow's lifeless body. He alerted the *Judenrat* executive and called for medical help, but there was nothing they could do. Dr. Milikovski looked at the cramped body, glassy eyes, mouth clamped tightly shut, and pronounced his verdict: death by poisoning. Adam Czerniakow, Kehillah and *Judenrat* President, had swallowed cyanide crystals and not suffered very long.

He left no will or suicide note, but in his notebook on his desk he had written the number 7000, which presumably meant he had to supply for extinction another 7000 souls immediately that day (that at any rate was how we understood it, erroneously as it later turned out). Until then Czerniakow had firmly believed — and often declared that belief — that we would outlive the German oppression and yet experience a better future. Now he had suddenly realized the gaping chasm yawning in front of his Kehillah. All his plans and hopes collapsed in front of the cruel reality. Rather than become a mere tool of the enemy, he took his life and died with honor.

Czerniakow had a multifaceted character. Though trained as an engineer with a precise eye for exact detail, he was also well read and a poet. Despite coming from an assimilationist background, he possessed a warm Jewish heart and never lost touch with the working classes, whom he represented politically, and always sought to better their lot. On the eve of the War, he was only a Kehillah board member, but when the previous Kehillah President, Mauricy Meisel, fled Warsaw in September 1939, he was elected in his stead. He stayed at his post from

November 8, 1939 to July 23, 1942, trying his utmost to prevent the worst Nazi excesses, rescue whatever could be saved, ease the unbearable burden, and above all "*a dorch tzukummen*" — somehow survive the terrible tragedy.

At his last meeting with the German Ghetto Commissar Auerswald (previously a well-known Berlin lawyer and the personal advocate of the famous Jewish industrialist Klausner), Auerswald had claimed that the "Jews are parasites," to which Czerniakow had replied (according to Dr. Milikovski, who was also present and repeated the conversation to me), "When we Jews arrived in Poland at the invitation of King Casimir the Great, there were only forests and empty tracts of land. Towns and cities, factories and blocks of houses, were built here with our inventiveness and energy. Take a look at the streets, industry, business, banking, or manufacturing — all were developed by the Jews. Our one mistake was to put all our efforts and energy into the land of our enemies. We built on a smoking volcano instead of directing our attentions to our own homeland."

Czerniakow the assimilationist had belatedly become a Zionist under the pressure of the German oppression. Earlier, on Sunday, July 5, he had told me privately, "All my life I worked hard and productively only to hear that I am a parasite, to suffer from those murdering beasts, and to witness such humiliation, persecution, and barbarism. If I yet could, I would tramp to Eretz Yisrael on foot to break stones like the lowliest *chalutz*. After this war is over, I will do just that and nothing and nobody will stop me...."

But the cruel foe put an end to his hopes and dreams, just as they had done to many thousands of others who had dreamt of a better future in Eretz Yisrael.

Friday, July 24

Early this morning, at 5:30 A.M., I took part in Czerniakow's *levayah*. There were very few of us — scarcely a *minyan* — since the Germans insisted on a top secret funeral. He was buried in a plot of many world famous Warsaw Jews. Nearby lay buried Professor Simon Ashkenazi, the Polish representative at the League of Nations. I read snatches of his tombstone inscription "Educationalist, Historian, Statesman... let us fight for an independent Poland and serve a free Poland." In the same row lies Ludwig Zamenhof, the inventor of the international language *Esperanto*, who fought for better understanding between nations. This is how Jews served the nations of the world, I thought to myself, and this is how their dream has been shattered.

Somebody else says *Kaddish*, as Czerniakow's son is serving in the Russian army — perhaps he will avenge his father's death. The widow, Felicia Czerniakow, a noted pedagogue, weeps quietly. But there is a great hurry to fill in the grave and return safely back to the Ghetto — who knows what might have happened in the meantime and what may await us. I leave the cemetery with the feeling that we have just buried not merely an individual but a whole epoch.

Returning from the funeral I find the burial carts of *Chessed V'Emes* busy plying their trade — Warsaw has already become a factory of death. And not a few of us envy these victims of the German murderers; perhaps their *mazal* is greater than ours. They suffered relatively little and were at least granted a Jewish burial, their final resting place is known — more or less — as is their *yahrzeit*, whereas those deported...who knows? People are scared to follow their terrifying train of thought. "And I praise the dead who have already died from the living who still live" (*Koheles* 4:2).

Meanwhile the machinery for our continuing destruction functions efficiently. Wagonloads of unfortunate Jews guarded by the militiamen trundle to the *Umschlagplatz*. The victims vary: women and children, the sick and the elderly. Some weep and beg for mercy, others produce documents, certificates, or try to explain their situation. However, some show no emotion at all and stand in the carts apparently totally apathetic. Those who have not completely lost the will to live try to send messages to friends and relations, hoping they will somehow save them.

But none of this is of any use; all are taken to the *Umschlag* — to destruction, as everyone instinctively fears, though nobody knows any details yet. However, some claim to have received letters from those first deported and a small chink of light is lit within the dark chasm of fear and despair.

At my office I find the depressingly usual bustle hither and thither, shuffling pieces of paper about in a mindless attempt to appear useful. Mrs. Sala Zeitlin (wife of the writer and poet Aaron Zeitlin), who runs the *Judenrat*'s taxation department, has "appointed" several more officials to send out tax demands to Kehillah members who have not yet paid (probably because most of them are no longer among the living). Among these new "officials" I recognize Elchanan Zeitlin, Abraham Walderstein, and Josef Wegmeister — all well-known communal activists.

Generally the *Judenrat* workforce has grown; in this way they hope to save Jews, since it is widely believed that *Judenrat* officials will not be deported. Now they are all busy sending out questionnaires that are no longer relevant, replying to letters whose senders have already been deported, and involve themselves in other totally irrelevant and unimportant work as long as it appears to the outsider they are doing something.

Nochum Remba (brother of the editor of *Hamashkif* in Tel Aviv) is busy with the *chalutzim* trying to get them positions in either the *Judenrat* or the workshops. The *rabbanim* use their influence to enroll their sons and sons-in-law in the *Judenrat*'s Religious Department, which I head. Though this section no longer has much practical application, its workforce has been considerably enlarged. When I took over in 1937 it had thirty-eight employees, now it has over one hundred and I am still recommending new appointees from among the famous *rabbanim*, activists, and religious writers — such as Yosef Moshe Haber (Kalisch Kehillah President), Wolf Lipsker (the journalist and satirist "*Lamed-Vav*"), Yitzchak Rabinowitz, and others.

Meanwhile, the *Judenrat* Board call a special sitting and elect a new Kehillah President: Mark Lichtenbaum, a well-known activist and architect who has built many of Warsaw's communal buildings. Who knows if he will be merely a passive witness to the impending catastrophe or if he will manage to save anything from the destruction? The architect and secretary of the Polish Central Jewish Businessmen League, Abraham Stoltzman, is elected vice president, as is Dr. N. Wileikovsky, a well-known Warsaw lawyer and now the president of ZSS (*Zydowska Samopomoc Spoleczna* or Jewish Communal Self-Help, which replaced the Joint).

7000 Victims Daily

The SS murder squads (or, to give them their official title, SS *Und Zicherheit-Politzei,* District Lublin, *Einsatz Reinhard*) have established an office — with Kehillah funds — which they call the "*Befehl-stelle.*" From their modern office — replete with telephones, typewriters, stencil duplication machines, and full-time shorthand typists — come all the latest decrees. The murder machine works with the latest modern technology: after all, we are in the twentieth century. Everything is working well according to the fiendish plan, already thought out and planned in advance according to the German system.

Brandt, the Gestapo officer, told me with satisfaction, "*Die organisation klapt, 7000 teglich* — the organization works well, 7000 a day!" Every day Warsaw loses another 7000 innocent victims. On the wall of the *Befehl-stelle* hangs a large street map of the Warsaw Ghetto, and every day they flag certain blocks for *einkesslung* and *reinigen* ("encircling" and "cleansing"). They use military strategy and tactics, employ military terms like "blockade," against women and children, the sick and elderly — their helpless captives weakened by years of starvation and continual terror.

At 6:00 in the evening there is a respite. The amount required — 7000 — has been supplied and the day's work is complete. Now it is safe for us to venture out onto the streets, look for food, and exchange news and information. Today 7000 souls have been taken away to the *Umschlag* and so it will be tomorrow and the day after and the day after that — when will it all end? Will the sword of the *malach hamaves* ever return to its sheath?

Opinion is divided over this. Some say "only" 50,000 will be deported and the rest will be allowed to stay. They even claim to have information that the deportations will end on August 1.

Others have better news — letters and greetings have been received from the deportees who have apparently been taken to near Brisk. I met the coal merchant and well-known benefactor A. L. Sviko and he shows me a letter from someone deported; I check the postmark — July 23, Treblinka. I share this good news with others and then we discover there is also a "Treblinka 2," a labor camp which has been there for some time (later, that camp, too, was wiped out). Nonetheless this information brings some relaxation of tension. Yet it also increases the uncertainty, until the uncertainty outweighs our composure.

The pessimists — or more correctly the realists — read the situation completely differently. They see us as being face to face with mass murder and recognize the deportees' fate as total extinction — for all of us. People whose relatives have been deported clutch at the forlorn hope that "they are still alive," for if they are not, then there is little value to their own chances of survival. We are driven not by cold logic but by the sheer instinct to live. Yet we can clearly feel our end rapidly approaching with giant footsteps, against which we are completely defenseless — and the World remains silent.

Tuesday, July 28

Hunger Claims Its Victims

Most of the "supply-shops" that sell bread for ration card holders are closed. Either the owners have been deported or they have taken safer employment in the German workshops. Besides, no bread has recently been allowed in the Ghetto. Even the smuggling of food into the Ghetto has been stopped completely.

The only meager source of bread are the labor brigades (Jewish slave workers supplied by the Ghetto for outside industries), who smuggle in a loaf or two of bread. Usually the

German guards confiscate this bread, but occasionally some is sneaked past. Today the price of a kilogram loaf can be up to 100 zlotys. (Before the War a loaf cost 30 groszy; in the Ghetto before the deportations the price fluctuated between 16 and 20 zlotys.)

People die from hunger — literally. They collapse at home or in the street. Without a fuss, quietly, weakly, and helplessly they succumb to their fate. They are too scared to approach any of the soup kitchens, since anyone taking public welfare risks being immediately deported as "non-productive." Anyhow, most of these soup kitchens are likewise closed, except for three which feed workers at the German factories.

So people collapse in the street from the great heat; men racked by hunger and fear flit through courtyards like shadows. Now we have a new dilemma: what is preferable, to die from hunger or in the death trains? The *navi* taught us (*Eichah* 4:9), "More fortunate were the victims of the sword than the victims of the famine." This cruel choice is laid before thousands of Warsaw's Jews, weakening their resolve and their will to survive or resist.

The hunger penetrates everywhere, into rich and poor households alike. Today I, too, felt the full weight of the famine. I had no bread and fasted all day. My head is heavy and my limbs feel like lead. I move with great difficulty and sit apathetically in my office. They tell me that nearby I can get a quarter-kilo bread for 25 zlotys, but I cannot summon the energy or inclination to go there. In the meantime I received a plate of soup from the Kehillah kitchen and begin to live again.

Only now can I comprehend what starvation is all about; the greatest writer cannot describe it adequately. I have read many books and novels on the subject but I never really knew what hunger actually meant until I personally experienced it first hand. Now I understand why the Talmud forbids us to fill our stomachs when a famine rages outside; we must empathize with the pain of our fellowmen and the community. And it is insufficient to sympathize in thought alone. Only by cutting one's own food intake can one unite with the communal sorrow. Only today did I fully understand and experience the suffering felt by hundreds of thousands of my brethren in the years 1940–42.

Wednesday, July 29

With Their Lives They Earn Their Bread

Today the following announcement was hung up on placards around the Ghetto:

> Anyone who voluntarily comes forward to the *Umschlagplatz* on the 29th, 30th, and 31st of July '42 will receive from the *Judenrat*, on German instructions, three kilogram of bread and one kilogram of marmalade for the journey.

Three kilograms of bread and a kilo of marmalade are a veritable treasure now when people are dying from hunger. Crowds stream towards the *Umschlag*. They persuade themselves, "Perhaps it is really only a resettlement from here to somewhere in the east." Many Jews creep from their hiding places after having reached their limit — both physically and mentally — and are unable to withstand any more.

I meet an old acquaintance on the street. His back is loaded with a heavy pack and he leads a young boy and girl by the hand. I take a look at these children. They have faces like skeletons, shriveled hands as thin as sticks, only their eyes glow with vitality — the deep, dark eyes of Jewish children. They do not speak, neither do they cry or complain. Yet they seem to understand everything. I can read it all in their eyes; such suffering and such wisdom in those so young. I recollect Bialik's aphorism: "There are no Jewish children; just underage Jews." On their young, weak shoulders lies the burden of a whole nation inflicted with so much recent pain. It appears that these tender souls can sense the approaching end.

"It is already three days that we haven't touched a crumb of bread or tasted a drop of soup," their despondent father explains, "so I have decided to travel."

"Travel?" I ask in surprise. "Travel where? The Ghetto is completely cut off."

"I will go with everybody else — from the *Umschlagplatz*!" he replies. I try to talk him round, somehow change his mind. I ask him where his wife and other two children are. "They are already *there*," he says, pointing. "They were caught last week. Now we will be all together. Besides I can't bear to see these children suffer anymore..." and the tears run freely down his face.

We see Rabbi Alexander Zisha Friedman, one of the most famous religious leaders in Poland, and my friend goes up to him — he wants to take his leave and hopes to hear a word of encouragement. Reb Zisha is struck dumb with overwhelming pain and instead he shakes the man's hand warmly. Then my friend turns and walks hurriedly off, as if he is in a hurry to receive the three kilogram of bread and one kilogram of jam — which in reality is an appointment with his murderers.

I exchange glances with Reb Zisha. He opens his mouth to say something, but he cannot say a word; he is completely dumbstruck. I have known him for a long time: he is one of the leaders of Agudas Yisrael, a great *talmid chacham* who has already compiled *sefarim*. Usually he is a brilliant speaker who can always hit upon the exact word, apt for each occasion, and his charismatic *drashos* captured the hearts of many. But now he stands before me helpless in shock, and he has not a word to say — "Even the wise are struck dumb...."

Today is also the 15th of Av. "There were no happier festivals for the Nation of Israel than *Chamishah-Asar B'Av*," says the Talmud, "when the young girls would go out to dance in the orchards." Ancient times, a bygone era. Could it be that the nation which is now being led like cattle to the slaughter once had a land and harvest festivals of its own?

Today our youth do not go dancing in the orchards, they run to the slaughterhouse — in pursuit of three kilograms of bread. In my ears ring the ancient prophecy, "And I will arrest the sounds of rejoicing and happiness, the songs of brides and bridegrooms from the towns of Yehudah and the streets of Jerusalem" (*Yirmeyahu* 7:34). Actually all these dire prophecies have come true more than once.

AUGUST 1942

Motza'ei Shabbos, August 1

Massacre in Nowolipie

What a day of terror and fear. The murdering demons run amok in Nowolipie Street where Shultz (the large brush factory) and Schilling (the shoemaking workshops) are situated. All the houses there were populated by workers and their families who were believed to be relatively safe. Did not the original *Aussiedlung* specifically promise that the workers would be spared? Yet particularly here, on this street, the barbarians vent their unbridled rage.

The Ukrainian militia — well trained in the art of pogroms since 1919 — arrived here early this morning, surrounded the buildings, and ordered all the inhabitants to assemble in the courtyards. The murderous beasts were too impatient to wait until Treblinka; they were eager to massacre Jews with their own hands. They chased after their unfortunate victims and entered the buildings, shooting and murdering. Tens of Jews were killed, including the Radomsker Rebbe, HaRav Rabinowitz, with his whole family and son-in-law, the learned Gaon Rabbi Moshe Rabinowitz. They were all shot in their flat, with their *talleisim* on in the middle of davening.

The wagons of Pinkert's Undertakers ply back and forth, but they cannot keep pace with the murderers. As the news of this massacre spreads, the panic and fear increases tenfold.

Among those who were deported today was Rabbi Avraham Mordechai Rogovy, the editor of Warsaw's *Yiddishe Togblatt,* with his whole family. The Kehillah tried to save him from deportation but he refused to part from his large family — eighteen souls, including his parents and in-laws.

Tuesday, August 4

How the Mighty Have Fallen

A sensation today in town! The Gestapo death squad sentenced Mr. Mauricy Kohn and Mr. Heller to death today. These were two young men from Lodz who established the business firm Kohn and Heller in the Ghetto and had very good contacts with the Gestapo. Many were the stories told about them; they even managed to import some Jews from Lodz to work for them (this was at the time when living conditions in the Lodz Ghetto were much worse than Warsaw's).

They also obtained the license to operate *kunke* (horse-drawn omnibuses), which was the only transport service in the Warsaw Ghetto. Generally they had all sorts of contacts and *protexias* and were the first to know of the impending mass deportations. During these deportations, many people — including friends and relatives — sought refuge and influence from them.

Yet, today, when the death squad arrived at the *Judenrat*'s police headquarters, these two men were shot and killed by Wande, the Gestapo head of the Jewish section. Their "crime" was described by the Gestapo as "helping to evade the *Aussiedlung* decree" (apparently mass murder of Jews has now been legalized into a statutory law, and evading it is now constituted a crime).

"Even among the mighty cedars, the flames have taken hold."

Sunday, August 9

Liquidation of Small Ghetto

Every day brings its own crop of "news." Today new placards were posted up in the Ghetto.

> The small Jewish Quarter (i.e., Ghetto) reaching up till the corner of Zelazna-Leszno streets must be evacuated by Monday, August 10, at 6 P.M. Its inhabitants must relocate their residences to the large Jewish Quarter. Any Jew found within the confines of the small Jewish Quarter after 6 P.M., August 10, will be shot.
>
> Signed:
> *Befehlshaber Der SS Und Zicherheit Politzei*

Verbally the reason given is "the reduction of Jews in the Ghetto." Apparently we must leave our flats — and without delay. This new decree affects the roads: Grzybowska, Zelazna, Twarda, Panska, Marianska, Sliska, Sienna, Komitetowa, Rynkowa, Grzybowski Square, and Niecala. Jews who have lived here for decades have to vacate their homes, shops, businesses, and synagogues within 24 hours.

Strictly speaking, they are allowed to take everything, but in reality they take very little. As there is no longer a removal service available in the Ghetto (besides a very few rickshaws drawn by humans), they take only what they can carry on their backs. Since early morning, crowds carrying their pitiful belongings stream towards Leszno-Nalewki: women carry children while men hold suitcases or small packs in their hand — all that is left after a lifetime of bitter struggle.

A few SS with Ukrainian militiamen stand at the corner of Zelazna-Leszno and every so often they drag groups of people — usually the elderly or women — out of streaming crowds and throw them into the trucks for transportation to the *Umschlagplatz*. Jews begin to circumvent the Nalewki crossroad, which leads into the large Ghetto, and wait until evening when one is safer from these snatch squads.

Before evening I walk through streets where the pulse of Jewish life once beat so strongly. But the "small Ghetto" is steadily emptying. I pass 26–28 Grzybowska Street, where the Kehillah buildings were located. Now they, too, are being moved to the old military prison in 19 Zamenhof Street. All that is left in this ghetto are German-owned workshops, such as Tenens and Dehring (in Komitetowa Street and the Kehillah courtyard), which employ Jews, and a few blocks of houses in Prosta and Ciepla Streets where their Jewish workers live.

The irredeemable optimists draw the hopeful conclusion that this signals the end of deportations and the situation will now stabilize.

Monday, August 10

Judenrat Moves

Today the Germans informed the *Judenrat* that to facilitate the evacuation from the small Ghetto to the large Ghetto, there will be a lull in the *Aussiedlung*, and in fact today there was no blockade on any streets or houses. But the Germans keep up their tactic of seizing Jews from among the crowds streaming through into the large Ghetto. These sudden swoops cause great panic in the Kehillah and the continuing hunger saps our strength further.

Today the Kehillah also moves to new premises. The imposing building at 26–28 Grzybowska Street, which for many years was at the center of Jewish life in the Polish metropolis, steadily empties. The typewriters, together with some of the furniture and files, are removed, but most of the equipment and papers are left behind. Time is pressing and we must hurry to complete the evacuation of the small Ghetto. Most documents are abandoned, since they are now irrelevant, and most of the Kehillah archives were also left behind.*

I take my leave from the place where I had worked for so long; the Kehillah hall and rooms are empty, the doors and windows thrown open to the elements. On the floor are scattered papers, papers, and yet more papers — the last remnants of the vitality which once coursed through these premises. Now despondency and disillusion reign supreme.

Peering down into the emptiness of the great boardroom hang the paintings of Reb Eliyahu Kirschbraun (a previous Kehillah President and the Aguda representative in the Polish Sejm, or parliament) and Y. L. Peretz (who had been a Kehillah official). Two paintings representing two diametrically different world perspectives — both of which are being destroyed with all their history. The black wings of the *malach hamaves*

---

* Only much later, due to the efforts of Professor Dr. Meir Balaban, were these archives moved across to the Kehillah's new premises at 19 Zamenhof Street, where they were burnt during the Ghetto Uprising on April 24, 1943.

still hover above the central flame of Warsaw's Jewish life, now rapidly being extinguished.

Tuesday, August 11

A Sign of Defiance

Today we find ourselves in new accommodation. I received a temporary flat in Pawia Street and my office, the Records and Archives Department of the Kehillah, is now at 19 Zamenhof Street. Slowly we acclimatize to our new surroundings. Perhaps the change will be for the better: "*meshaneh makom*...a change of venue heralds a change in *mazal*." But so far our luck has not changed. After a half-day lull, the deportations resume with a vengeance.

In the afternoon we had two unpleasant "surprises." Dr. Meir Tauber (previously director of the State Seminary for Religious Teachers and now deputy head of the Kehillah School network) was leaving the Kehillah entrance, when Brandt from the Gestapo Jewish section was just passing. He seized him together with his wife and his only son of eighteen and sent them off to the *Umschlagplatz*. This was the first time that such a prominent *Judenrat* official was snatched on the street. This is extremely depressing for all of us, and his daughter, Channah, "rents the heavens" in her efforts to rescue her parents and brother — to no avail.

Also seized outside the Kehillah was the eighty-two year old Rav, Rabbi Yitzchak Meir Kanal, one of the most energetic and active of Warsaw's *rabbanim* and vice president of Agudas Rabbanim in Poland. Only yesterday, as the small Ghetto was being closed down, I overheard the elderly Rav, who had lived in Twarda Street, tell Rabbi Zisha Friedman, the famous Aguda leader, "I will never allow them to take me away from here — whatever happens. Here at least I will have a Jewish burial!"

Towards evening, a request came from the *Umschlag*: send a hearse for Rav Kanal, *zt"l*, who had been shot and killed. Afterwards we discovered that the elderly Rav had put up some resistance by trying to snatch a revolver from the German soldier guarding him.... Obviously he was shot and murdered on the spot. But he achieved his aim, he was not deported and received a decent burial.

As the first sign of resistance, his action receives respect, but it also causes fear in the Ghetto. Apparently there is little hope at the destination of the deportees, otherwise the wise and elderly Rav would not have acted the way he did. If so, our situation is as bad as it possibly can be.

Wednesday, August 12

Death March of Korczak's Orphans

Today they deported the orphanages. The number of orphans in the Ghetto is by no means inconsiderable. The German massacres, the hunger, and the typhus epidemic have all combined to produce many *yesomim*.

Dobra Wola (Good Will) was one of the larger orphanages in Warsaw and run by Abraham Gefner (previously president of the Businessmen Central Association and now director of the *Judenrat*'s Supply Department). However the oldest and largest of Warsaw's orphanages was the one run by Dr. Janusz Korczak-Goldschmidt in Krochmalna Street (recently relocated to Sliska Street.)

Janusz Korczak was famous throughout Poland and beyond — a first-class writer and the pride of the Polish *literati*, he had written many books both for and about children. An expert pedagogue, an exceptional educator, and a brilliant speaker — he was above all an endearing personality who radiated a unique blend of generosity and charity. Originally he had been a pediatrician with a large successful practice. But he gave up his profession, abandoned his rich clients, and sacrificed his career and prospects for the poorest of the poor and those unfortunate to have no parents.

To his orphans, he was both father and mother, granting them a home and surrounding them with love and affection. These children instinctively recognized his warm heart, and they showered "the doctor" (as they insisted on addressing him) with their undying gratitude. In this atmosphere of mutual affection, Korczak educated generations of pupils and closely followed their future progress with advice and practical help until they were capable of standing on their own two feet. From all corners of the globe — America, Eretz Yisrael, England, Australia, and New Zealand — letters arrive from his former pupils expressing their heartfelt gratitude as well as their longing to meet again their model and teacher.

His present pupils display a similar admiration — and no wonder. During the most difficult phases of occupation, as the hunger and suffering increased, all Korczak's thoughts were directed to one end alone: how to provide "his" children with a slice of bread, a plate of soup, or a cup of milk to sustain their life. Daily he knocked at the doors of the rich and powerful, activists and heads of various committees, to obtain bread for his beloved orphans. Their pain was his pain, and he did everything to provide them with some vitamins or fat; and when he finally managed to obtain something, his face would light up with joy. This was his only reward for sleepless nights and days full of worry.

Today he was ordered to "vacate" the orphanage. Korczak himself could really stay, since doctors are considered essential, and the *Judenrat* still retains enough clout to save him.* But Korczak refuses to save himself alone. He cannot bear to leave his orphans and decides to accompany them on their final journey.

All the children assemble in front of the orphanage in Sliska Street — so many children, from the almost adult to the very tiny — and though they are starved and weak they remain disciplined and well behaved. Some carry small packs while others clutch textbooks or notepads under their arms. None cry, but here and there a silent tear rolls down a famished cheek. They slowly descend the steps and line up in rows with a discipline wonderful to behold.

All eyes follow the "doctor"; with him at their side they feel almost safe. Korczak attends to his children with a frightening intensity: he buttons up the coat of one child, straightens the cap of a second and adjusts the satchel of a third — then he goes up to another child and carefully wipes away his tears.

The column of children begins to move, marching to their unknown destination. Many sense this is their final journey from which there is no return. Who knows how much potential, skill, talent, and Jewish treasures are contained within these precious young souls, now condemned to death. Yet they march so quietly, so purposefully towards their untimely end. Though the children are quiet they must instinctively realize what the future holds. Why else those silent tears on the faces of so many? Why else the frightening seriousness on their pale, starved faces? Yet still they march slowly, passively, and in line.

---

* Incidentally, doctors' repreive was only temporary and later doctors were deported, too.

At their head marches Janusz Korczak — the symbol of selfless love and charity overwhelmed by the cruel and evil enemy who knows no mercy. Humanity has been beaten by the beast of prey.

Monday, August 17

Kalischer Rav Deported

News spreads of a "blockade" on the streets of Pawia and Dzielna, and those seized are now being marched to the *Umschlagplatz*. Those captured include the Rav of Kalisch, Rav Mendel Alter, who was the president of the Polish Agudas Rabbanim. The *Judenrat* leader Lichtenbaum phones the Jewish police force and orders them to rescue Rabbi Alter. Rabbi Avraham Hendel, the director of the firm Schultz, sends couriers to the *Umschlag* to try and save the famed rabbi and *gaon*. No money or influence is spared.

Meanwhile the captives from Pawia Street are marched down Zamenhof Street and I see the Kalischer Rav marching among thousands of other Jews. He marches proudly, almost indifferently — he seems lost in deep thought. Around him walks his sons and daughters-in-law, his daughters and sons-in-law, including Rav Horowitz, the Rabbi of Bilchatow, and Rabbi Justman. Recently the Kalischer Rav has become the central figure in religious Jewry. From all over Poland people turn to him for advice and comfort. Important meetings were held in his fourth-floor flat at 11 Pawia Street. Rav Mendel Alter is an important religious leader exuding *emunah* and *bitachon*.

Now, on his behalf, every exertion is made to save him; Rabbi Zisha Friedman uses every avenue of influence and *protexia* open to him — Rabbi Mendel Alter is, after all, the most important religious authority left in the Ghetto. Everything possible is done to rescue him. But at 6 P.M. word comes from the "front" — the most frightening front of all — that it was all in vain. He had already been forced into one of the boxcars; and from there it is impossible to save anyone.

The brilliant mind, the great religious leader, the Rabbi of Kalisch, is with us no longer.

Tuesday, August 25

Ghetto Leaders "Selected"

"Selection" — that terrible word spreading so much dread, terror, and fear. Originally it meant the release of those with work cards from the deportations, but very soon "selection" came to mean something far worse. The SS would suddenly swoop on a factory or workers' dwellings, herd them out into the street, and line them all up into rows — and then decide the fate of each individual. Some would be sent to the *Umschlag* and the rest would be released for another day.

This "selection" could take hours, while the panic-stricken victims would try to weigh up their chances for life — or death. Feverishly they gather their official papers, work cards, and documents until the executioners finally arrive. One casual wave of the whip and their fate is decided.

Today I, too, savored the bitter taste of a selection. We were sitting in the offices of the Warsaw Kehillah archives — a group of writers and intellectuals masquerading as officials so as to shelter under the "protection" of the *Judenrat* — when I received an order from *Judenrat* president Lichtenbaum to assemble with my officials in the Kehillah courtyard. Immediately afterwards a second order from the Germans: anyone who remains behind in the

Kehillah building will be shot on the spot.

We all hurried downstairs, Dr. Schipper, Prof. Dr. Meir Balaban, Prof. Dr. Nachman Stein, Y. L. Orlean (director of the Beis Yaakov Seminary), Dr. S. Schimkovits, the editor A. N. Friedensohn, Dr. Mordechai Rosner, among others. Some of the *rabbanim* who have survived earlier purges — such as Rav Pinchas Ziemba, Rav Eliyahu Patman, Rav Yaakov Zamestchik, Rav Shloma Marker, Rav Pinchas Warsabiak, and Rav Leib Biderman — hide in an attic.

But two elderly *rabbanim*, Rav Noach Rogozinsky and Rav Zvi Yechezkel Michelsohn, come down with us. Apparently they believe that despite all their excesses, the Germans will not deport elderly *rabbanim* with such a long experience in the Kehillah.

In the courtyard we find a whole platoon of Ukrainian militia, together with chiefs of the Nazi death squad and "Jewish experts" from the Gestapo such as Brandt, Handke, Witos, etc. They rush us into line yelling, "*Schnell! Schnell! Schnell!*" Whoever is not fast enough gets hit with a whip. In the courtyard we stand on parade under the sweltering sun, bathed in sweat, and clutching pieces of paper. Eventually, we file singly past those evil murderers — Brandt, Mende, and Handke — their cruel eyes fixed on us.

They are not interested in our papers but in our appearance. If someone is young, tall, good looking, or even well dressed (somebody was saved by his leather coat), they send him to the right where those allowed to remain are gathered. If, however, they are not enamoured with his appearance, he is shown to the left together with all those destined for the *Umschlag*....

I wait for a long time with the others awaiting their destiny.

It is doubtful if my pale, tired appearance will earn me much credit. I watched how a famous personality like Professor Balaban passes their scrutiny; only after much discussion and thought is he allowed to stay. After him Dr. Schipper, Dr. Stein, Orlean, and Friedensohn step forward in turn. A *Judenrat* representative accompanies each with entreaties and they are all waved to the right. But no plea will suffice to save the two elderly *rabbanim*; I see Rav Michelsohn and Rav Rogozinsky among those on the left — sentenced to deportation from the *Umschlag*.

Rav Michelsohn stands in front of the killers, his back straight and his head held high. It looks as if he is totally indifferent to his situation, but in reality he is lost in thought. The eighty-six year old Warsaw Rav was previously the Rav of Plonsk for many years (indeed he was popularly known as "*Der Plonsker*")and had already authored forty-three *sefarim*, besides unpublished manuscripts. Now he stands abandoned, forlorn, and helpless within the Kehillah confines; he has been sentenced to destruction and calmly awaits his slaughter.

Besides him stands Rabbi Rogozinsky of Lithuanian extraction, a Rav with noble character. The fate of both has apparently been sealed.

Now Dr. Mordechai Rosner steps forward, pale, weak, and exhausted, and finds little favor in their eyes — to the left! With one wave of the hand the great *talmid chacham* and academic is condemned to death. After him a number of other officials are likewise removed from our ranks. I begin to scribble a note to my family in Lwow:* "*Know, dear Father, that I have been deported to an unknown destination and I wish to take my leave*

* This was Lemberg. Only afterwards did I discover that by then my father had already been taken.

from you all: from my brothers, sisters, and brothers-in-law. Live in peace and may Hashem be your Savior." A Jewish policeman promises me that if "something happens" he will send the postcard.

Meanwhile, I feel a strange calm creep over me, and my turn comes. I step forward apathetically as if I am strolling for pleasure. I catch a glimpse of Brandt's evil staring eyes. He stares at me angrily, like a wild beast of prey, and the awful thought crosses my mind — I am lost! Already he begins to wave his whip to the left. Just at that moment Mark Lichtenbaum, the *Judenrat* president, speaks up for me: "But this is Seidman, the director of our Archives..." and the *Judenrat* vice president Stoltzman interjects, "He is also the director of the Civil Bureau," and the other vice president Dr. Wileikovsky chimes in: "He is *unentbehrlich* — indispensable!" Brandt waves his hand to the right, and I am saved.

In the crowd on the right I had nearly all my colleagues, "only" a few are missing. Strangely I feel no happiness at being saved, just apathy. After about an hour the selection is over; about half of the *Judenrat*'s officials have been taken to the *Umschlag*. Those officially recognized by the Germans (how invidious is that recognition) return to their offices, and the Ukrainian militia depart.

The other *rabbanim* finally leave their hiding place, but some Ukrainians who had secretly concealed themselves notice their appearance and drag them away to the *Umschlag*. This was how the *rabbanim* Rav Shloma Marker, Rav Yaakov Zamestchik, Rav Eliyahu Patman, Rav Pinchas Warsabiak, and Rav Leib Biderman were seized — Rav Pinchas Ziemba was saved by a miracle. So, at the tragic end of our shocking selection, most of Warsaw's *rabbanim* — eight in all — were taken away in one day.

Slowly, painfully slowly, we return to our senses. Each of us begins to recall his own personal miracle — saved, but for how long? Will this be the last selection? We have survived for the moment but we are badly shocked and very much ashamed. With our own eyes, we watched as our brethren were dragged away to the slaughter. In our concern for our own survival, we were forced to be mere passive onlookers. How pitiful our lives now seem by comparison. Is this, too, called living?

Wednesday, August 26

Rebbe Moshe Betzalel Seized

In what has become an almost daily occurrence, today another famous religious personality was caught — Rebbe Moshe Betzalel Alter, brother of the Gerrer Rebbe. And once again great efforts were invested in saving him. Couriers were dispatched, money was laid out — Rabbi Avraham Hendel himself put forward 8000 zlotys.

Finally, after much exertion and perseverance, they managed to have him returned from the *Umschlagplatz*. But he did not *bensch gomel* (recite the thanksgiving blessing) on his escape from death. He returned to his "work" among his pliers, nails, and old shoes at the shoemakers' workshop where he spends most of the time reciting by heart *Mishnayos*, *Zohar*, and *Tehillim*. He works at Schultz on the same bench as Rav Klonimos Schapira (the Piasznow Rebbe and author of *Chovos HaTalmidim*), the Alexander Rebbe, and Rav Meir Alter, the eldest son of the Gerrer Rebbe.

Thursday, August 27

On the Death March

Today I am caught among the multitude being taken to the *Umschlagplatz* for deportation to... I am scared to continue that train of thought.

And so we march — *binoreinu ub'zekenenu,* "with our youth and our elders" — old and young, women and children, rich and poor. "*Alle zenen gleich*" as Rubinstein the town *meshugene* used to chant; now we are all indeed equal (perhaps Rubinstein was not so mad after all).

And so we march — in lines of eight abreast, according to the German system, in our many thousands, and the crowd stretches back as far as the eye can see. How often have I heard the cliché "the Jewish masses," but never did I really feel this so tangibly until today. Everybody presses tightly together, so united in suffering, so totally an *am echad.* Never before have I sensed so palpably the strands which bind us Jews together, our common cause, and our united purpose like I do today on the death march.

How much potential, elemental strength, and vitality; how many hopes and dreams are encapsulated within this marching multitude, now helpless and numbed to the point of apathy. (Suddenly a wild thought flits through my mind: what if we marched to the Promised Land instead of towards our likely fate? There used to be a revisionist lawyer called Riffel before the War who actually advocated a massed public march to liberate Palestine. But everyone dismissed him as a crackpot.)

And so we march — in our thousands, in our tens of thousands or perhaps even more. Side by side they march, elderly Jews and gnarled, bent Chasidim alongside young erect workers, intellectuals, and simple folk, a saintly aesthetic next to a well built *chalutznik*, the coarse "*goldene yugend*" and refined *yeshivah bachurim.* Here and there I recognize familiar faces: a famous Warsaw Rav with the workers' leader Zagan, the respectable Chasidic *baal habayis* Rabbi Avramele Walerstein and a simple Jew from the ranks of "*amchah,*" the famous doctor Siegmund Braustein and the young businessmen's leader Neufeld. There are grown-up adolescents and tiny babies accompanied by countless shocked and overwrought mothers full of maternal love — and pain without end.

And so we march — a veritable army of women and children, the ill and the weak, and all of us completely helpless. (All thought of resistance vanishes in the final analysis with the realization of how totally helpless we are; as well as the very real fear of the inevitable repercussions the Germans will take on those left behind.) Many of us feel this is "probably" our last march, our march unto death — and not a few realists would dispense with the caveat "probably."

And so we march — eventually my gaze strays from those marching in front and behind me. Another strange, wild thought occurs to me: only this week in *Pirkei Avos* (3:9) we learnt that if somebody studies Torah while going on a journey and then interrupts his study to exclaim, "How beautiful is this tree; how fine is that field," he deserves to lose his life. And what if somebody is journeying to his own slaughter — is it then permissible? Does such a *halachah* exist? Did the *Tanna* in *Pirkei Avos* foresee this, too?

Yet the view today is so enticing: the clear blue skies without a cloud in sight, the air clear to the horizon. It is a midsummer's day and nature is at her best. The earth is in full bloom. Even in our wretched Ghetto at Nalewki Square (or rather where Nalewki Square was before it was destroyed), a few vegetables sprout forth and glisten in the brilliant sunshine. On this glorious summer's day the sun pours down its bountiful rays and bathes the world in a golden glow.

Has the sun, too, donned festive clothes for our funeral? Does it, too, laugh scornfully at our suffering? Is it not ashamed? Could it not conceal itself behind thick, black clouds as dark as Hell? Has it, too, abandoned us just like the rest of the world? If the sun stopped at midday over Givon, why does it not halt its playful progress across the skies as we are herded towards the *Umschlag* and on to we know not where.

Eventually I tear my gaze away from the cheerful sun, serene among beautiful blue skies, above the hapless victims marching inexorably to their final appointment with their slaughterers. Never, I think to myself, will I ever again enjoy the gentle caress of the bountiful sun without reflecting on its indifference to our sorrow.

At the last moment I was rescued (who knows for how long), but I shall never forget the forsaken feeling that everyone had abandoned us — even the world and inanimate nature — and I recalled Bialik's poem (written after the Kishinev pogrom:)

> For God called to spring and the massacre together
> The sun shone, the flowers flourished
> And the murderers slaughtered....

Friday, August 28

Rescued from Extinction

A miracle happened to me yesterday and I was saved — though I do not know for how long. Still I must thank Hashem, even for life in the short term. It all started in a fairly ordinary way. Yesterday morning I set out from my flat at 6 Pawia Street to the Kehillah offices at 19 Zamenhof Street, a walk of barely five minutes. But en route I stumbled across a German "blockade": all the buildings from 13 Gesia Street down to the Jewish cemetery were surrounded by the accursed Ukrainian militia led by SS officers.

A group of captured Jews were already held at the gate; they were waiting for more victims. As soon as I turned the corner at Gesia/Zamenhof Streets and noticed the blockade, I tried to withdraw — but it was too late, and Ukrainian militiamen dragged me into the crowd.

Meanwhile, more captured Jews were marched in from the streets of Karmelicka/Nowolipki/Nowolipie — there had just been a "selection" at the factories and workshops around there, and the gang of murderers had reaped a rich harvest: thousands upon thousands of Jews. Now our captors did not bother to wait for any more fish to fall into their net, and they started the large crowd off on its final march.

And so we marched — in our thousands upon thousands arranged in rows. I looked around me, in front and behind there was a sea of heads: bareheaded and with hats, caps, *kashketelach*, and *kapalishen*; grey heads and black heads with *chupiks, sheitels* redolent of *yiras Shamayim* as well as modern hairstyles.

And so we marched — young and old, strong and weak. We all dragged ourselves along apathetically with all our thoughts and instincts apparently extinguished. Even the instinct for survival died within me. Only my sense of curiosity was still alive (a legacy from my training; after all, I was once a journalist) and I constantly gazed about me. I also hoped to see an acquaintance or a friendly policeman through which I may perhaps have got a message through to my friends in the Kehillah so that they could find a way of rescuing me.

Meanwhile, the large crowd marched on as apathetic as I was. Above us hovered the specter of death and we sensed that all was already lost, so why bother to resist. Our only thought was that the end should come soon without any more pain and suffering. Among the eddies of my tortured mind floated a scrap of half-remembered *Midrash* in *Bereishis: "ki tov meod,"* and it was exceedingly good... that is death!

Near me marched an elderly Jew, tall, with a beard as white as snow. He was bent a little, and he carried his *tallis* and *tefillin* under his arm. He reminded me a little of Hirschberg's famous painting of "*Galus.*" Only that portrayed a wintry scene, while now we are in the middle of a glorious summer. Suddenly, my thoughts were rudely interrupted by the German officer barking "*Stehn-blieben!*" and our large column comes to a halt. (What is the difference, we all thought to ourselves, if death comes a little later?)

Surprisingly, he then ordered "*Ausruhen!* — Rest!" and people sat down on the sidewalk or even in the road. Unwillingly a thought crossed my mind — so the Germans do retain a spark of human decency after all. But I am soon disabused. The SS officers strolled among us scrutinizing our footwear. If they noticed anyone with expensive shoes or boots they pulled these off our feet immediately, and those Jews were forced to continue their march in their socks. So this is what the Germans called "*Ausruhen.*" I examined my own shoes; they are nothing special to look at, so I am safe from them for the moment.

And so we sat — squashed, hungry, and completely cowed — all of us had surrendered to total despondency and apathy.

Suddenly, my elderly, white-bearded neighbor with his *tallis* and *tefillin* straightened up and began to speak: at first quietly, but soon with growing strength.

"*Yidden! Zorgst eich nisht! Fall nisht arein in a marah shechorah! Fahrlir zech nisht in atzvus — chalilah!* Jews, do not worry yourselves! Do not fall prey to depression or sadness. Can't you see we are marching towards *Mashiach*? Can't you see that? If only I had a glass of *mashkeh,* I would drink a *lechaim,* here and now! *Lechaim Yidden! Nor nisht kein yiush!*"

Meanwhile I noticed another character, the *chalutznik* Shoshana, who was homesick and returned to visit her mother just before the outbreak of the War. Around Grzybowska Street where she lived she had become quite famous for the Hebrew songs she had brought back with her, and she never stopped pining for her beloved Emek Jezreel, planning to return there with her mother, brothers, sisters, friends, and acquaintances. Now she, too, was caught. Leaning on her brother and leading her little sister by the hand she marched proudly forward, humming her Hebrew songs and dreaming of marching on to Emek Jezreel. And then I lost sight of her. (Only much later did I discover that her friends managed to rescue her by disguising her with a white gown as a nurse.)

By this time my own friends had discovered my predicament and made great efforts (particularly Professor Balaban) to save me. I was rescued with another *minyan* of Jews, including the elderly Mizrachi leader Rav Yitzchak Nissbaum. But I did not feel greatly relieved and cannot bring myself to *bentch gomel* since I remember that the *halachah* also stipulates that thanksgiving is in order "when the danger is past," and that is hardly our own unfortunate situation. Constantly I am haunted by terrible dreams and cannot understand why we deserved this terrible punishment.

The *chalutzniks* did not march towards Emek Jezreel just as the elderly Chasid with his *tallis* and *tefillin* did not march towards *Mashiach*. Their dreams were cruelly shattered as were the dreams of thousands upon thousands. The hopes and aspirations of the three and a half million Jews in Poland went unrealized.

SEPTEMBER 1942

Tuesday, September 1

War's Third Anniversary

Today marks the third year in which the War has raged. Its military echoes seem to come from a long way away — almost from another planet. Certainly this War is not being waged for our sake; whatever happens we are lost forever. No victory can save us now. The oppressive enemy is too near us, his deathly weapons are pressed close against our flesh. The majority of Warsaw's Jewish population have already been murdered, yet still the Germans' blood lust is unsated.

Tsudner, the Hebrew author, asked me, "*Vos vell ich fardinen,* what will I gain if I am not alive to see it and somebody whispers into my grave that Hitler has finally been beaten? By that time I, too, shall have been long murdered."

I remember the day, when this War broke out in 1939. Naturally there was a deep sense of foreboding, and we were especially frightened about the bombing. But then I firmly believed that we Jews would outlive this turmoil, as we had survived so many earlier upheavals in the past. I had hoped we would emerge strengthened, free perhaps from the chains of *galus*, and might finally be granted a Jewish homeland, a land of our own.

But now? Can any of our previous ambitions ever be realized? Now that Polish Jewry — central to the most powerful strand of Judaism and its largest treasure trove — has been completely destroyed, are any of our aspirations within the realms of reality? As *Achad Am* once wrote, "When a land is ruined, its sons can restore it. But when a nation is obliterated, who can rebuild it?"

At 11:30 P.M. tonight, the air sirens sounded. Allied aircraft were attacking Warsaw. It has been a long time since we heard these sirens, not since September 1939. At regular intervals, the bombs drop nearby: the walls shake and window panes shatter. Surprisingly none of us show any fear, not the slightest tremor of fear at all. Quite the reverse, the bombing gives us a warm feeling of revenge. Let the bombs fall, we think, and wipe everything out — even ourselves! — as long as our accursed murderers be punished. These bombs have no built-in prejudices, they know of no "selections," they won't particularly choose Jews.

The bombs continue to fall for a long time. If only they destroy at least one SS Extermination Squad. Perhaps they have been sent to deliver us from evil. Let them fall in their hundreds! "*Ribono Shel Olam,* throw on them Your arrows of wrath and temper" (*Tehillim* 144:5). Similar verses from *Tehillim* also echo through my mind.

The bombs mainly fell outside the Ghetto but they also landed in Pawia Street and on a house at 7 Dzielna Street. The Moriah Synagogue caught alight but was put out. There were no casualties in the Ghetto.

Wednesday, September 2

Welcome "News"

Spirits rise today in the Ghetto, it is almost a *Yom Tov* as we hear good news. From where, from whom do these stories originate? Nobody knows. But none questions their validity, since "everybody knows":

> "America will recognize all Jews residing in the Warsaw Ghetto!" (Another version even amplified this to ".... all Jews remaining in Poland!")
>
> "England will consider all Jews left in Poland as citizens of Palestine!"
>
> "There will soon be a population exchange between Polish Jews and Christian civilians living in the U.S. and Britain."
>
> "President Roosevelt announced today that he is warning the Germans against the destruction of Poland's Jews. All Germans resident in America will be held as a surety for the fate of all the Jews remaining in Poland!"

These stories rapidly pass from person to person, from flat to flat, from building to building. A small beacon of hope lights up the darkness of the Ghetto, and everyone begins to analyze the latest news. In my office this sparks a heated discussion. Some recall a similar proposal in the English parliament put forward in 1937 which actually passed its first reading, but it failed to get through the subsequent votes and never came into effect. Dr. Yitzchak Schipper, the confirmed optimist, first began to examine the declarations from a legal standpoint (bearing in mind that he holds a doctorate in law) and comes to the inevitable conclusion that these announcements are perfectly feasible in International Law.

Then he considers the political implications (after all, he had also been a parliamentary member of the Polish Sejm) and once again concludes that it is not only politically possible but even very likely. After that he begins to look for historical precedents (he is also an eminent historian), and then finally he examines the affair from the background of a seasoned activist (not forgetting his position as president of the Polish Zionist Federation), and proves that Jewish leaders in the West would never sit back quietly or rest; they would storm the heavens in both America and England, and he quotes various names: Weitzman, Ben-Gurion, Greenbaum, Harold Laski, Bernard Baruch, Morgenthau, and Herbert Samuel. They must have aroused the world's conscience and this is undoubtedly the result: these declarations we have all just heard about. The news must be 100 percent accurate.

Dr. Edmund Stein (director of the Warsaw Seminary), however, is sure the credit must go to the Jewish intellectuals who must have influenced the American and English statesmen. "Our cry for help," he insisted, "did not go unanswered. The world finally heard us. Humanity is not entirely dead...."

R. Yehudah Leib Orlean (dean of Cracow's Beis Yaakov Seminary) enters the discussion by quoting a *pasuk* from *Yeshayah* (6:13) "...but a tenth remains." The mathematical analogy is remarkably accurate: There were originally 450,000 Jews in Warsaw, now only 45,000 remain. I rejoin with another *pasuk* from *Amos* (5:3) "...out of a town of one thousand will only one hunderd remain; from a population of one hundred will only ten remain to the House of Israel...."*

However, Professor Balaban tries to introduce a note of caution into our debate. "I don't believe in World Opinion," he declared dismissively. "I do not understand the nature of this creature nor do I expect to see it in my lifetime!"

Rabbi Menachem Ziemba is sure it is the *rabbanim* who have fought for those declarations. He knows scores of *rabbanim* in the free world, and he is convinced they did not rest day or night until they achieved success. They must have *ubergedreyt velten* (caused a world upheaval) to influence this decision. Dr. Schipper does not entirely dismiss this line of argument and also mentions Chief Rabbi Hertz of England and Dr. Stephen Wise of America.

"What is the difference whose work it is?" asks Rabbi Shimshon Stockhammer seeking to strike a balance. "As long as somebody is finally taking some decisive action on our behalf. And whoever does anything should be blessed for his efforts. Personally I am sure that everybody must be doing something. What Jew possessed of a warm Jewish heart can sit back quietly and do nothing — not hammer on the door of the world's conscience — to save the last remnant of his brethren? *Is dos meglech,* is this possible?"

Internally I feel the stirrings of my journalistic training, urging me to uncover the prime source of all these stories, as well as the precise details (I am an archivist, too). Someone tells me they come from the British radio service, the BBC. But who actually heard it? I turned to the principal source for

---

* Later, incidentally, I used this pasuk (I wrote "*Amos* 5:3") to smuggle the information past the German censor, to alert the free world that only one-tenth of Warsaw's Jews survived. My contact, the Agudist Rabbi Chaim Yisrael Eiss of Zurich, wrote that he understood the hint.

wireless news, Mr. Papower the Kehillah registrar, who sends me to Dr. Wildkovsky, the lawyer. However, he has been confused with the medical doctor Dr. Milokovsky. But this gentleman directs me to a second source, who in turn sends me on to a third, and then to a fourth... until I eventually come round full circle.

For all my efforts I cannot find out — nor can anybody else — where on earth these wonderful stories came from. I return home feeling completely drained; apparently they are merely the fruit of false expectation and wishful thinking inherent in our situation. By nightfall all these stories have withered and died. We return to the dark reality, to the demoralized state of slavery. We have been deprived of yet another avenue of hope and awarded with yet another deep disappointment.

Religious Personalities

"Reb Don" of the Warsaw Rabbinate was a legend in his own lifetime. All sorts of almost unbelievable stories were circulated about him by Jewish journalists. He was known as a "*pikeach,*" being unusually smart, and was armed with all sorts of certificates: he was simultaneously registered as a Kehillah official, as an employee at a German workshop, and as a specialist skilled in brush manufacture. Besides, he was extremely careful and avoided the murderers throughout the occupation. But today, while on the way from home to the Kehillah, he stumbled across a German "blockade" and fell into their trap.

I ran into the *Judenrat* President Lichtenbaum to see if he could do anything. He phoned Jacob Leikin (head of the Jewish police) and Schmerling (in charge of the *Umschlagplatz*), but it was all too late. Both M. Posner and Mottel Pinkert (who officially ran the cemetery and the undertaking service respectively) returned from there, very upset, and told us that "Reb Don" Wolkenbreit had already been forced inside the boxcar. One of the beloved characters in Jewish Warsaw was with us no more.

Also caught today was another interesting personality, Rabbi Yaakov Gesundheit, a grandson of the famous Warsaw Rav of the same name. He was employed as the Rabbinate secretary for many years and saw his position as a holy duty at which he worked day and night. Possessed of a generous heart and an open hand for every unfortunate, he was particularly concerned for the plight of *agunos* (abandoned wives).

Though he constantly carried a heavy burden of work and responsibility, he made do with a low wage, never sought any financial advantages nor took a holiday, and carried out his task without favoritism or for personal considerations. During the occupation he refused all hand-outs and subsisted in great poverty. Unusual in carrying out his responsibilities according to traditional values with such total dedication, his capture leaves another void in Warsaw. Certainly it is difficult to find his like among the present *Judenrat* officials.

Heights of Heroism

We decided to bury our most important archives: documentation of the Ghetto and the deportations, leading manuscripts from the Chasidic Rebbes of Ger and Chabad (the "*Baal HaTanya*"), as well as the writings of Prof. Balaban, Yaakov Ben-Yaakov, Ghetto plays, and other literary efforts. We chose a suitable area of the Kehillah courtyard, and at 2 o'clock in the morning we cautiously creep out with two large sacks full of writings. Besides myself there were Dr. Tulu Nussblatt, Nochum

Remba, Shmuel Horenstein, Dr. Samuel Schimkovits, Dr. Nachman Kuvalsky, and the academic Rassin. We bring the sacks down slowly, with great care, listening out for the slightest sound — even a pin drop.

When we are already halfway across the courtyard, we hear soft footsteps. Our hearts contract with fear and we stand stock still, listening for further developments. The indistinct footsteps come ever closer. Who else could possibly be out at such a late hour. We confer in hushed whispers and conclude that these are not the heavy, self-assured tread of Germans. Nevertheless, we are extremely afraid. We remove our shoes and fearfully creep back to the Kehillah building in our socks.

Suddenly we see three figures approaching through the open gateway at Wolynska Street. Staring at them against the darkness I can just about make out that they are wearing long coats, *kashketlech*, and *peyos*. If so, they must be *yeshivah bachurim*; no one else still dares to wear the traditional dress.

"Who is there?" I call out, but nobody moves or answers. I repeat the question but again the only reply is silence. Finally I called out, "This is Hillel Seidman — what do you want?" and the strange figures come up to us. I stare at them closely, a mixture of fear and determination is reflected on their thin and wasted faces as they tell me the purpose of their night's visit. These *bachurim* are part of Rabbi Avramele Weinberg's group (the famous Warsaw Rav who has already been deported; they are now under the auspices of the Kozieglower Rebbe, Rabbi Yehudah Leib Frumer, previously the *rosh yeshivah* of Lublin).

They are living and learning at 14 Mila Street — actually underneath Mila Street, since their secret bunker is below ground — but their food supplies ran out a week ago. They have not been out during the daytime since the panic first began in the Ghetto. Without being registered with the Germans and never receiving documents or official numbers from them, it was too dangerous for them to be seen on the streets. At night they are less scared to wander about looking for food.

Usually they enter abandoned apartments whose owners have already been deported to search for leftover flour, potatoes, beans, or whatever is now considered *hefker.* They also appeal to Jewish householders who have stocks of food and often receive small amounts. There are even provisions of cooked food — a few Jewish women collect food on their behalf, which they cook or bake and then await the *bachurim*'s night visits. Though there is a strict curfew from 7 P.M. onwards, the *bachurim* ignore it; they feel safer at 1 or 2 A.M. Since the Germans regard all those unregistered as "wild ones" or "illegals," they are anyhow condemned whatever time they are found. Besides, at this time of night, even the German thugs are tired.

Their group has nineteen *bachurim* and two or three go out each night to find food, which is shared collectively. This is their only alternative to perishing from hunger. Naturally they know of the soup kitchen at 38 Nalewki Street, but the food there is not kosher. Though a reliable Rav has permitted the weakest among them to eat non-kosher food, "must we do everything that is permitted? Besides it is not only a question of *kashrus*; according to the Rambam, *treifah* foods can glut the heart! As you can see we'll find some alternative. A good night to you, or rather, since dawn is beginning to break, a good morning...."

Our nocturnal visitors vanish as quietly as they arrived, but we remain in our places, our minds in a whirl — particularly Dr. Tulu Nussblatt, who can get very emotional. These brave youngsters have made an indelible impression on him, and he turns to me and remarks, "Only generations of Jews who have been *moser nefesh* for their Torah and beliefs could have possibly produced such remarkable personalities. All the stories I have read in the past about Marranos and other martyrs have been brought of life at this moment! Now I have seen it all with my own eyes!"

We return to our own mission, but slowly and without enthusiasm. That unworldly night encounter still casts its spell over us, and everything else pales into insignificance.

News from Treblinka

I had a visitor today. A "guest" enters my office — torn and bedraggled, weak and exhausted, and there is a strange wild look in his eyes. I remember him from some time ago: he is Yaakov Rabinowitz, the Parczewer Rebbe's son and the brother of the young Munkatcher Rebbe. He is a "*yeshiva-man*," about twenty-five years old, and a member of the religious organization Haboneh in Warsaw. He used to live at 7 Gesia Street, but hadn't I heard that he had been deported? If it wasn't true, where had he been until now?

He looks at me strangely for a long time without answering. Suddenly he blurts out, "From *there*...." I was not quite sure what to make of this but instinctively I ask him, somewhat tentatively, "From Treblinka?"

"Yes!" came the abrupt answer. I remembered then that I had vaguely heard of someone from *there* — so this was the man. I did not want to speak about it in the office and he, too, was very circumspect. There were countless officials wandering through my office and many of them had relatives who had been deported eastwards, "*Nach Osten*." So we arranged to meet later at my apartment. He arrived exactly on time, and this is what he told me (I wrote it all down to ensure I did not leave out any particulars from his report):

> As you know I was grabbed during the "blockade" on the Landau workshop at 30 Gesia Street. As soon as we arrived at the Ghetto railway station we were loaded into boxcars — freight wagons normally used for transporting animals — about a hunred people into each boxcar. Old and young, healthy and sick, men, women, and children were all forcibly pushed into the wagons.
>
> The crush was awful, the heat stifling. Everybody stood pressed up against one another unable to move even an arm or leg. Rivers of sweat ran down our faces, and it was difficult to breath. I experienced an unprecedented thirst; my tongue felt glued to my palate and my body cried out for water, just a little water. This sole urge dominated my thoughts, but it was a waste of effort; there was no water provided for anyone, none at all.
>
> We stood like this for about four hours. How long would they keep us in these conditions? Will we be able to withstand it? Next to me stood a mother with three children, all of them crying pitifully, enough to break one's heart. The youngest one especially, a boy of about two years old, would not stop sobbing, "A drink! A drink!" I soon forgot my own unbearable thirst and began to worry about this poor child — where to obtain just a little water for this tiny toddler. I just couldn't bear to watch his suffering, but what could I do? The boxcar was locked, bolted, and completely closed. Only a small vent above our heads allowed a few beams of sunlight to penetrate, as well as the screams of women and children still being

forced onto other wagons. Somebody suggests I take a look through this vent, and so I perch on the back of my neighbor — and witness a horrifying scene.

The large square is filled with thousands of men, women, and children carrying their pitiful baggage. They are being forced mercilessly forward by the SS. The Ukrainian Police push and shove at them ruthlessly, lash out indiscriminately with whips and clubs at those unable to run fast enough, while screeching, "*Schnell! Schnell!*" in tones menacing enough to make your blood run cold. I cannot watch this any longer. Better to be crushed together inside the boxcar than to witness what is taking place outside. Though I slip off my neighbor's back, I cannot blot out the terrible scene I had just witnessed. For how long will we have to endure these insufferable conditions?

Finally after four hours we move off. Even though we have an idea what this train trip entails, we still feel some relief. Let whatever is due to happen, happen — as long as it is soon. By now the sun is setting. A cooler wind wafts into our sealed boxcar and the pastoral scent of fields and farms reaches us. Outside the Ghetto, nature still smiles on Poland; the fields and forests, birds and flowers, still thrive in the large — and free — world.

Now I no longer resent the crush, though the boxcar is as crowded as before. I no longer feel thirst or hunger even though I have tasted nothing yet. What I do experience however is a sudden urge for survival. *Davka* today, *davka* here in this wretched boxcar I have this urgent desire to live. Though there is apparently no escape, nowhere to run to — yet I repeat to myself: I want to live! I want to live!

Meanwhile our train proceeds very slowly...we have time, there is no hurry, we shall not miss our appointment.... The engine moves forward only grudgingly and stops at various stations for many hours. Nobody knows where we are going but in everybody's head hammers the dreadful destination: Treblinka. Then we are distracted by "minor incidents": an old man faints, they try to revive him but to no avail — he has just died.

Nobody grieves over his death. Some even envy him for coming to the end of his life; Heaven has obviously decreed an end to his torment. "A lucky Jew," someone remarks. "*Yiddishe mazal,*" rejoins another. Suddenly a woman starts laughing and crying simultaneously — an attack of hysteria — and a young man collapses. They shake him vigorously and he revives, his suffering is destined to continue.

Beside me the children continue to cry but their wailing has grown weaker and intermittent. By now I have lost all account of time; it was a fearfully long night and it is already morning when we reach our final destination. Next to the railway line, the sign on the outbuilding reads "Treblinka." So we have arrived.

Nothing happens for about half an hour, then the doors are unlocked and the wild yelling begins: "*Araus! Araus!*" Soldiers of the Wehrmacht and SS haul us out of the boxcars and march us off — where to? "To the showers!" comes the reply. They bring us into a large building without windows and order us "to undress for the showers." Everybody undresses slowly, apathetically, almost indifferently. I myself am in no hurry, I only take off my coat and loosen my shoelaces. Meanwhile they begin to lead people towards another hall. Suddenly an SS officer appears and signals for a few people to follow him. He chooses eight of us from among the youngest there who have not yet undressed — and I am among them.

We are taken outside and ordered to wait. We look around us. The large area of land contains four long buildings without windows and slightly pitched roofs. We stand waiting for about two hours. Suddenly we hear the most frightful screams. Sobbing cries and desperate calls for help force their way through the walls and roof, reaching for the very heavens. Our hearts turn to stone within us, our numbed brains refuse to function, and we stand frozen like marble pillars. But our ears continue to receive those agonized, unearthly sounds. (In fact those terrifying screams still echo within me until this minute; they give me no rest by day or by night, haunting my dreams and every waking moment. I shall never be able to put them behind me — never!)

The shrieking lasted for about fifteen minutes and then there was a terrible silence. No sound or echo. At that moment the SS officer reappeared and ordered us to reenter the first hall where we had begun undressing. This hall was now completely empty of people, there were only baggage and pathetic bundles of clothes lying where they had been left on the floor. Some of the clothing had been folded neatly with little notes on top stating their owner's name to ensure these not be exchanged or taken by mistake. Apparently some people had allowed themselves to believe and hope until the very last moment that they would yet be permitted to return to reclaim their belongings.

Now we are ordered to collect their orphaned clothing and transfer it to the boxcars. I fulfill these commands like a mindless automaton, all emotion and personal feelings totally numbed. I begin by collecting footwear: girls' shoes, children's shoes, men's shoes, ladies' shoes, elegant shoes, expensive shoes, battered shoes, torn shoes, large tall boots.... How many footsteps had these countless shoes traveled — tap-tapping, scurrying, rushing along life's highway until they reached this abrupt barrier. Helping us collect these belongings was a team of Polish workers. When the German overseer moves away to a safe distance, I take the opportunity to ask: what exactly is going on?

"These hair-raising screams we hear a few times a day, every day!" the Pole answered. "My hair has turned white from hearing them. I have long wanted to escape from here but it is impossible, I am myself a political prisoner. Now I am already a little used to these screams but I still cannot sleep nights — these heartrending cries even intrude into my dreams!

"There's nothing more to be said," he added brutally, pointing at the third building. "From *there* nobody escapes alive. Ten thousand a day, that's the daily total of people murdered with gases there for many weeks now...."

From that moment, only one solitary thought possessed me — I would not enter *there* on any account. I will have to get away from here somehow. But the Poles explain to us that after we have finished transferring all these clothes, we too would be forced into the third block from which there is no escape. Above the doorway of that apparently innocuous building ought to be fixed the slogan from Dante's *Inferno*: "Abandon hope all ye who enter here!" As I stare at the accursed place my mind is firmly resolved: I will not go *there*, I just will not go....

I abandon collecting shoes and rush to gather clothes together like a madman. With sudden reserves of superhuman strength, I stagger to the train with huge bundles of clothes and fling them inside. I work at a furious pace like one possessed, throwing bundle after bundle into the boxcar until it is almost full. Then I jump in myself and burrow deeply down beneath the many loose bundles.

Though I am almost suffocated down there, I am simultaneously gripped by relief and hope, "I have saved myself and shall yet live for another day...." I lay there motionless for some time until I hear faint noises and sense the bundles being moved about, fortunately not near me. The Germans are searching for me and I can hear them becoming very angry before they abandon the chase. Finally there is a welcome silence, but it is broken by more sounds — not of one of the Germans returning but the spine-chilling screams of my workmates being murdered. Their death cries reach my ears and penetrate deep into my soul, to remain imprinted there for the rest of my life.

I lay in that boxcar for a whole day without food or water. As I sense my last reserves of strength draining away, a new terror looms: death by hunger. But suddenly there is a large bang as the door is closed and the train finally moves off. After about half an hour I try to extricate myself from the bundles. After a brief struggle, I manage to free my head and then my arms; soon I am sitting on top of the baggage. The door is only partly closed and through the large crack I can easily see outside.

The sun is shining brightly and the clear blue heavens are not dark black. On the contrary, everything is wonderful and idyllic in Hashem's world as the annual cycle continues and the farmers gather in the rich harvest. Only for us have the heavens darkened and the sun set at noon.

By now I can recognize some of the areas that the train is passing through, the orchards and small parks on the outskirts of Warsaw. I push at the half-closed door with all my strength and force it open wide enough to slip through; I jump from the moving train and roll down the grass — I am saved! I lose consciousness and lie there senseless all day until nightfall.

It is not important how I managed to hide with non-Jews or how I managed to return to the Ghetto. It is sufficient that I am safely back. But do not think that I am truly saved. My life has been totally ruined by the harrowing scenes I saw and witnessed. The brutal deportation of thousands onto the death trains; then to be murdered by poison gases. I have heard the last cries of the dying, their screams torment my soul, day and night.

I come from Treblinka and just as surely I will return *there*!

These were the words of someone who had somehow returned from *there*. To the casual observer he may still look young and healthy, but how many years has he aged in a few days? His lifespirit is broken and destroyed. Despite his youth he will never again trust another human being; to him abstract concepts like humanity or world justice have been exposed as a sham. Our eyes meet, and I can see the strange, wild fires of *gehinnom* raging in his eyes.

I can only record dryly what he has told me but I cannot speak — words fail me. All I want to do is to cry, and cry, and cry, until there are no more tears.

"Who will turn my head to water and my eyes to a source of tears, and I will cry day and night over the slain victims of my people..." (*Yirmeyahu* 5:22).

Motza'ei Shabbos (1st day *Selichos*), September 5

A Fresh Selection in Warsaw

About 2 A.M. there was a commotion in our block at 8 Pawia Street. Special messengers from the *Judenrat* arrived to awaken two members of the *Judenrat* executive — Rosenthal and Horowitz — and summon them urgently for an extraordinary meeting. By 5 A.M. the news was out. All remaining Jews still living in the Ghetto would have to assemble within the streets of Wolynska/Mila/Stawki/Niska/Szczesliwa by 10 A.M. Sunday morning. Any Jew found after that time to the north of Gesia Street would be immediately shot.

What is the reason for this new order? Nobody knows, not even the *Judenrat* — they, too, received these instructions from the Germans without any explanations. Feverish thoughts flit through our minds: mainly that this must be the end, no one will survive. We are all condemned to extinction.

Sunday, September 6

From early morning, large crowds assemble in Zamenhof Street, everyone carrying a pitifully small bundle. That tragic scene repeats itself — of women and children, elderly and sick, the weak and emaciated. Shoving and jostling each other in an effort to get there first, the crowds file towards Wolynska/Mila according to the German instructions — and factory workers from Schults, Tennens, and Dehring join the throng. What will happen next? Still nobody knows.

Kehillah officials and their families gather in the Kehillah building and courtyard at 19 Zamenhof Street. My office in the Kehillah archives too is suddenly full of people. On the floor, on the desks, and on the bundles of documents sit prominent members of the Jewish intelligentsia. Until now people of the caliber of Prof. Dr. Meir Balaban, Dr. Issac Schipper, Dr. Edmund Stein, Jonah Schefer, Elchanan Zeitlin, the director Brandstetter and A. G. Friedensohn from Lodz, were "employed" by the Joint or various workshops. Now they seek safety under the *Judenrat* umbrella. Here, too, are the few surviving Warsaw *rabbanim*, R. Menachem Ziemba, R. Shimshon Stockhammer, R. Dovid Shapira, with their families. All the other *rabbanim* have already been deported. (Later other *rabbanim*, Rabbi Eliezer Yitzchak Meisel and Rabbi Simcha Treisman from Lodz, joined them, and these were the last *rabbanim* remaining in Warsaw.)

The crush in these tiny rooms is oppressive, it is impossible to move. (The building had first been a palace during the 17th century, and later it served as a military prison before being allocated to the *Judenrat*.) The children cry for food but there is no food. People overcome by hunger gnaw at raw vegetables since there are no cooking facilities.

Schipper sits on a bundle of files and conducts a philosophical discussion with Rundstein, a young academic from Lodz — on Spinoza. Every so often Balaban interjects a word or two and Schipper replies. I had to go hunting for chairs for my new "assistants" whom I feel morally bound to minister to. By the time I returned half an hour later, there was a spirited discussion on the origins of Polish Jewry. Schipper furnishes new proofs to his theory that we are all descendants of the Khazars, but Balaban remains adamant that we migrated westwards into Poland from the Rhine Valley.

If I am not mistaken, this debate had already been going on for some thirty years and was fully discussed at a scientific Historical Conference in Warsaw during 1935. But the *rabbanim* listen to this argument in amazement. "Dr. Schipper is unfortunately becoming deranged!" Rabbi Shapira says. "According to him we are all descendants of *geirim*. This is the first time in my life I hear such crazy theories!" I, too, allow myself to interrupt the argument. "Perhaps, gentlemen, instead of concerning ourselves "*m'ayin basah* — from whence we came," I venture we should try and discover "*l'an atah holech* — until whither are you destined?"

The intelligentsia rapidly descended from the lofty heights of academia to the black depths of present existence. "We shall have to ask the *Judenrat* President Lichtenbaum, perhaps he will know," they decide; and they send Schipper, for whom Lichtenbaum has much respect. Tensely we wait until he finally returns, but his face does not betray any good news: The SS *vernichtungskommando* extermination squad has assembled all the Jews in order to carry out a new selection or, as they prefer to call it, "*durch-kemung*" (comb-out). Only those deemed economically necessary will be allotted numbers, and as for the rest — we already know what will happen to the rest.

Monday, September 7

We have just sat through an awful night of terror. All night long we could hear frightening noises and echoes from outside. At regular intervals we hear the heavy tread of the SS guards, and every so often we hear the crack of a rifle shot and we know full well what that means — yet another Jewish soul has been murdered. Throughout, the children whimper pitifully. Poor things, they are starving. Their mothers have nothing to give them and try to quiet them with words alone. "Soon my precious, soon it will get light and then we will have food and drink...."

But no one really knows what the morrow will bring. True, they promise us that some will survive but does anyone still trust their promise? We, the *Judenrat* officials, are also trapped within the "*einkesslung*" the blockade. Does the *Judenrat* itself have a future existence — is it still considered indispensable? And even if it should be, does there remain any need for the archives? How many of its officials, whose ranks have suddenly blossomed so substantially, will be spared?

The older officials, those who had been employed previously, are furious with me. Why have I foolishly accepted so many new officials? Did I not realize that by so doing, I was endangering them all, and now we shall all be deported. How can I explain to them that I felt a duty to the academics and *talmidei chachamim*?

As morning dawns and people begin to move about, a relative calm descends, I am not sure from where. Dr. Schipper, the eternal optimist, begins to hold forth on his most recent trip to Eretz Yisrael in 1939. In his unique manner he describes the view from Mount Scopus. The young historian Dr. Samuel Schimkowits, who had also visited Palestine, chimes in with the vivid description of the roads to the Dead Sea and Jericho where the ancient biblical scene is coming alive again. Schipper talks of his future plans and whispers to me his secret — he has been promised a position at the Hebrew University. He also speaks glowingly of his political hopes for the future. Now after everything we have suffered, he asks, can anyone dare deny us a Jewish homeland?

Rav Menachem Ziemba is meanwhile writing his *chidushei Torah*. As he explains to me, "If not for Your Torah which is my pleasure, I would almost surely be lost through my suffering" (*Tehillim* 119). He shows me a responsa on the *Minchas Chinuch* which he has headed with the words: "*B'ezras Hashem Yisbarach, during the days of wrath and destruction. Will You destroy the remnants of Israel? Second day of Selichos. To Your Judgment we stand today, for we are all Your servants.*" Then he turns to his son-in-law Rabbi Behr from Ozrakow to argue in learning. Afterwards in a discussion with Rav Shimshon Stockhammer he elaborates on the *Rambam*'s view (in *Hilchos Deos)* on the duty to stay alive.

Later I hear him discuss the *Sefas Emes,* and he repeats the previous Gerrer Rebbe's explanation on the Divine promise to redeem the Jews from the "*Sivlos Mitzraim* — the tortures of Mitzrayim." "*Sivlos*" can also mean acceptance and resignation. But one must not accept the situation, one must not become resigned to one's fate.

The *rabbanim* immerse themselves in Torah study, the academics in various scientific disciplines, and Schipper, the inspired orator, vividly describes his future visions from Eretz Yisrael and the free world. But meanwhile an extremely difficult and depressing morning awaits us.

Tuesday, September 8

Into the Trap

We discovered that a number of prominent people have been caught in the blockade around Wolynska and Mila streets: Dr. Emanuel Ringelblum, the religious leader Rabbi Zisha Friedman (the general secretary of Agudas Yisrael in Poland), the Piasznow Rebbe Rav Klonimos Schapira, the Bundist leader Mauricy Orzech, the author Isaac Bunim from Lodz, the Hebrew poet Yitzchak Katzensohn, the families of Rabbi Menachem Ziemba and Dr. Edmund Stein (these last two are here with us in the Kehillah building). Approaches are made to the *Judenrat* President Lichtenbaum that attempts should be made to rescue them. He agrees, but who should venture out to save them?

The choice falls on the Deputy *Judenrat* Secretary Nochum Remba, an energetic youngster full of initiative. He dons a white coat and pretends to be a doctor — though he has no medical training, we all address him as "professor" — and he begins negotiating with the Jewish ambulance driver. But he also insists on being accompanied by an archive official since he hopes to rescue those trapped by issuing them with false archive employment certificates. Since I am the archive director, I was volunteered for this dangerous mission.

The *Judenrat* issues me with a special document designed to protect me from the SS and their underlings. It soon transpires, however, that this document is absolutely worthless. Though we enter the *einkesslung* trap guarded by two *Judenrat* policemen, in reality their protection is useless and the two Jewish policemen fear for their own lives.

The scene that meets us is horrendous. Thousands of

weakened people, half-fainting and stricken with hunger, are sprawled in the narrow alleyways, in filthy rooms, in cellars, in courtyards, on the steps, or in the roadway. The children lay crying, the old folk lay groaning, the sick lay abandoned without any assistance, and everyone is beset by fear and despondency. And above them all stalks the relentless specter of hunger — there is not a piece of bread to be had. Even for all the wealth in the world one cannot obtain a slice of bread or a plate of soup.

The debilitating hunger dulls all other instincts and destroys every feeling. There was not much food at the Kehillah from where we set out, but the situation was nowhere near as bad as it is here. At least there we receive a quarter kilo of bread a day, whereas here they receive nothing at all and only a few privileged individuals have some meager food stocks. I can sympathize with their plight since I, too, have had nothing more than a plate of watery soup for the last two days because I arrived late for the bread allocation. I, too, feel very weak on my legs.

As we begin tentatively searching for the whereabouts of those we had come to save, the news suddenly spreads that a "selection" is about to take place. We all know what this really means, how one casual wave with a whip can decide one's fate for life — or death. This selection is centered on Zamenhof Street near Muranowska, and consecutive groups are led there. It is only 10 A.M. but the sun beats down mercilessly. People stand bathed in sweat and fear for four hours, until 2 P.M., when the Extermination Squad leaders with officers of the Gestapo Jewish section — Brandt, Mende, Vitusk, and their friends — arrive.

They all carry whips in one hand and some also carry

revolvers in their other hand. They are all in a jolly mood, laughing among themselves and cracking their whips against their shiny boots. They look content, well fed, and energetic.

They select people by their looks alone. All their victims show their various documents, identity cards, and work permits; but the murderers do not spare these a glance. Instead they scrutinize each victim. If he looks young, reasonably healthy, and still capable of work, they send him to the right. He is saved and destined for the factories. But otherwise — and there are very few remaining in the Warsaw Ghetto who can still appear healthy and strong — he is shown to the left, destined for the *Umschlagplatz* and extermination.

The German factory owners assist in the selection process. A good recommendation from them can save their workers, but these are offered very sparingly. Their recommendations are extremely expensive. These German citizens have now accumulated vast riches in bribes offered by their desperate Jewish slave workers.

Officers of the *Wehrmacht* and SS keep "*ordnung*" among the waiting crowds by sadistically striking out with their whips indiscriminately. Their whips land on the old, young, and children, drawing blood from the face, head, or shoulders. And if anyone falters behind the running crowd or topples over, one of these officers approaches to shoot him dead with his revolver. Parents are murdered in front of their children; children are killed before their parents.

Near me stands a woman whose daughter works in the *Judenrat*. A German officer pulls her out of the ranks and shoots her dead in front of everybody. And throughout this terror the murderers rush the crowds along shouting, "*Schnell! Schnell! Schnell!*" The lifesaving order to "step to the right" becomes ever rarer.

As people realize that their chances of coming through this selection are extremely slim, they begin to slip away. They conceal themselves in cellars, attics, and the filthiest of hiding places. These houses in Wolynska/Mila had been inhabited by the poorest segments in Warsaw under the most unhygienic and crowded conditions. Despite the unbearable crush of hiding fugitives nobody wants to deliver themselves over to the murderers, and so they hide. But the babies among them beg for non-existent food and begin crying and whimpering. This is extremely dangerous, for it can attract the attention of the Ukrainian militiamen who search these houses.

Anyone they discover in hiding is either shot there or dragged straight off to the *Umschlag*. Sometimes they toss grenades into cellars which arouse their suspicions, and those trapped inside cry out for help but no one comes to their aid.

Our rescue mission no longer has any significance, we have no chance of carrying it out. How stupid we were to assume that the *Judenrat* documents would protect us. We will be lucky if we can escape from here alive. But we do not manage to evade the "*kesl*" — the trap. We, too, are caught in their accursed net together with all our unfortunate and despairing brethren. Despair grows by the minute, and we can see no avenue of escape from the merciless sun, the debilitating hunger, and the dreadful sight of the trapped children.

Children Caught in the Kesl

So many countless children. We would never have believed that the Warsaw Ghetto still housed so many children. In all my years I have never seen such remarkable children, their faces aglow with a pure light from another world. And those haunting eyes — the eyes of young Jewish children. All the bitter tragedies that we have yet lived through are totally reflected in their eyes. How true was Bialik's description that these are "underage Jews" rather than mere "children." All the immense Jewish suffering presses down on their young, emaciated shoulders. By now I am apathetic to my own fate and surroundings, I can only feel for these children. If only, I think to myself, all these youngsters were miraculously transported to live under the hot sun of Eretz Yisrael. These children don't cry, even the youngest among them are totally disciplined.

Finally the angels of death appear in Mila Street — the Gestapo, the SS, and the Extermination Squad. Their fearful names are whispered through the ranks: Brandt, Mende, and Globocnik. Complete silence reigns in the street as everybody holds his breath; even the children do not make the slightest sound. Suddenly a fusillade of shots ring out nearby followed by groans — obviously somebody in his death throes. Apparently a number of elderly Jews were murdered because they were too weak to walk to the *Umschlag.* Some even envy them, at least their suffering has ended.

Thursday, September 10

It was difficult enough to enter the *kesl*, and it is harder still to get out. I failed in my rescue mission completely. Besides, those we came to save believe that there are even less chances of survival at the *Judenrat*. It is already too overcrowded there with nowhere to hide. So this is the second day that I lie in some attic. Not having eaten for two days, I experience a tremendous weakness. Finally I hear that the Germans are sending a team of Jewish "work-guards" (who usually keep order at the factories) to the Kehillah building to bury those who had been shot. I manage to join this team and finally return to the *Judenrat*.

Life or Death for Judenrat Officials

I enter my office in the archive section where Prof. Balaban, Dr. Schipper, Director Brandstetter, R. Menachem Ziemba, R. Shimshon Stockhammer, R. Dovid Shapira, and others await my tidings with bated breath. They are desperate to know what is going on "there" at the *kesl*. But I remain silent. Since I do not have any good news, I do not want to increase the despair. Besides, I am so weakened from hunger that I can hardly speak; indeed, I feel my last reserves of strength ebbing away. Everybody is sunk into the slough of deep despondency. Only R. Yehudah Leib Orlean, who paces the courtyard, refuses to succumb. He calms the others down and tries to infuse them with strength and *bitachon*.

Dr. Schipper is also optimistic. He does not actually talk about it, he just refuses to admit any news of our imminent destruction. Ignoring the bitter reality, he takes refuge either in the future or in the past (he is, after all, an historian). He is busy combing through the Kehillah's old files and is as comfortable as a fish in water. He can sit among the Kehillah archives delving and researching to his heart's content without disturbance — what more could he want? Why should he worry that we are surrounded by death?

He is totally immersed in the 1870s and the battles between the Warsaw Rav, Rabbi Yaakov Gesundheit, and the Nathansohns, who led the Kehillah council. Schipper is about to complete his book on the history of the Warsaw Rabbinate, while the Germans are preparing to "finish" both the Rabbinate and the community altogether.

Rav Menachem Ziemba, too, is sitting and writing. Now that he has been freed from the regular distractions of the Rabbinate, he has ample time to write *chidushei Torah.* I glance at the heading: "What I have been *mechadesh, b'ezras Hashem,* during the days of wrath under the heat of oppression on the subject of *Kiddush Hashem* according to both the *Rambam* and *Raavad, zt"l....*" Nevertheless he is not divorced from the present reality, and he encourages me to approach the *Judenrat* president again to see if there remains any chance of rescuing anyone from the *kesl* and bringing them to the Kehillah. Then he tells me a *vort* from the Kotzker Rebbe: both *eruvin* and *netilas yadayim* were enacted by Shlomo Hamelech. "*Eruvin*" also refers to involving oneself in worldly affairs, while "*netilas yadayim*" also refers to withdrawing from worldly affairs. Shlomo Hamelech was teaching us that one has to know when to apply each approach at the right time and place.

Rav Shimshon Stockhammer, who officially is also the *Judenrat* Rabbi, enters with the information that the *Judenrat* has been allotted 2800 "numbers" and only holders of these numbers will be allowed to live. I run up to the *Judenrat* president's office to inquire what will happen to my assistants (only a few of whom are genuine archive officials, while the rest belong to the rabbinical and intellectual professions). I discover that they are all on the list to receive numbers, and so we are saved.

Suddenly my physical strength returns, and I race back with the glad tidings. But nobody is particularly overjoyed. The instinct for self-preservation may be foremost, but the concern for the general majority is also running very strong, particularly now when everyone is concerned for friends and relatives trapped outside. Fear stalks us all — fear for our families, ourselves, and everyone else. What will happen today and what will the morrow bring? Even if we are saved today, we are still haunted by the perennial burning question — for how long?

At 3 P.M. the order comes: all of us are to assemble in the courtyard. The large palatial courtyard was remodeled in the 18th century by the last Polish monarch before it was converted into a military prison, and now we officials of the *Judenrat* assemble here in ranks of four abreast. Every section stands separately with its leader in front, who is to present his team of workers to those dreaded angels of death. So I stand at the head of my "assistants," to whom, in normal times, I would bow my head in deference. These are the remnants of the Polish intellectual elite whose names are famous throughout the Jewish world. My sudden "elevation" above them only fills me with grave disquiet, especially now that I have to come face to face with the most sadistic and terrible murderers the world has ever seen.

After standing and waiting for nearly three hours, Professor Balaban feels very weak. This is hardly surprising since he is nearly sixty-five years old and the enforced poverty and famine have taken their toll. He asks me if he may sit down on the ground, but I do not advise him to do so. According to our instructions we have to "stand vigorously erect." Displays of weakness do not invite their sympathy — just the opposite.

Finally at 6 P.M., Brandt the Gestapo head arrives together with a group of SS, while the Ukrainian militiamen search every nook and cranny of the Kehillah building looking for fugitives. They discover a few Jews, including Mordechai Langer, Yitzchak Ravitz, Zev-Woolf Lipsker (all journalists of the *Yiddishe Togblatt*), and Rabbi Shalom Mordechai Hakohen from Drabin — none of whom had been allotted "numbers." When I had pleaded their case, Lichtenbaum had replied, "We don't have enough numbers." The *Judenrat* also did not provide a number for the widow of Rav Meshulam Kaminer, and they are all taken to the *Umschlag* for extermination.

Brandt inspects each *Judenrat* group individually, including my own. He stares murderously at me and then at my "assistants." Then he commented, "Ahh, you have that Balaban..." and wanders off. To him the greatest Polish historian is "that Balaban," just another "number." This spine-chilling farce lasts for about half an hour, and then the order is given: "March forward!" And so we march four abreast, in military style, until they tell us to go home, each to their own apartment. Is that still possible?

I return to my flat in 8 Pawia Street and throw myself onto my bed. I fall into a deep disturbing nightmare with my head still reeling with pictures from the *kesl,* that terrible cauldron of murder and mayhem. Those scenes will remain forever imprinted on my memory; I will never be able to erase them for the rest of my life.

Friday, *erev* Rosh Hashanah 5703, September 11

"Every day's *k'lalah* is greater than the curse from the previous day." Can each day bring a new horror? What can still happen that has not already taken place? Surely there must be some limits to our oppressors' sadism. But their cruelty breaks even their previous records.

Today they deported sick patients from the Jewish Hospital in cattle trucks — 120 to a truck. Why should they bother to take them? Are they, too, being "resettled" in labor camps? They are far too sick to work. They can only be destined for... but none dare complete that particular train of thought. Who can still summon up the moral reserves to draw the correct conclusions?

Among these latest deportees was Hillel Zeitlin, the doyen of famous Jewish writers and thinkers. Much was done to prolong his survival. His daughter-in-law Tala Zeitlin held an important position in the *Judenrat* running the tax-collection department, and she "employed" him as their "messenger." He sat in their office in Grzybow Street — and studied *Zohar.* The genuine tax officials were loutish and non-religious and scornfully turned up their noses. This long-bearded Jew will endanger us all, they claimed. But their protests were ignored.

After his wife was deported, his life was shattered and he aged tens of years overnight. He grew progressively paler by the day, and when his family noticed that the butchers spared the Jewish Hospital (then at 1 Leszno Street, at the former spirits factory) they transferred him there over a month ago, on August 10th. Both Dr. Stein, the hospital director (even though he had been baptized) and Dr. Wahl, brother-in-law of the famous Mizrachi activist Dr. Oscar Yeshiah Wolfsberg, put themselves out to make life easier for him. When the hospital was periodically searched — and those considered healthy, arrested — he was carefully concealed. For a short time, his son Elchanan stayed with him. (Elchanan took ill when the mass deportations began, and, despite his wife's dedicated nursing, succumbed on September 4 and was buried in the writers' section of the Warsaw cemetery.)

Now despite all their best efforts, the eighty-year-old leading Jewish thinker and writer was deported together with his younger brethren. Many recollections of Hillel Zeitlin flood my memory. Whenever I visited him during the War, I always emerged feeling encouraged and uplifted. One particular occasion just over a year ago made a significant impression.

I received a written invitation to visit Zeitlin during the last Shabbos of that year — for a period of introspection before we entered the new year of 5702, whose Hebrew acronym also spelled "*Shabbos.*" Subsequently, when I arrived at 4 P.M., I found about a *minyan* of religious Jews, including some famous *talmidei chachamim*. Zeitlin sat in his chair, white with emotion, and his voice was fiery as he spoke of his mystic hopes for the coming year.

"Precious Warsaw Jews," he proclaimed, "can you not see the old world disappearing in flames and a new world order arising? The Creator is once again destroying worlds and rebuilding them. The new Year of Redemption is at hand; a whole year of "*Shabbos,*" a microcosm of *Olam Habah*! Shall we ignore the footsteps of *Mashiach* because of the backbreaking slavery and shortness of spirit?"

In that small room, dark with shadows, I felt a mystic elevation and could almost imagine the approach of the long-awaited Messiah. But Zeitlin's dream was shattered, and we did not merit to greet *Mashiach.*

"They only gave my father-in-law five minutes to collect his belongings," his daughter-in-law Tala Perlmutter-Zeitlin (who went to the *Umschlag* in an unsuccessful attempt to save him) told me. "He put on his *tallis* and *tefillin*, took the *Zohar* in one hand, and went."

"What an impressive march that was," Nochum Remba later told me. "He walked firmly and erect among his unfortunate brethren. His tall figure, princely bearing, shining eyes, and firm tread demanded respect. Even the barbaric Ukrainian militiamen were impressed. They left him alone and did not try to rush him. He walked slowly, his lips constantly moving, his eyes staring at the far distance."

Today is *erev* Rosh Hashanah. A year has passed on and with it about two million Jews. As usual Jews still wish each other "*A gut yahr,*" but they say it with little conviction or hope. What sort of a year can a young man look forward to, after having lost his wife, his four children, his parents, his brothers, his sisters, and now is left alone and forlorn in the world? Yet still the instinct for self-preservation reasserts itself. At least there should be an end to the ongoing destruction; at long last the *Ribono Shel Olam* should decree an end to our *tzaros*.

When I meet Rav Menachem Ziemba, he quotes the *Gemarah*, " 'Even when the blade of a sharp sword rests against one's neck, one must still not despair from Divine Mercy.' There is still hope... *A gut yahr*! Besides, I can prove to you that this year has to be an improvement on the last. Simple! There no longer remains three and a half million Jews in Poland to be tormented and murdered. So this year cannot possibly be as bad as the last. Let us hope it will be a better year!"

Yet when I repeated these comforting words to Dr. Schipper, he refused to accept them. "This is not true," he protested. "The remnants are still in mortal danger, terrible catastrophes are still possible. But I remain confident (Schipper is an incorrigible optimist) that those who have survived until now will live until the end! Why else have they carried out all these selections?"

Professor Balaban is busy organizing communal prayers for Rosh Hashanah at the *Judenrat*. Since the Ghetto has been reduced to only a few streets, all the synagogues are now situated outside the walls. Balaban, the great historian, had always dreamt of being a religious minister like all his colleagues. Then he was ordained by Dr. Leo Baeck from Berlin, and the previous *Judenrat* president Czerniakow had appointed him to a position. So now he is busy collecting *machzorim* (of which there is no shortage in the Ghetto), *talleisim*, and a *shofar.* He has invited Mr. Sherman, *chazan-sheni* from the Tlomackie Street congregation, to serve.

Meanwhile the terror at the *kesl* continues. Terrified people are still in hiding in cellars and attics. Officially the "selection" is over and those who have been condemned have been taken away to the *Umschlag*. But these fugitives remain in hiding, since the area is still surrounded by Ukrainian auxiliaries dressed in German uniforms. Generally nobody here in the Ghetto really knows what has been going on between the streets Wolynska and Mila. We still have no clear idea who remains there and where they are. But everybody realizes that a great tragedy has taken place.

Sunday night, *motza'ei* Rosh Hashanah 5703, September 13

Rosh Hashanah also had its share of events. On the first day, the Kehillah Hall at 19 Zamenhof Street was filled to capacity as Chazan Sherman led the prayers. The congregation was mainly comprised of non-religious and assimilationists, but all were obviously deeply in earnest. I myself davened with a private *minyan* organized at Rav Menachem Ziemba's apartment. Our group included the remnants of the Warsaw's *rabbanim*, R. Stockhammer, R. Shapira, R. Yehudah Leib Orlean, R. Eliezer

Gershon Friedensohn, and Mr. David Guzik, the acting director of the Joint. Rav Menachem himself davened with great fervor and R. Yitzchak Rosenstreich davened at the *amud.*

All of them were broken men who had lost all their relatives. Every so often, silent weeping broke out or deep sighs, which can break a person in two. After davening we began discussing our future prospects. What particularly concerned us was: why were we being punished like this? Even Rav Menachem Ziemba, who can usually find a *tirutz* to every *kashye,* cannot provide us with an adequate answer to this question.

Guzik turns to me and asks "*Nu ?*" I understand the full significance of this wordless question. Guzik had survived alone, bereft of wife and children. But during the three years of brutal occupation he had excelled himself in charity and kindness. Despite his non-religious background, he ensured *rabbanim* and *talmidei chachamim* were not discriminated against. He helped them to the best of his ability and saw to their needs from the Joint's funds. Rabbi Zisha Friedman helped him in this vital work with all the power at his disposal. He supported *bachurim* who studied Torah with great *mesiras nefesh.* And now he asks me wordlessly — what now? What will the future bring? They all ask me to enquire what is going on at the Kehillah.

I enter the Kehillah building and meet Mark Lichtenbaum on the stairs. He urges me to join the prayers — as do all the other *Judenrat* officials. He has a religious streak and is proud of his rabbinical lineage, a descendant from the *Megaleh Temirin.* So I enter the Kehillah Hall where the services have nearly ended. Suddenly a young German SS official enters and points his revolver at the congregation. He orders everybody to pass slowly by, showing him their "numbers" that everyone has pinned to their lapel. We pass by in single file like the proverbial

"*B'nei Moron*" of the *tefillos*, until the turn came for Rav Yosef Konigsberg.

He was not allotted a number since he is officially incarcerated in the Jewish prison (which is how he escaped the deportations), where he is being continually interrogated by the Gestapo about the Lublin Yeshivah, of which he was financial director. Now he was brought by a Jewish warder to join the Rosh Hashanah prayers.

The SS official demands to know what he is doing here. The Jewish guard tries to give some reply, but he is brutally beaten for opening his mouth. The SS official aims his gun at Rav Yosef Konigsberg, who goes as white as a sheet — seeing death staring him in the face. All of us stand rooted to the spot, struck dumb by fear. But the SS official changes his mind and instead hauls him off to the *Umschlag*.

A great commotion breaks out at the Kehillah: some run to the Jewish prison governor who is officially responsible for Rav Konigsberg; others plan different strategies. A. B. Ackerman arrives, a bottle of whiskey is produced from nowhere and after a suitable bout of bargaining Rav Konigsberg is returned from the *Umschlag* back to the prison, and his life is saved.

On second day Rosh Hashanah, there were no official prayers at the Kehillah. But there were a number of organized *tefillos* at the Shultz factory at Nowolipie Street. The largest *minyan* was led by Rav Zisha Friedman who *leined* as well; his heartfelt *tefillos* sent a shiver through everyone present. Officially work was to continue on Rosh Hashanah, but ways were found round that restriction. Looking for friends and relatives, I visited there on second day Rosh Hashanah, and I found the Piasznow Rebbe, Rav Klonimos Schapira, the Pavianitz Rav, Rav Avraham Alter, and Mottel, Yosef, and Leib Lewin, as well as Yaakov

Rudzinski (the last surviving Mizrachi activist).

On this day, too, the Ukrainian militia were withdrawn from the *kesl* and it was finally possible to freely move to and fro. People begin to emerge from their hiding places, at first hesitantly and later with growing boldness. The first small groups are soon followed by larger crowds openly returning to the factories and workshops. I meet Rav Behr (Rav Menachem Ziemba's son-in-law) from Ostrow, Rabbi Yosef Frankel from Bilitz, and many others. They had all been hiding until now with their lives hanging by a thread. They are exhausted, emaciated, and tremendously weak; yet they are all relieved for the moment and each tells of his own personal miracle. There is a definite surge of optimism and a small flame of hope is lit within browbeaten hearts.

Monday, *motza'ei* Yom Kippur, September 21

Yom Kippur 5703

The Germans have decreed that work must continue through Yom Kippur but the Jews seek strategies to circumvent this. All the factories and workshops organize their own communal prayers, where they daven with broken hearts and great *kavannah.* In one workshop the famous *chazan*, Gershon Sirota, led the prayers. Even in the years preceding the War, his voice had become weak and lost its previous resonance. Now, in his old age and under the most oppressive conditions, his voice amazingly returned with all its former vigor and charm. His congregation listened in surprise and wonder as the talented but aged *chazan* surpassed all his previous performances, and many an eye ran with tears.

The small room was tightly packed, but Sirota's sweet

melodious voice enraptured them all, as he implored, *"U'malei misha'aloseinu*... And fulfill our desires with good measure, deliverance, and mercy." His enunciation of that last word, *"rachamim,"* mirrored simultaneously both the sobbing plea of a child and the desperate cry of an adult: all the many echoes of those sadistically persecuted and brutally murdered — could be heard in that word.

Sirota's composition for *Avinu Malkeinu* was heartfelt and plaintive, but it was not his normal *nusach.* Generally, according to his regular congregation, he never sang this section. But today a beautiful improvisation burst forth and truly tugged at our hearts. A particularly moving moment came near the end of this piece, when Sirota broke down as he sang:

"Avinu Malkeinu... Act for the sake of those slain for Your Holy Name!

"Avinu Malkeinu... Act for the sake of those slaughtered for Your Unity!

"Avinu Malkeinu... Act for the sake of those who have been through fire and water to sanctify Your Name!"

These poignant words accurately reflect our national catastrophe and penetrate deep into our soul. We all burst out weeping as we remember precious family and relatives. No longer was this a regular *tefillah* from the standard *machzor* text, but the bitter personal tragedy of each one of us. That ancient hallowed prayer was now totally relevant to the very hour. But what will our Father in Heaven do? Will He yet revoke the evil decrees against us? After such an enormous cataclysm, a spirit of bitterness holds sway everywhere.

All of us want to live, to escape, to survive until the end, but not on the basis of such a mass slaughter. What adequate redress is there for this horrendous bloodbath? We know that good outweighs evil and Divine reward is far greater that Divine retribution, but what possible good can result from this raging calamity?

"Avinu Malkeinu... Avenge the spilt blood of Your servants!"

Revenge is all that can bring us some comfort now. Finally we appreciate — today more than ever before — the potency of revenge. "Great is revenge," says the Talmud, "that it is enclosed between two Holy Names: *Kel Nekamos Hashem*."

Indeed, though the *Tanach* is full of kindness and mercy, we find that the avenging spirit is not lightly dismissed. "To Me belongs revenge and retribution" (*Devarim* 32:35). "He shall avenge the blood of his servants" (ibid. 32:43). "And I shall avenge the blood of those not avenged" (*Yoel* 4:21). "O Earth do not conceal my blood!" (*Iyov* 16:18).

In Poland now, every house, every brick, screams for revenge. All our own instincts in common with millions of our murdered brethren, the persecuted, the tortured, and the innocent children — all demand revenge.

Even so, what possible vengeance can outweigh what we have suffered in its severity, in its barbarism, in its enormity? After a far smaller catastrophe than ours, the poet wrote, "Satan has not yet devised the appropriate reprisal for the innocent blood of a child."

In the late afternoon I was davening *Neilah* at Rav Menachem Ziemba, when my friend Pinchas Wasserman, who was on the *Judenrat* executive, told me, "There is an *aktion* at Shultz!" I hurry to the *Judenrat* to discover more details and hear that this was "merely a sequel to the large *aktion* which just ended on Rosh Hashanah — only a few hundred Jews!" Through the *Judenrat* windows at 19 Zamenhof Street we can see groups of Jews being marched off to the *Umschlag.* It is already dark but I can recognize some of them.

I see Rav Meir Alter, the firstborn of the Gerrer Rebbe. Although he is dressed in ordinary working clothes and apparently lost in thought, his princely countenance betrays his lineage. Next to him walks Yitzchak Eisner and behind is Rav Meir's son-in-law Woolf Landau with his wife and their twin sons — thirteen years old and handsome, they were well known in the Ghetto for their maturity and diligence, having already absorbed much Torah (as well as foreign languages).

Dr. Isidor, the lawyer, is among the deportees as is Pulman, the secretary of the Tlomackie Street synagogue. (Only two days ago, Pulman told me about a letter he had received from his daughter who had escaped during the War to the Hebrew University.) I also notice Marissa Eisenstadt, the famous daughter of the Tlomackie Street choirmaster, who also has a beautiful voice; now she walks apathetically and alone to the *Umschlag* clutching her music notes. Her parents and family have already been deported. One can apply to all these unfortunate captives Eisenstadt's favorite song: "With fire and water we are killed for You."

Wednesday, September 23

More bad news. During the night four Jews were shot dead. The German pattern is recognizable. After midnight there is a hammering on the door, some Jew is dragged out at random, and his dead body is discovered next morning lying outside in the street. Before the mass deportations began this used to happen regularly.

Last night's events bring to mind how in the spring of 1942 the lawyer Menachem Linder was murdered by the same method. He was a friend of mine. Born in Soniatin on the

Galitzian-Romanian border, he studied in Warsaw, and by the time he was thirty he had the reputation of a serious academic, publishing a number of scientific papers in the *Yivo-bletter* for whom he was very active. Prof. Balaban predicted a great future for him as a sociologist. During the occupation he directed the statistical section of the Joint; together with Rabbi Huberband, Dr. Ringelbaum, and myself he also compiled archival evidence on the German persecution and decrees. In addition he organized cultural activities under the *Yikor* group, which he founded.

I once joined his group with Dr. Ringelbaum, when a discussion took place on Jewish writers such as Sholom Aleichem, Mendele Mocher Seforim, and Peretz. But I must confess I was not that interested since I knew full well that even then in Warsaw over 2000 *yeshivah bachurim* were diligently studying day and night *Gemara* and *Tosefos* in depth. Culture, science, and intellect began long before Mendele Mocher Seforim. But then it was not the time nor the place to engage in that age-old argument, especially since no one was likely to be persuaded either way — so I remained silent. But I could not help admiring their enthusiasm and spirit, and I agreed to supply Linder with any evidence available in the *Judenrat* archives under my care. (Though Czerniakow was not prepared to grant official permission, he was usually quite happy with these projects on a de facto basis.)

When I showed Linder what I had collated on Vilna, Lvov, Tarnopol, and Kolomia he was very appreciative, and I was greatly impressed how this earnest young man possessed both the cold analytical approach as well as so much energy and enthusiasm. But the barbarians cut his young life short. His young widow showed me a whole suitcase of his writings, scientific thesis, and sociological and statistical data on Warsaw's Jews. I placed all these into the underground archives, hoping one day to publish some memorial to this talented young man with so much potential — alas destroyed by the accursed enemy.

Thursday, September 24

Outside Help

Every letter from abroad brightens our dismal existence in the Ghetto. Today a letter arrived from Switzerland mentioning "a present like that sent to family Weingurt" — and the Weingurts have received South American passports. Similar letters have been sent to a few other families, including the Frankel-Rapaport family from Bilitz as well as Aaron Blumenkopf (from his son, a Swiss doctor). These passports are now our only lifeline in the Ghetto. Everybody is searching desperately for relatives, friends, or acquaintances living abroad — particularly in Switzerland — to whom to write coded letters containing the urgent message: send passports!

A great deal of effort and ingenuity is put into these letters to get them past the German censor and yet be understandable to the recipient. People employ vague hints or quote *pesukim* from *Tanach*, but very often these have precisely the opposite effect to what was intended. The German censor does suspect the underlying message — which can cause all sorts of problems — whereas the distant relative completely fails to comprehend our real needs. So in answer to urgent requests for "presents," small parcels arrive from Portugal containing packets of figs and tea! It is easy to imagine the bitter disappointment.

But, generally, no replies at all are received or else an answer which is worse than useless. Here in the Ghetto —

oppressed, imprisoned, and frightened — we wait eagerly for a letter with a foreign stamp. And when it finally arrives we read empty, meaningless promises written with no sense of urgency. They are, thank God, very well in Switzerland. It is already holiday time so they are leaving for a short break. On their return they will look into the matter, get some more information, and write again. Here the ground burns beneath our feet, every day feels like a year, but our relatives are calm and relaxed — they are going on holidays!

Only the closest of relatives are spurred into activity. Passports and letters were recently received by the Posnansky family from Lodz. Their son, Dr. Julius Posnansky in Basel, wrote, "I hope that you will soon enter a camp to be exchanged for other citizens from South America." Since this letter was written in French, which his mother cannot read, Mrs. Posnansky comes to me to translate it into Yiddish for her.

I was happy to do so the first time she asked me, but she is not content with that first session and she returns at regular intervals, nearly every other day, until I know the letter by heart — and so does she! I caught her in my outer office — her eyes running with tears — reading the letter aloud in Yiddish from the French words!*

A number of religious Jews, including prominent activists attempting to obtain foreign passports via the Swiss Aguda office, write to Rabbi Chaim Yisrael Eiss in Zurich. Since I have a permit to cross from the Ghetto to the "Aryan" (i.e., non-Jewish) areas of Warsaw, I am involved in this correspondence.

---

* This whole family transferred to the Vittel Camp in France for foreign Jews. But later they were deported (some on April 18, 1944 and the remainder on May 16, 1944) to Drancy and then on to Auschwitz, together with another 175 Jews. None of them returned.

We write a great deal about the remaining Warsaw *rabbanim* and religious activists.

I myself write to Rabbi Toviah Lewenstein in Zurich (whom I personally met in Warsaw when he was touring various *kehillos* in his campaign against the League of Nations' proposals to alter the secular calendar, which would have endangered Jewish festivals and Sabbaths). But they do not always answer, though we discover from other sources that our letters and pleas have arrived (such as when Rabbi C. Y. Eiss replies that he has shown my letter to Rabbi Dr. T. Lewenstein, who cannot take up this matter at present). Dr. A. Silverstein in Geneva does not reply to either Prof. Tamar Shorr's letters or mine.

We were not writing on behalf of ourselves, as we already have the necessary documents. We are more concerned for the plight of Dr. Schipper, Dr. Stein, Abraham Gefner, and others. But we receive neither a reply nor passports. Mr. Schwalbe, the *chalutz* leader in Geneva, does reply and, judging by the correspondence shown to me by Mr. Alexander Landau, appears to fully understand what is at stake and will send what is necessary. Rabbi. C. Y. Eiss also sends some passports to a select few religious Jews, but he seems to work extremely slowly and without warmth. Rabbi Dr. Saul Weingurt in Montreaux has sent passports to his parents and relatives, including Rav Shabsi Rapaport, the well-known author of *sefarim* from Widislav-Pinzov, and Rav Chaim Leibush Berglas from Crakow.

Foreign passports are now our only means of escape. We are desperate for one, for a promise of one, or a warm word of encouragement from abroad. The Sejm Representative Yaakov Trokenheim, R. Zisha Friedman, R. A. G. Friedensohn, and R. Yehudah Leib Orlean have all received firm promises, but for the moment they still have no passports. Meanwhile the ground literally burns beneath one's feet.*

These passports alone are not in themselves the complete salvation. One also has to employ the services of a great many brokers and intermediaries as well as utilizing every influence and *protexia*, which all costs a lot of money. Only after much effort and influence is one officially recognized as a foreign resident, and not everyone attains this goal.

Friday, September 25

I had a visit today from Dr. Lipman Tzumberg, a teacher at one of the schools run by the anti-religious Bund workers' movement. He related to me many of the activities carried out by former Bundist teachers on behalf of the poor. Officially they are under TOZ *(Towarzystwo Ochrony Zdrowia,* or the Society for Health Preservation) and are only involved in public health and sanitation. But effectively they are running schools for children between the ages of seven and fourteen, with food supplied by the Joint. They also have soup kitchens, which I have visited and are efficiently run — with great ingenuity exercised in converting pitifully small amounts of vegetables into nourishing meals. Dr. Tzumberg claims that the Bundists are also secretly involved in social work, again with the Joint's support.

When our discussion turned to Eretz Yisrael, I reported some news I had heard through illegal channels, that Rav Shloma David Kahana (who had escaped to Jerusalem) has — together with the lawyer Shimon Seidman — established a

---

* Later in March and April 1943, they received these foreign passports, but it was already then too late to transfer to camps for "foreign" Jews. Only Rabbi Y. L. Orlean and the Rapaport-Frankel family managed to enter these camps but they were later deported.

special office to solve the *agunah* problem. At this, Dr. Tzumberg trots out all the Bund's anti-religious propaganda, but eventually he admitted, "If we only outlive these butchers, surely we will find some common ground. We cannot continue to go on in the future like we have in the past. All those many socialist workers, members of the Bund, must finally take a part in rebuilding the Homeland, which also comprises so many socialist ideals."

We discuss avenues of escape and resistance. Nearly everybody else senses a common purpose, but a few Bund leaders — generally those who have little knowledge or contact with the outside world — still naively wait for "outside help." Dr. Tzumberg is not numbered among these. He is too wise to be taken in by empty promises of solidarity and brotherhood from the Polish socialist movement, and he rebuts such wishful thinking with a dismissive wave of the hand.

Monday (1st day *Chol Hamoed* Sukkos), September 28

While walking through the Ghetto, I meet Dr. Esther Markin, previously a university lecturer on psychology, and she informs me that together with her former colleagues she is still giving lectures to private audiences. Apparently there is a great thirst in the Ghetto for academic knowledge and foreign languages. There are also a number of mobile libraries usually operating via each block of buildings. Clandestine schools exist, too, with quite a large spread of subjects. In addition, the previous *Judenrat* president, Czerniakow, set up laboratories so Jewish university professors could continue their research. Among them was Professor Zentenrswer, a famous chemist, and the two biologists Professor Hirschfeld and Professor Sweibaum; somehow they have even made some important scientific discoveries despite the impossible conditions and severely limited funds. What a waste of talent!

Wednesday, September 30

Rav Treisman's Wife, H.y.d.

Yesterday, as I and Nochum Remba cautiously emerged from the Revisionist bunker at 21 Zamenhof Street and were gingerly approaching the exit to the street, we noticed a commotion opposite in Kopeicka Street. We withdrew and waited in the courtyard as night fell. After about half an hour we summoned up our courage and ventured out onto the street, where we found Rav Simchah Treisman and Rav Eliezer Yitzchak Meisel from Lodz running frantically.

"What's happened?" we ask.

Rav Meisel replies, "We have had a 'guest.' Meisinger's just been!"

We all know instantly what that means. Meisinger is one of the Gestapo's sadists. Every alternate day he drives into the Ghetto in his small car and fires at any Jew he finds on the street. He has just shot another four victims, and now at the corner of Zamenhof and Kopeicka Street there lies the body of a murdered woman — the wife of Rav Shalom Treisman and the mother of four children. Her brother-in-law Rav Simchah Treisman rushes to arrange a Jewish burial with the help of Yaakov Mintz from Mottel Pinkert's Undertaking Service.

"Now," says Rav Simchah bitterly, "I have another three young children to cope with besides my own." His brother, Rav Shalom Treisman, has been exiled by the Russians to Siberia, together with his son.

"Do you remember," Remba remarks to me, "the authoritative, almost regal impression Rav Treisman would make when he appeared at weddings in an official capacity? How he would love to lead the Jewish revolt against the Nazis!"

"If he was here," I replied, "he would certainly have joined the resistance movement. In the past he had helped establish the Revisionist religious group Yeshurun. Now he has another reason — avenging his wife's murder."

We enter the *Judenrat* archives and pass on the latest outrage. Knowing that many presently at the archives have an avid interest in historical papers and footnotes, I show them copies of letters received from Rav Shalom Treisman. (I saw this as a sort of memorial or *Kaddish* for his murdered wife.) I open the folder and read aloud:

> "*Today is erev Rosh Hashanah*," writes Rav Treisman from Archangel, "*but we have to work in the forests, cutting down trees — today, tomorrow, and the day after — encircled with the freezing cold and starvation. There are no Yomim Tovim here. But I was lucky: I had wounded my leg! A special mazal, I am temporarily off work. To quote the Chumash on Yaakov Avinu: The sun shone on him as he limped on his hip; there is a special brightness for those that limp. Yet I have no shofar, no machzor, not even an ordinary siddur. David Hamelech had blended a special medicine for every ailment. As a last resort we will have to use his medical compound today: Ribono Shel Olam, witness my affliction, my hard labor, and forgive all my sins. Let that suffice this year instead of*

the many piyutim, selichos, tefillos, and techinos."

There is another letter in this bundle from the Bucharian exile written by the world famous *gaon* and *tzadik* Rav Berish Weidenfeld, the Rav and *rosh yeshivah* of Tschebin. This letter was written to my relative Leah Turkel of Warsaw, now deported:

> *"I was forced to work throughout the Holy Day in my new profession — shepherding the sheep. There was no machzor or siddur, so I pointed to my flock of sheep and chanted 'Kevakoras Roeh Edro...' (as the shepherd checks his flock) with such great kavannah, I have never before experienced. Ribono Shel Olam, witness how faithfully I look after the sheep in my care. Your Nation Israel are Your sheep!"*

And another letter from Rav Shalom Treisman written on *erev* Sukkos:

> *"Today is erev Sukkos but we have no sukkah, no lulav or esrog, no meat or wine. We do not even have two white challos — merely coarse black bread and watery soup. The pasuk commands us 'ulekachtem...vesimachtem....' Easy enough to say 'Take and be happy,' but overwhelmingly difficult to carry out in our present circumstances! I remember from our stetl a former photographer who later practiced as a dentist. When patients would arrive after a sleepless night wrestling with the pain of an abscessed tooth, the dentist (and former photographer) would gather up his intimidating instruments and announce (out of force of habit) — smile! This is almost our experience today... Be happy! Nonetheless we*

> *must not lose our bitachon. Times will improve. The world must celebrate its Yom Tov and we are commanded to be joyful. So let us rejoice. This too is for the best."*

These letters unveil an unusual *bitachon*. And in his circumstances it was indeed for the best. His deportation to Siberia saved his life. Jews in the frozen faraway northern wastes are relatively safe; probably the only ones among the Polish Jews. Their terrible "disaster," which they fought so hard to evade, was actually their *mazal* — "*Hashem chashvah letovah,* Hashem planned it for the best."

OCTOBER 1942

Thursday, October 1

Ghetto Institutions

Since the Germans could not be bothered with too many separate organizations or institutions, they instead grouped them together under one central umbrella in order to keep them under closer scrutiny. All individual trade or economic federations were — like charitable organizations — arbitrarily closed down and placed under the *Judenrat*'s jurisdiction. (Political parties were banned completely.) As far as possible, however, these groups continued to function independently with many of their former officials in place, though officially they were operating from the Kehillah.

For instance, Abraham Gefner, the former president of the Businessmen's Central Federation (in Senatorska Street) now became the president of the *Judenrat*'s Business Department — just as Abraham Shtolzman, the former director, still retained his old position, now though, officially under the *Judenrat*. The same applied to the president and director of the Central Federation for Young Businessmen (at 40 Leszno Street) and the directors of the Artisans' Central Federation, which now operated officially as Kehillah departments.

Effectively these all functioned independently with their own committees and staff. However, because of the dismal circumstances in the Ghetto, they were now far less concerned with previous organizational affairs and more immediately involved with mutual assistance. By being cut off in the Ghetto, they ceased to have a national role throughout Poland and were primarily limited to Warsaw.

TOZ (the hygienic and sanitation organization) and CENTOS (*Centrale Towarzystwa Opiekinad Sierotami* — The National Society for the Care of Orphans) were within the *Judenrat* umbrella only as far as the Germans were concerned; they were, in fact, completely independent bodies, funded by the Joint. These two groups established and ran hundreds of children's shelters, where thousands of children were fed, cared for, and educated and received all forms of aid. These shelters formed a vital function in the Ghetto. ZTOS (*Zydowskie Towarzystwo Opieki Spolecznej* — the Jewish Society for Self-Help) also operated on its own, eventually growing so large that it overtook the *Judenrat* in the scope of projects undertaken and the number of employees on its payroll. It ran 141 communal kitchens feeding tens of thousands a day, and also organized dozens of charitable institutions and supported thousands of needy individuals.

As a result of ZTOS's growth, it inevitably took over many of the Kehillah's functions and functionaries — becoming in the process a serious rival to the *Judenrat*. And while the *Judenrat* was led by relatively new faces with no previous political affiliations, representing nobody but themselves, the Joint and ZTOS were headed by veteran activists from the larger pre-war National parties: in particular the Zionists (Dr. I. Schipper), Agudas Yisrael (Rabbi Alexander Zisha Friedman), the Bund

(Mauricy Orzech), and the left-wing Poalei Zion (S. Zagan). Lower down the ranks many of their departments were staffed by activists from other parties.

Due to their influence, ZTOS greatly enlarged their number of employees — enlisting mainly the *literati* and intellectual elite — by inventing new positions or establishing new institutions with the Joint's support. They preferred to give the intelligentsia official employment rather than distributing handouts.

At the outset of the War, as journalists rapidly lost their jobs and livelihood, a self-help organization was set up by B. Chilinovitz, N. Gavza, and in particular the young Moshe Mark (later known as Moshe Prager) who displayed enormous enterprise, organizational ability, and great personal bravery, often risking his life on his forays between institutions and activists. Later, this mutual aid organization for authors and journalists was incorporated within the Joint, and its numbers were recognized as Joint officials.

Such "employment" not only provided vital salaries but also a modicum of protection against deportation, labor camps, or conscription into the slave labor brigades. As their numbers swelled, the Joint used them to manage various communal kitchens, children's shelters and other welfare agencies. Generally, these authors and artists did not receive very high positions, but in order to justify their salaries they would mount shows, concerts, exhibitions, and the like. All this activity was usually carved out between two rival cultural groups: Tekuma (Zionist-Hebrew) and Yikor (Socialist-Yiddishist). Despite the dire reality in the Ghetto, these cultural efforts continued with great tenacity, a symbol both of defiance and the fervent desire to outlive the enemy and experience a better future.

Friday, *Hoshanah Rabbah*, October 2

Torah and Avodah at One Bench

Today I toured all the workshops and factories in the Ghetto. Although I had received an official permit only to search for books and *sefarim,* I was really looking for people. And I found a number of personalities whose life is a book in itself. "How foolish of the Babylonians to stand up in respect for a *sefer Torah* and not for a great man learned in Torah," says the *Talmud Bavli.*

Our expedition should be uncovering rare books; instead we discover rare human treasures amid the poverty and oppression. I arrive at the Schultz factory when the assembled "workers" are davening and reciting *Hoshanos*. By the efforts of R. Avraham Hendel, one of the managers there, the Schultz works now "employ" the cream of Orthodoxy — Chasidic Rebbes, *rabbanim, talmidei chachamim*, religious activists, and prominent Chasidim. At one workbench, officially repairing shoes (actually the "work" only involves removing nails with pliers), sits the Kozielglow Rav, R. Yehudah Arieh Frumer, formerly *rosh yeshivah* at Chachmei Lublin.

He might be sitting here but his mind is miles away; his lips are constantly moving, obviously he is studying Torah by heart. Every so often, he throws a question to his neighbor opposite, the Piasnow Rebbe, Rav Klonimos Shapira, author of the *Chovos HaTalmidim,* and they begin a whispered dialogue in Talmudic study quoting *Chazal* and *Poskim*. The spirits of the *Rishonim* and *Achronim* hover above this workbench — for these "shoemakers" are really *gaonim* and Talmudic giants. Who worries about the German overseers or the SS? Rapidly, they forget the continual hunger, the ongoing persecution and oppression, the ever-present threat of death. They are no longer in a factory at 46 Nowolipie Street, but inside the Temple's Hewn Chamber at a sitting of the *Sanhedrin*. While some succumb to their maltreatment, these *gadolim* rise to new spiritual heights.

As I sit at this table, I notice my old friend Moshe Pinchas Hertz, the Biala *ilui*; despite his young age, his mind races like a raging fire which cannot be contained. Throwing all caution to the wind he quotes *Rambams, Rans*, and *Tosefos* at all comers. But there is an urgent need to restrain him — any minute the SS may reappear. Nearby "works" another young man, Avraham Shloma Rabinowitz, son of the Niestadler Rebbe and son-in-law of R. Avraham Ostrover. Next to him sits R. Avraham Alter (the Rav of Pavianitz), R. Dovid Halberstam (the Rav of Sosnowitz), and R. Blumenfeld the Mizrachi activist. Every so often R. Rabinowitz bashfully adds his own contribution to the discussion, which his neighbors on the workbench pass on until it reaches the Talmudic giant, the Rav of Kozielgow, and others who listen eagerly.

"This young man talks to the point!" they exclaim, and the Talmudic debate switches tack. Afterwards, Rabbi Frumer tells me, "This young man will be a great *gaon*, I had no previous idea of his potential!"

Here at the Schultz factory I meet Rivka Alter-Rapaport. She has only one worry: how is Rabbi Y. L. Orlean, the Beis Yaakov director, getting on and what are his views? Others tell me that she works in the factory kitchens for twelve hours at a stretch. She also works a couple of nights in lieu of working on Shabbos. Furthermore, she works an extra night to free Yocheved Lewin-Alter (Reb Itche Meir Lewin's sister) from having to work on Shabbos.

"As you see, my mind is made up," she tells me simply but

firmly. "I shan't work on Shabbos. What can already happen? *Mus ich den leben* — Must I live? Whatever the consequences I shall not barter away my Shabbos!"

Obviously the *rabbanim* could permit her to work on Shabbos on the grounds of *pikuach nefesh,* but she prefers to ask no *shailos.*

Rabbi Yehudah Leib Orlean still teaches Torah subjects to those few Orthodox girls still surviving in the Ghetto. In his lessons he also discusses the problem of Rivka Lewin-Alter. She possesses both a wide knowledge and profound comprehension which earns her respect from all quarters, even the non-religious. Not everybody accepts her strong views but they can recognize greatness in this short woman who has grown old before her time. (Her sixteen-year-old son Pinchas, too, has exceptional knowledge and the understanding of somebody extremely mature.)

The Schultz factory is a whole world on its own, providing a sanctuary for religious Jews. I find here Rav Sender from Posen, Rav Simchah Treisman from Lodz, Rabbi Dr. Glitzenstein from Grodzivondez, the young genius Aaron Ziemba (the son of R. Menachem Ziemba), Radomski the Mizrachi activist, the Rapoport brothers from Bilitz, and the brothers of R. Itche Meir Lewin — Mottel, Yosef and Leibel. Previously were also here R. Moshe Betzalel (the Gerrer Rebbe's brother), R. Meir Alter (the firstborn son of the Gerrer Rebbe), R. Bunim Lewin from Lodz, and R. Zvi Gur-Arye and sons, all of whom have already been deported to Treblinka.

The remaining survivors sit and study. Despite privation, starvation, and fear, they rise above their dismal surroundings and soar to great spiritual heights.

Tuesday, October 6

Apostates

I had a strange visit today — the widow of the author Leopold Belmont (who died in the Ghetto during the summer of 1942 and was buried in the Christian Evangelical Cemetery). I am interested to discover the position of the Polish Church on all the persecutions and massacres.

"They are sympathetic," Mrs. Belmont informs me. I ask in surprise, "That's all? And do they aid any of the baptized Jews in the Ghetto?" But Mrs. Belmont does not know, since she is an Evangelist and the Evangelists are also persecuted — the Germans regard them as traitors. (As Protestants they share the German cultural background, yet they remained loyal Polish patriots.) I can actually confirm this: I remember the Polish Evangelist leader Senator W. L. Awart telling me that the Nazis imprisoned all the Protestant priests and refused them permission to conduct services in public.

And what of the Catholic Church? There are about 3000 Jewish Catholics in the Ghetto and they have their own church in Leszno Street with their own clergy — also renegade Jews. It was claimed in the Ghetto, with some justification, that Czerniakow treated them favorably, giving baptized Jews positions in the *Judenrat*. Indeed the Jewish Police was headed by Josef Szerynski, a Catholic *meshumad*. Other apostates, for instance Prof. Zentenswer, received privileges from the *Judenrat* presidency. Had the Catholic clergy helped any of these baptized Jews? It turns out that they had not.

Jews would always remain Jews in their eyes — even after they converted. And an antisemite remains an antisemite even with regard to the sons and grandsons of renegade Jews —

unofficially the Polish Church had accepted the racist criteria.

Some time ago, a priest from a village near Cologne in Germany came to see me. He was the grandson of a *meshumad*; neither he nor his parents had any connections with Jews. Yet somehow the Nazis had discovered his parentage and exiled him to Warsaw with the other Jews. He was in a difficult position — from where should he receive support? So he appealed to me in my position as head of the *Judenrat*'s Religious Department. Certainly he had a religious connection, but I felt uneasy: should the Kehillah's Religious Department fund priests? What will our expenditure accounts look like in the future when this strange item appears? (It will surely make an odd historical footnote.) But on the other hand, one should not check too closely when it comes to "*mezonos*" — providing vital food aid. There is also a question of promoting peace between religions and people.

So I suggested he appeal directly to the Bishops' synod and other priests from his church. I took on myself the responsibility of delivering his letter to the correct address when I next crossed over to the Aryan side. The German priest was not much impressed by my suggestion, but he wrote out a letter all the same and handed it to me. Since I was apprehensive about personally entering Christian institutions, I had the letter delivered via a Polish friend. After a week the priest returned with their reply — a blunt refusal with no explanations. The priest was nonplussed by this but I understood it only too well. In their eyes he remained a Jew.

We found a solution to his particular problem: he would be supported by the *Judenrat*'s Social Welfare Department run by my good friend M. Lustenberg. When I was being marched to the death trains, I noticed the Cologne priest among the crowd.

The same fate awaited all the other apostates in the Ghetto.

Somebody had once suggested that I should advise these apostates to seek shelter with their Aryan co-religionists or within the Polish monasteries. But I had hesitated. Since childhood I had felt a particular abhorrence to Jews who had baptized out of their faith. I felt they were the greatest abomination to our nation. In the Ghetto my antipathy had only grown worse, and I could not bring myself to approach people like Szerynski, Natanson, or Luxembourg. Later I felt deep remorse for my reluctance. This was a matter of saving lives.

Now I can see we had not missed an opportunity. The Polish Church, which had always been antisemitic, did not improve during the German occupation. Even during the mass slaughter they remained hostile neutrals.

Friday, October 9

I went on another book-seeking exercise around the Schuling carpentry workshop in Nowolipie Street, where I discovered some old acquaintances. Actually, I arrived during a heated discussion between the Hebrew author M. L. Tsudner and the Hebrew poet Yitzchak Katzenelsohn regarding the merits and motives of Sh. Y. Agnon, before they begin debating the Hebrew translation of Homer's *Iliad*. Do they have no greater worries at present?

Katzenelsohn does have another concern — what will happen to his play *By the Waters of Babylon*? He wrote it in the Ghetto before the mass deportations began, and I have heard a few very powerful scenes at a secret venue organized by the Revisionists. He wants to place the original manuscript at the Kehillah archives for safekeeping, and I agree. Tsudner has a request of his own: he wants employment and safety at the *Judenrat*'s Archives Department. The carpentry workshops are busy shaving down the same wooden beams until some are as thin as cigarette paper. How long can that charade continue before the Germans discover that their work is is not productive. And then what will happen to them?

"And our work at the archives is more productive?" I retort sceptically, but Tsudner insists he cannot abide the company of common carpenters who have not the faintest inkling about the finer points of Hebrew literature. After I finally agreed to take him along, he explains his true reasons. Already he has lost his whole family and now he is starving. His situation was never too brilliant in the Ghetto — subsisting from the sales of his books off a wheelbarrow — now he is completely alone.

"Nonetheless, I have no wish to become one of the nameless millions," Tsudner continues earnestly, "for whom American and English Jewry will organize impressive memorial services in their synagogues and their leading cantors will serenade them with '*...b'avur shenehergu al Kiddush Hashem...*' and the *Yehudim* will proudly nod with their top hats. No, it's not worth it. Nor do I need the Archbishop of Canterbury to conduct prayers on our behalf so that the hearts of the Anglo-Jewish leadership will melt at the noble compassion shown by the Nations. I cannot be happy after this war is over if somebody will shout into my grave the glad tidings that Hitler has finally been defeated. No, what I want is to live and see it all for myself! Do you understand?"

I do understand. This is one of the most powerful sentiments in the drive for survival in the Ghetto. Why else should those callously condemned to extinction display such superhuman efforts to stay alive?

Only the fundamental belief in the ultimate triumph of Justice. They know, they are convinced, that this evil regime will be destroyed, and they are anxious to see this for themselves. In the words of the Talmud, "*Yeisi v'achiminei* — Let the liberation come so I should see it."

Low Suicide Rate

This is probably the underlying reason behind an amazing phenomenon. Despite our awful suffering there are hardly any suicides in the Ghetto — neither before the mass deportations, not even during the deportations, nor in this relative lull afterwards. In fact, the suicide rate before the War was higher. I can only think of two cases in the last few years, and neither were Zionists or religious Jews. Czerniakow's suicide, by contrast, was an act of heroism. If the suicidal urge results from depression, despair, or a form of escapism, then nobody in the Ghetto has lost faith in the eventual defeat of evil. The oppression has only strengthened their will to live.

The director of the Statistical Department showed me the astonishing fact that between 1940 and 1942 the suicide rate fell by 65 percent compared to pre-War statistics! My own theory is that in the face of such a colossal communal calamity, personal problems fade into insignificance. Above all, everyone wants to survive until the end. After that the future will undoubtedly be better, more promising, more secure, more pleasurable.

Monday, October 12

The Jewish Police

Had two guests today: the young Josef Tennenbaum (son of the late Mizrachi *parnas* Eliyahu Tennenbaum) and Jacob Ehrlich. Both are Jewish policemen, but what a difference between them — literally worlds apart. While the former is an intelligent young lawyer, always ready to do a favor or save a fellow Jew, even at risk to life and limb, the latter is an underworld scoundrel and a merciless extortionist. And yet both are Jewish policemen. Which of them best typifies the true face of the Ghetto police force; which of the two is more representative?

Now perhaps is an opportune time to finally evaluate this hybrid institution and its function within the Ghetto.

The Jewish police force is a difficult, painful chapter in the annals of the Ghetto. History will pass its own severe judgment on this strange creature, and I shall not attempt to defend it. I will merely try and answer the awkward question: How was it that some Jews were prepared to hand over their brethren to the murderers? But first we must ask how it all began. For the police force was not originally established to collaborate in mass murder. Indeed when the Jewish police were being created, nobody then in their most pessimistic, wildest nightmare could have dreamt of the forthcoming ruthless program of extinction.

Its early role was in maintaining *ordnung* after most of the Polish police force was withdrawn from the Ghetto. From the beginning the police hardly became a haven for the best elements. But when it became obvious that the job included extra income and privileges, there was soon a great demand for employment there. The *Judenrat*'s representative on the Jewish police was the lawyer Bernard Zundelovitz (a weak individual who soon lost all influence) and Kupshitzer, a small man blessed with neither intelligence nor communal responsibility who had suddenly climbed to the top. Appointed to head the police was the apostate Szerynski, previously a colonel in the Polish police force. Though the police staff did contain a number of honorable people, it did not take long before the lowest elements took over.

Many of the leading positions were held either by assimilationists — mostly lawyers — or baptized Jews like Szerynski. All of them were far removed from Judaism and the Jewish masses, looking down at them with disdain and often palpable hate. To this motley crew were added groups of swindlers, youths from the "*goldene yugend*," and others of the lowest class. These all undertook their allotted tasks with great gusto and enthusiasm; and therein lay their central defect and *aveirah.*

They swaggered to their appointed role and revealed unnecessary diligence and persistence — far too much diligence and persistence. Many possessed a great deal of energy and enterprise, and they used these where they were least welcome: in carrying out the German decrees. Since the vast majority of police officers came from an assimilationist background and disliked the Jewish masses, they often performed the German's dictates willingly — instead of unwillingly, with a broken heart.

At first they received no wages from the *Judenrat* and carried out their tasks voluntarily, as if they were honorable idealists and it was a privilege. But since they needed money to live, they would seek out profitable sidelines, particularly in the smuggling of food into the Ghetto. This actually had its positive side — even if the police did make some money on it — since otherwise we would all have starved to death on the regulation daily ration of 12 dekagram (i.e., 120 grams) of bread each.

It was worse when they invented their own decrees (sometimes in conjunction with other institutions). For example, the communal bathhouse decrees. Whenever a case of typhus was discovered in an apartment block, they would seal the block, letting no one in or out before marching everyone off to the bathhouse (where they were most likely to become infected with the disease). Nobody could then leave their house until they paid the police a certain sum. They had many other similar schemes. However, there were still a few honest policemen who behaved honorably.

This was the situation prior to the "*aktions*," as the Germans called the mass deportations to the death trains. When these began, the police force underwent a fundamental change in character and function.

But a few words of warning. It is wrong to measure events in the Ghetto, particularly during the deportations, with the regular yardstick; nor should one be in any hurry to judge certain individuals.

Generally Jews in *galus* reflect the external pressures which are not of their own choosing. Now our surrounding circumstances have been deliberately engineered by the Germans to wreak havoc on normal modes of behavior. So those with a weak personality descended yet further, the wicked became worse, the corrupt became even more venomous. (By contrast those on a high spiritual plane soared to ever greater heights.) Just as the ancient Egyptians not only behaved badly towards us but also "*v'yoreyu osanu hamitzriim,*" which also means, as the Sefas Emes explains, they forced us to act more wickedly and descend towards ever greater evil.

This also accurately describes the German system of oppression. They used every satanic method to break the Jewish spirit and release the most inhuman instincts. They made our struggle for survival so harsh and subhuman that eventually we could only live at the expense of our fellow Jews.

Since the police were anyhow not guided by the best of motives or personnel, during the deportations they were totally dominated by the renegade Jews, extreme assimilationists, swindlers, underworld gangsters, and the "*goldene yugend*" devoid of any morals. No religious Jew — whether affiliated to Aguda, Mizrachi or non-political — held any position in the police.*

Nor, incidentally, were there any well-known Zionist activists among the police. The police force was made up of alien elements, enemies to their own people, and these were unable to rise to the test. When the opportunity came to save themselves at the expense of others (or so they believed) they did not hesitate. Some acted as the Germans' hangmen with alacrity and initiative, looking down at the Jewish masses as being lower class. And they regarded religious Jews with scorn and even hatred. Indeed, they had scarce brotherly feeling towards any Jew and showed very little humanity in general. (However, a select few policemen did save a large number of Jews at grave personal risk.)

As the pace of the deportations quickened, some of the police degenerated even further. Besides saving their own families, many amassed great riches and lived a life of wild hedonism, drinking themselves into stupor. (Because of the prevailing insecurity, there generally existed in the Ghetto the philosophy of "Eat, drink and be merry, for tomorrow we may die.")

Recently on passing the entrance to 11 Zamenhof Street, I heard cries for help. Investigating further I discovered an elderly Chasid struggling with a policeman. The policeman was

---

* Later, too, in the camps, the *kapos*, the guards, and other oppressors were not religious Jews.

trying to drag him away and the Chasid was resisting. Where was he taking him to? To the deportation area!

I could not contain myself any longer and asked for an explanation. It appears that the policeman discovered the Chasid in hiding without an official "number" and wanted to march him away. The Chasid had agreed to go quietly but he insisted on fetching his *tallis* and *tefillin*, and this the policeman would not allow. I tried to persuade the policeman to relent; I begged him for mercy but to no avail. I introduced myself as a well-known journalist, but he was an assimilationist and had never heard of me. Eventually a hundred zlotys gained the release of that elderly Jew, at least for the moment. Since this all took place two days ago, after the deportations had already stopped, that policeman was acting voluntarily!

Those who had previously tried to cut their links with the Jewish people continued their alienation in the Ghetto. Vainly they believed this was the way to save themselves.*

As to the question how normal morals and suitable behavior had deteriorated so rapidly, this was mainly due to German machinations which had set in motion the conditions to drive those of weak resolve even lower. People who under normal conditions might have been ordinary, law abiding citizens were unable to withstand the abnormal and awful circumstances we now faced.

---

* Later the Jewish Resistance carried out the death sentence on the collaborators Jacob Leikin, Josef Szerinsky, Israel Fuerst, Firstenberg, and other police officials.

Motza'ei Shabbos, October 17

Child Smugglers

While I was walking down Franciszkanska Street, I heard shots. Immediately there is panic, people running in all directions to hide in apartments or cellars. Within seconds the road is empty except for the body of a murdered victim, left lying in the street. I enter a nearby apartment and find a group of people trembling with fear. Somebody plucks up enough courage to peep out of the window but there is no movement outside. Everyone stands back waiting for further developments.

Does this herald a new *aktion* or is it an isolated incident? One hour and then another slowly passes in fearful apprehension before a tall youth in a leather coat goes down to investigate. After about ten minutes he returns to reassure us. "It's nothing — two smugglers have been killed." This is what we have become used to: two men are killed and it is "nothing," a daily occurrence.

Smuggling in the Ghetto is an important activity, and it is worthwhile recording this for posterity. Under normal circumstances it would hardly be considered an honorable calling. But now it demands a great deal of courage and fulfills a vital role in the beleaguered Ghetto — possibly as important as that played by any of the official or unofficial welfare agencies. True, the Ghetto smugglers carried out their clandestine activities for personal gain (as, indeed, did some of the welfare workers and their benefactors, who also had ulterior motives), but without the smugglers' cunning exploits, starvation would soon have killed us all. Never did the epigram "*B'nafsho yavo lachmo* — with his life he earned his bread" apply so aptly as it did to these intrepid smugglers.

The Ghetto was surrounded by walls three meters high, which were topped by barbed wire and shards of sharp glass. Both sides of these walls were patrolled by watchful Polish policemen and German guards. Merely approaching the walls or gates was a risky business; the German guards would shoot at the slightest suspicion. Some guards fired even without suspicion. One particular German guard — nicknamed "Frankenstein" — would regularly shoot down Jews for no apparent reason; it was claimed in the Ghetto that this man had a daily compulsion to fire at Jews. Effectively, the Ghetto was as sealed and closely guarded as a prison for dangerous criminals.

Yet despite this strict blockade, various products were smuggled in from the Aryan side: primarily foodstuffs such as bread, flour, vegetables, potatoes, sugar, jam, and butter. Without these, the German-imposed starvation diet would have carried us all off, long before the program of systematic liquidation began. It is difficult to describe all the tricks and inventions these cunning Jews needed to bring in a sack of flour, a few loaves of bread, and some kilos of potatoes.

Originally, the Germans constructed the Ghetto by blocking off streets and splitting adjoining homes so that one house belonged to "Jewish" Warsaw and the other was on the "Aryan" side. Soon secret openings were made through party walls into neighboring apartments or attics to facilitate smuggling. When the Germans discovered this stratagem, the walls were rebuilt to encompass whole blocks of houses and hermetically seal off the Ghetto.

Even so, the Jews found ways of outwitting the German scheme by bribing Polish policemen — and even German guards. Every hole or break in the walls was exploited, as were the dark alleys. Official import licences from the *transferstelle* (the German customs post in the Ghetto) were amended to bring in other merchandise. One of the main centers for smuggling was the cemetery in Gesia Street where the surrounding walls had many holes. Much food was brought in through there and even, on occasion, live cows!

The most interesting yet saddest aspect of these smuggling exploits was the part played by children. Young children, thin and wiry, aged between six and eight years old, would slip through the tiniest gaps or holes in the walls and with a few precious zlotys, would buy small amounts of food — usually bread or potatoes — which they would conceal in their clothing. But now they could no longer squeeze through those tiny gaps. So they would loiter around one of the guarded entrances to the Ghetto until the German guards were momentarily distracted, at which point they would hurry through without a body search. (Generally the checks on entering the Ghetto were relatively less stringent than on the way out.)

Usually these child smugglers were successful, but every so often a Polish detective would prowl around (either voluntarily or as a duty) and would catch Jewish children acting suspiciously. Either he would ask the German guard to beat them savagely or he would beat them himself — or even shoot them dead. For the crime of trying to feed themselves and their families with a slice of bread, these brave children would pay with their young lives. Often these courageous children were the sole breadwinners for their parents, as well as older brothers and sisters, who were too large to squeeze through these tiny gaps. The families were left at home waiting in hungry anticipation for the pitifully small amounts of food their savior — a seven-year-old child — could bring them.

Tried and tested by cruel circumstance, these tender young

children rapidly matured into seasoned businessmen. Their brains were sharpened by the complicated give and take in the Ghetto, their mental arithmetic was phenomenal and it was not easy to fool them. They had become old before their time; speaking and acting like grown-ups and carrying on their thin shoulders the whole burden of Nazi oppression.

In the mortal battle with our ruthless enemies who plot to starve the Ghetto into extinction, they are the central heroes. Many fall in this harsh, unequal struggle but they fall as heroes fighting to sustain their starving families — and often they will supply food to total strangers, too. Even though they receive no medals or publicity, their heroism deserves respect no less than other fighters in the Ghetto. They might even have beaten the German plans if not for the mass murder which destroys all resistance.

The Jewish Ghetto children, who act as breadwinners, importers, smugglers, and, above all, fighters against the German-imposed starvation, are soldiers without uniforms or weapons. Tiny soldiers, yet huge heroes constituting one of the saddest but also one of the most amazing chapters in the annals of the Ghetto resistance.

NOVEMBER 1942

Friday, 1st day Chanukah, November 4

Ray of Hope

A sensation yesterday in the Ghetto — entry certificates from Palestine arrived. A tiny flicker of hope is lit in each heart, everyone thinks: perhaps there is one for me, too? Later it transpires that only fifty-four certificates were sent, mostly for wives whose husbands were already in Eretz Yisrael. The head of the Jewish postal service, M. Yashunsky, brings the letters and documents to my office in the archives to ask advice on how to deliver them. All of the addresses are totally out of date; most of these streets have already been cleared of Jews and "Aryanized." I examine these letters carefully.

All the certificates were sent by the Eretz Israel office in Istanbul, Turkey, and most have photographs of the women and children for whom the certificates are destined. Each certificate has an official cover letter signed by Dr. Goldin, which confirms that after exit visas are provided by the German authorities, the recipients are guaranteed transit visas through Turkey and travel expenses to Palestine.

I run my eye down the list of names and recognize some friends and acquaintances: the wife and daughter of Rabbi

Pinchas Lewin (Mindel and Sarah), the wife and children of Shmuel Rotstein (editor of the *Warsaw Togblatt*), Family Kaminer (from 9 Ceglana Street), and many others. I happen to know the whereabouts of some of them — they are working in the German workshops — and I inform Yashunsky.

But before it is possible to deliver the letters, the recipients themselves hear about the certificates. (The Ghetto's internal "news broadcasts" work perfectly; within a half-hour all information flashes through to every corner of the Ghetto.) Immediately they arrive at the Ghetto *Judenrat* to ask advice. Do these documents have any validity? And how should one use them? Soon it becomes clear that no more than ten out of fifty-four women destined to receive certificates are still alive in the Ghetto; the rest have already been deported.

The *Judenrat*'s vice president, A. Shtoltzman, asked at the Gestapo — what was the point of these certificates? He was told they were to be used "in exchange for German citizens in Palestine." Shtoltzman further discovered another interesting fact: the Gestapo also have a list of twenty-one men who are eligible to be exchanged, and the Gestapo urged Shtoltzman to search for them. When Shtoltzman pointed out that many of the names on their list have been deported, the Gestapo replied with broad hints: "You can send substitutes. Who will check their credentials?"

So a tiny escape hatch has been opened for some of us still penned up in the Ghetto enclosure; activists plan to allocate the unclaimed certificates among prominent personalities in the Ghetto. An ad-hoc committee is instantly set up to choose the names with great deliberation — this could be a matter of life or death. After a lengthy sitting they choose for a possible citizen exchange: Dr. I. Schipper, Senator Yaakov Trokenheim, Dr.

Emanuel Ringelblum, Yitzchak Giterman, Pinchas Kirschenbaum, R. Zisha Friedman, David Guzik, Mauricy Orzech, Shmuel Horenstein, R. Menachem Ziemba, R. Shimshon Stockhammer, Dr. Jesi Hirschfinkel, R. Dovid Shapira, Mrs. Nechama Rotner, Nochum Remba, Joshua Perle, Avraham Gefner, Dr. J. Rotfeld, Dr. N. Wahl, R. Yosef Konigsberg, and myself.

Then began the scurrying and scraping in front of the German authorities, but later that night we were informed that "the whole matter is not relevant at present." At present...and what of the future? Will it have any relevance then? Meanwhile, some of us dream of escaping from the bitter reality to the warmth and safety of Eretz Yisrael. Will our brethren in Eretz Yisrael extend a fraternal hand and redeem the last remnants? Will our dreams ever come to fruition?*

Friday, November 27

A Breathing Space

The *Judenrat* President Mark Lichtenbaum today summoned directors of the various departments for a meeting with national activists. I met there a number of men and women who had previously been involved in education. Since there are many children in the Ghetto who have nothing to occupy their time, lessons should be organized for them. This would also give former teachers some useful employment. Lichtenbaum claims he can obtain permission for this from the *Befehl-stelle* (the German section effectively in charge of the Ghetto).

But some delegates hesitate. Is it safe to gather all the

* Later, the Germans transferred many of those holding certificates to Bergen-Belsen near Hanover, and most were saved. But the dreams of salvation of the last survivors were not fulfilled.

children together under one organization? What can one teach them? What can we answer when they ask where are their parents, brothers, sisters, or former classmates? What should we say when they ask us that perennial question: Why?

I raise my own objections: Why have none of the famous religious pedagogues (such as R. Zisha Friedman or R. Yehudah Leib Orlean) been invited? Why, for that matter, have no *rabbanim* been invited? Lichtenbaum promises to invite them to the next session and asks me to contact them meanwhile and ascertain their views. He also promises to enroll religious activists in any education project.

I return home to my apartment, which I share with Rabbi Y. L. Orlean and Rabbi A. G. Friedensohn, and I report to them on the meeting. Their first conclusion is that the "situation is stable." In other words, if they are talking about children there is unlikely to be any more German *aktions* in the near future. Then they begin debating the actual problem of schooling.

Rabbi Y. L. Orlean argues that there are very few children left to religious families in the Ghetto. Most of these did not have any money or *protexia* and were therefore unable to save their children. Those children who have survived are mainly from the assimilationist ranks, who had both the means and the influence. They had "safe positions" in the police force, in the *Judenrat*, or in the supply departments. Their children are naturally under the care of Mrs. Natanblut, a good woman and teacher but an assimilationist, too. So why should we get involved?

Then I spoke to Dr. Edmund Stein, who is as optimistic and enthusiastic as ever. Now that every attempt at assimilation with the non-Jewish nations has failed so miserably, he argues, we will teach the children *Ivrit* and educate them to life in Eretz Yisrael.

Rabbi Zisha Friedman tells me he has already organized illegal *chadarim* for those few religious children who are left. He does not want help from the *Judenrat*. He has funds from the Joint and he is suspicious of any "legalization" from the Germans.

Finally I contact members of the Resistance Committee, and they are totally opposed to any organized courses, in any form. Their fierce arguments convince me if we have to "wield the sword, then there is no book learning" (*Avodah Zara* 17b). I decide to persuade Lichtenbaum to withdraw from the whole project — it is not the right time, especially if we are to depend on the goodwill of the Nazi gangs.

Yesterday, incidentally, the Gestapo spokesman on Jewish affairs, Mende, publicized the following proclamation:

> Since irresponsible elements have been spreading rumors of an impending clearing-out of the Ghetto, we are therefore informing you that those who spread these baseless rumors will be punished.
>
> *Signed: Mende*

This notice stuck up round the Ghetto, combined with the *Judenrat* plans for children's education, has partially succeeded in calming the atmosphere in the Ghetto — though the public harbor a great deal of suspicion about German proclamations. Unfortunately they have already had many opportunities to judge the value of such promises. Others claim that in fact it's a bad sign: German promises are normally followed by fresh oppression.

There was yet another event today — the workshops were asked to supply a number of master tailors with sewing machines for labor needs in Lublin. Forty tailors left for Lublin, and there is no anxiety as to their fate, though there is no shortage of pessimists. Generally an uneasy calm reigns in the Ghetto, there has been no Nazi *aktions* since Yom Kippur. Yet nobody knows if this is really the end of the genocide program or merely a temporary lull.

The news reaching us from the provinces about continuing *aktions* is naturally not at all comforting. So everybody makes plans commensurate with the opportunities and means at their disposal. Those who have contacts with the Aryan side, and a lot of money, lay plans to smuggle themselves out of the Ghetto. Architects and technicians build underground "bunkers" equipped with all conveniences: electricity, light, water supply, etc. All store up stocks of food according to their abilities and prepare for battle....

Monday, November 30

Provincial Tales of Woe

I visited Niska Street where the *Werterfassung*, the German agency, processes the systematic plunder of Jewish property. All belongings of deportees (as well as those remaining in the Ghetto) are collected by the Nazis and despatched to Germany. Many of Warsaw's Jews are employed on this job — as are some Jews who have recently arrived from the neighboring towns. I have specially come to speak to these latter Jews to discover what has been going on in their areas. Furthermore, my friend, R. Yehudah Leib Orlean, asked me to find out information particularly about the village Wengrov, where his wife and five children are sheltering.

I find one Jew from Wengrov who claims to be the only survivor from his entire family — and from the whole *kehillah!*

According to him, on Yom Kippur (Monday, September 21) an SS squad descended on the village and ordered every Jew, of any age or gender, to appear in the marketplace. When they were all assembled, the Nazis shot, there and then, the elderly or sick who were unable to walk. Others were dragged off to the Jewish cemetery and killed there — and the rest were deported. Where to? To the place where all Jews are sent to!

Was there nowhere to hide? I asked in surprise. Yes, a small percentage did conceal themselves in cellars, attics, or forests. But the Germans then offered a reward — a quarter kilo of sugar — for every Jew found. At once the Polish Catholics joined the hunt; children and adults alike began searching every nook and cranny for hidden Jews. When they found a Jew, they dragged him from his hiding place by force (any attempt to resist them was met with savage blows) and delivered him up to the waiting Nazis. No amount of pleading or offers of money could assuage their blood lust — those Poles knew no mercy.

When they "smelled" a young Jewish boy of twelve hidden in an attic, the house was surrounded by "*skotzim*" who threw stones and set wild dogs on him. They tried to set the house on fire, until they forced that Jewish boy to descend. Then they brought him with whoops of triumph to the German commandants — in front of the whole village!

Not a single Pole lifted a finger to protect that poor defenseless child. The Germans took him to the Jewish cemetery and murdered him there, in front of the crowd who had come to watch the "execution." Not one other Jew survived in the village of Wengrov. Even those who had hidden in the forests were betrayed by the peasants and handed over to the Germans.

Miss Zakon, a young girl who comes from Minsk-

Mazoveicik, described the end of her village. Most of the Jews were already deported during July to September. Only 180 were left working outside the town. However, her family, who owned a vinegar factory in town, continued to work there. The rest were in huts outside town. One day, typhus was discovered among the Jewish workers, and a Nazi squad was immediately sent for. They forced all the Jews into one hut and set it alight — all were burned alive.

In Otvosk, so I was told, the massacres followed the classic Nazi pattern. The extermination program in Warsaw was interrupted for one day in August and the whole squad descended on Otvosk. The only drawback, as far as the Nazis were concerned, was that many Jews had already managed to hide in the forests (as Yechiel Zalberg, the son of the Chasidic hotel owner told me). The Poles began immediately searching for hidden Jews and handing them over for a reward. Some peasants preferred to kill the Jews themselves so as to plunder their belongings. A few Jews managed to hide in Rambartov or Kolbeil and later escape to Warsaw. The young Rav Yisrael Wiedenfeld (R. Menachem Ziemba's son-in-law), who had been in the Otvosk convalescent home, also managed to escape to Kolbeil. But all the Jewish patients in the Brios convalescent home were deported.

The young intellectual, Dr. Bruno Weinabar, who recently headed the Natural Science faculty in the Ghetto University organized by Czerniakow, was also murdered during the destruction of Otvosk. Earlier, Otvosk had absorbed Jewish refugees from Shrodborov, Shveider, and other places. The Jews of Palnitz had already been deported to Warsaw during the last winter.

Rav Zemelman, the Rav of Pesheitz, is another recently

arrived refugee who describes the destruction of many provincial *kehillos*, both large and small. An Aguda *askan* and a great *talmid chacham*, he has made attempts to establish links with left-wing Polish partisans. He regularly smuggles himself over to the Aryan side, where he masquerades as a pure "Aryan" to acquire guns and ammunition. Now he constantly calls with great fervor for resistance.

Today I heard him hold forth at a secret meeting in a bunker. He is a talented speaker and describes in harrowing detail the barbaric scenes perpetrated during the extermination of the provinces. He issues a clarion call for revenge and quotes the *Chazal*, "Great is revenge, an attribute which is mentioned between two Holy Names — *Kel Nekamos Hashem.*" He lays down a detailed plan for an armed revolt and takes responsibility for providing weapons and ammunition. He does not make empty promises; what he has already achieved is quite substantial. Today, for instance, he handed over twelve pistols and cases of cartridges.

He has also visited all the *rabbanim* and Rebbes in the Ghetto to demand that they support calls for a revolt. I am told that yesterday he appeared at a meeting of the *chalutzim*, the central powerhouse for resistance, and roused the young *chalutzim* to tremendous enthusiasm. Last week he had a blazing row with Bund representatives. They claimed they were waiting for signs from London and their socialist comrades in the Aryan quarter, but he reprimanded them for relying on vain hopes.

DECEMBER 1942

Tuesday, December 8

Every so often a Gestapo officer appears in the Ghetto and shoots down Jews at random. Today seven Jews were murdered. Two days ago, this murderer himself came into the *Judenrat* to telephone his superior and report, "I have shot five Jews." Apparently it is some sort of tactic. We are afraid to walk in the street; we wait until twilight when it is less dangerous. So we sit in the archives, nobody leaves or enters. Time passes slowly, as heavy as lead. The *rabbanim* peruse *sefarim* while others pace nervously waiting for evening to arrive.

In this tense atmosphere a single word can unleash an avalanche of emotion. Somebody asks his colleague, "Where will it all end? What can the future hold?" Typically his neighbor replies with yet another question, "And how do you understand the present?"

In the archives are gathered men of many disciplines, great *rabbanim* and intellectuals who view the world from different perspectives. Yet no one can now find an apt analogy or the appropriate precedent in either history or politics, logic or emotion — not even from the Torah. We are too upset; it is all too fresh. The debate rages fiercely as they attempt to grapple with our dilemma, plumb the depths of our predicament, and perhaps glimpse behind the dark curtain obscuring our future. Gathered around are people who in normal times are brilliant thinkers and profound speakers, yet now they cannot find the right words to categorize the catastrophe we are living through nor discover any hint of it in our history.

Before our troubles began, there was a huge reservoir of Judaism here — perhaps half a million Jews in the Ghetto — and now only a small, emotionally battered remnant exists. Men whose lives are shattered, who are only half alive, whose existence lies only in the past — they have no present and precious little hope for the future. The tragedy is still far too large for any of us to grasp; the pain cuts too deep. No *midrash*, no commentary, no *pasuk* in the *tochachah* appears sufficient to sum up our present tragedy. We are still too overwhelmed. Any attempted comparison with a historical precedent seems absurd, without relevance. Is the Armenian genocide comparable to what we are suffering? The *churban* of both Temples, the Spanish Expulsion, the massacres perpetrated by the Crusaders or the Cossacks, or any of the other tragedies throughout our long history soaked with the tears of centuries, all appear dwarfed in comparison with our present calamity — it has a unique dimension all of its own.

Other nations have suffered, too. But at least their inner core was spared — weakened, perhaps, but ultimately spared. Whereas here, the very heart of the Jewish people has been destroyed. It harbored so much spiritual potential, such a richness of culture, a wealth of financial clout. The Jewish population in Poland and Lithuania in all its varying strands and hues, with its many manifestations, was one organic whole. A separate nation in its originality and a boundless reservoir for all other centers.

And now it has been systematically, cold-bloodedly, brutally destroyed.

I remember, at the old Kehillah, I used to receive notices to publish that were addressed "To the Jewish Nation in Poland." But I would amend these to read "To the Jews in Poland." For I felt the customary wording was wrong — we were not a separate nation. Judging by today's discussion I realize I was in the wrong. The Jews in Poland possessed all the necessary national characteristics in their own right. So there was indeed a Jewish nation in Poland, perhaps the most powerful Jewish nation ever. Never before in our long history — at least according to the present renowned historians — has so much nation-building potential, with so much talent in so many fields, been gathered together in one area. This is not merely the *churban* of one Jewish center — but *the* center of Jewish life, a national calamity.

During our discussion, Dr. Schipper speaks of the Jewish influence on Polish culture but R. Orlean interjects that he cannot abide any mention of "culture," whether Polish or European, since the Germans were the greatest advocates of culture.

I mention that our revenge on Poland was that the three greatest Polish poets were all Jewish. When I studied at Warsaw University and witnessed the antisemitic outrages of the Polish students, my own consolation then was that the three most illustrious professors there were all Jews. That is our revenge.

Our long discussion is interrupted by the entrance of Josef and Irene Tannenbaum, Anielewicz, Miss Tusia, Miss Landau, and Yechiel Reisman.

These *chalutzim* have more practical concerns. They, too, talk of revenge — but pure and simple, without any literary flourishes. I had promised them to negotiate for weapons, and they have come to check on my progress. What can I tell them? For the last ten days I have been busy with this matter. I first made contact with a Polish acquaintance, a ministerial advisor who before the War was the expert on Jewish affairs in the Education Ministry. But he is a very frightened man, and no wonder — he was imprisoned in Pawiak and only extricated himself with great difficulty. More recently, I contacted Vladislav Vilkosch, a businessman, and haggled with him for a full week. I even paid over an advance sum of money — and all for no results.

These *chalutzim* explain in brutally simple terms that they are not interested in heroism for its own sake or "impressing the world." For all the practical consideration and help "world opinion" has so far offered us — they can all have a *schvartzen sof*, a bad end! Currying world respect can also lead only to a *schvartzen sof*, it is a useless activity that interests journalists alone, they add sarcastically, with a dig at me. If we are destined for the slaughter, they want to taste the sweetness of revenge before they die, to see the blood of those wild beasts flow. If we can get guns for them, all the better; if not, then sharpen some knives!

They tell me I am not the first to suffer disappointment. Countless times so-called friends have taken money yet done absolutely nothing. Sometimes these cheats have even extorted yet more money by threatening to betray the Jewish contacts to the Germans. One Revisionist member of the Jewish resistance, Saltzwasser, was negotiating with an arms dealer and set up a meeting — from which he never returned! He was too enthusiastic and not careful enough. So I must try other avenues. They are only asking me to make contact — the rest, including smuggling the arms into the Ghetto, they will see to themselves.

We arrange that tomorrow I shall cross over to the Aryan side, where I have an "address" in Vidka Street. I manufacture some non-existent request to copy material from the municipal population archives in Dluga Street and will leave the Ghetto at 8 A.M. the next morning. Thus the *chalutzim* group from Grochov have brought me down to earth, from that lofty discussion to the practicalities of pure revenge without histrionics or literary flourishes.

Wednesday, December 9

The Polish Underground

After crossing over into the Aryan quarter I met various Poles. Some are former acquaintances, and I have recommendations for the others from the ZKN (*Zydowski Komitet Narodowy* — the "Jewish National Committee" which oversees the resistance). I visit "Victor" and "Stashak" and others with underground pseudonyms. They have contact with London and are not doing very much at the moment. They claim they are waiting for a "signal." For the present they distribute clandestine magazines and newspapers, and they give me a few to read. As I flip through the pages I come across openly antisemitic articles!

"How is this possible?" I burst out. "Even now? When Jews are being murdered in their thousands? When we both have a common enemy? Even now you are running antisemitic campaigns?"

They look a little embarrassed and attempt to explain it away. "These are only from the NDK (members of the prewar nationalistic antisemitic party). Old habits die hard. But we are not prepared to split the Polish underground arguing about the Jewish question! It was hard enough combining together to form a common front against the Germans."

I try to explain the tragic danger implicit in these antisemitic diatribes. The Jewish nation is being exterminated, and if anyone manages to escape and throws himself on the mercy of the Polish population, they promptly turn him over to the Germans!

Then I confront them point blank: "When the Polish Underground do carry out acts of sabotage, why do they never blow up the railway tracks leading to the death camps? Why has no railway worker employed on the death trains to Treblinka or Belzec ever sabotaged anything? Why is no effort made to alert the Allied Powers? How can the Polish clergy still remain silent? Where are the Polish intelligentsia? Can't you at least save individual Jews — intellectuals, prominent personalities, or children?"

But these questions remain unanswered. Meanwhile other socialist activists and underground leaders arrive for a secret meeting. I report on events inside the Ghetto and the ongoing bloodbath. They all look shocked, but confused. They condemn the barbarity — but what can they do? I tell them of the death trains, how passengers expire from thirst and children suffer dreadfully in the suffocating crush and relentless heat. But according to those few who escaped, the Polish populace remains hostile and "neutral." Nobody ever comes forward to offer water to the suffering passengers!

They listen silently and nod in agreement. They will discuss the problem and give me their considered reply. So I wait in an adjacent room until they finish.

But the meeting drags on and on. One hour passes and then another and I begin to get nervous. It starts to get dark, it is already 6 P.M. and Jews in the Ghetto must not be out after curfew at 7 P.M. I am joined by another young man whom I eventually discover is a Jewish messenger from the Cracow Resistance. He tells me that Dr. Michal Weichert, the Cracow welfare representative, asked Prince Runiker, the Polish Welfare Committee president, to approach the Archbishop of Cracow, Count Sapeiha, about the possibility of hiding Jews.

But Prince Runiker dismissed the request, adding that the Archbishop would never lift a finger to save Jews. Earlier, in 1941, a rabbinical delegation, including Rav Shmelke Kornitzer and Rav Rappaport, met the Archbishop, and the only concrete result was that the Germans found out and all the *rabbanim* were sent to Auschwitz and shot. (I know this for a fact since Rav Kornitzer's wife, my cousin Perel Kornitzer, received a telegram that her husband had "died" and later received a casket of ashes.)

I also discovered another disagreeable piece of information. Once, before the mass deportations, I had been sent by *Judenrat* President Czerniakow to the Polish Senator Vladislav Ludwig Awart (the Polish Evangelical Church president and a friend of both Senator Yaakov Trokenheim and Prof. Dr. Moses Shorr). I had written request from Senator Trokenheim that he should approach his friend the senator, Prince Janusch Radziwil, to use the network of Catholic clergy to rescue Jews. Though Senator Awart himself was being hounded by the Germans, he promised me he would see what he could do.

Now this messenger from Cracow's Underground tells me that the senator, Prince Radziwil, who wielded great influence over the clergy, had instructed Vatican circles and Catholic leaders not to protect Jews, as this might harm Polish interests under the Germans.

Finally after three hours the underground meeting draws to a close, and "Victor" informs me that there were more important items on their agenda and they had not yet reached the Jewish problem! It has been left for another meeting. I quickly took my leave and ran as fast as I possibly could for the Ghetto entrance. It was already 6:50 P.M. and the German guards subjected me to a very thorough search. They confiscated my gold wristwatch, a fountain pen, and 180 zloty. But who cares for financial losses now? It is no longer important.

More significant is the knowledge that the hopes of the Bund activists in the Ghetto are without foundation. Their dreams that their Polish socialist comrades will respond to Bundist requests and somehow help us are shown to be a sham. All promises of outside assistance are hollow; there are no probabilities of help arriving from outside the Ghetto. Other members of the ZKN Resistance Committee had suggested we should approach the Polish clergy for assistance, and that avenue, too, has been exposed as worthless. Not one strand of Polish society bothers to reply to our frantic calls for help. They are all enemies; some openly, others less openly, but we can depend on none of them.

On my return to the Ghetto there happened to be a meeting of the ZKN Resistance Committee, and I patiently listen to the empty prattle. Mauricy Orzech, the Bund representative, repeats yet again the hollow slogans about the solidarity of the proletariat — but without much conviction. Then I report what I had witnessed, factually and without much elaboration.

A deep depression settles on the face and hearts of the delegates. It is all so painfully simple. Our Polish neighbors are not all that unhappy to see the Jewish Problem "solved" for them. The new Polish Republic that will eventually rise from the ashes will not have to contend with a Jewish Problem. This is *realpolitik* — Polish style.

Sunday, December 20

Musical Delights

The young Marcel Reich comes rushing into my archives office looking very distraught. Since he is in charge of the *Judenrat* internal post and is always the first to know of any impending calamity, I fearfully ask him, "What's happening?" But as it turns out he has different problems altogether: important musical compositions from Jewish composers in the Ghetto have been discovered in the apartments of the Hebrew conductors Pulman and Pormansky (by now the composers themselves are no longer there). Reich insists that the team involved in collecting *sefarim* and literature for the archives should also take care of the musical treasures. He knows where the compositions are, he promises to help us and will assist setting up a musical section in the archives.

This talented and engaging young man, normally so cool and earnest, is now so excited and impassioned. Obviously the matter is very close to his heart. But it strikes me as rather incongruous. Is this his only concern? Is this all that's missing in the Ghetto?

Surprisingly the Ghetto has, in the past, displayed an enormous interest in music. Even large symphony concerts were organized. Members of the various Ghetto orchestras may have been literally starving, but the concerts were on a high enough standard to rival the music capitals of the world. Many Jews who had been exiled from Berlin and Vienna, and later languished in dismal hovels within the Ghetto, attended these concerts and were amazed at the musical talents displayed — which they insisted were as good as any of the world famous orchestras. Some of the Ghetto's composers and conductors had already earned both fame and a following before the War. Unbelievably, others within the Ghetto made their name during the War.

One might have thought that nobody had much time now for such trivialities, but Ghetto "concert halls" were filled to capacity and even non-Jews smuggled themselves in from the Aryan quarter to feast their ears. Perhaps people are anxious to forget the present reality for a few hours.

As with all musical circles, intense rivalries and bitter quarrels broke out between the old guard and younger members. Fortunately, the Germans did not interfere, they only forbade the playing of "true Aryan music" by German composers like Beethoven, Mozart, or Bach. The Jews were content to play Halevi, Mendlesohn, Meyerbeer, Bloch, and others. Actually, there was other entertainment in the Ghetto — plays, choirs, oratorios, and musicals — but none reached the high standards achieved by the orchestras. This was mainly the legacy of top-class Jewish musicians who had either been deported from Germany and Austria or Polish-Jewish musicians who were now confined to the Ghetto.

But none of these towering talents are with us still. When everybody was trying to save themselves from mass deportation by enrolling in the German workshops and factories, there was no place for the refined hands or sensitive fingers of violinists, harpists, pianists, or conductors. They were considered "parasites" who were not "productive" for the German war machine. So they were among the first to be deported. Now we are only concerned about saving their compositions for posterity, hoping that one day the world will recognize their genius if their works are not destroyed.*

---

* The *Judenrat* archives were later destroyed by the Germans during

Thursday, December 31

I feel like an antiquarian explorer searching for ancient manuscripts among various faraway *kehillos*. Similarly I, too, am out collecting *sefarim*, and my expedition is likewise hedged about with uncertainties and danger. Generally, however, I find the personalities more interesting than the *sefarim*.

Today I was in the former "small Ghetto" (which had been linked by a footbridge to the larger part of the Ghetto). This small Ghetto has now shrunk to a few German factories and workshops: Tobbens in Prosta and Ceglana Streets, Dehring in Komitetowa Street and in the former Technical College (of Dr. Ludwig Natansohn) situated in the courtyard of the Kehillah at 26–28 Grzybowska Street.

Everywhere I find good friends. At Tobbens I meet Miss Halprin, the former secretary of the Jewish group at the Polish Parliament from the time of Y. Greenbaum. She tells me that Greenbaum found her a position in Palestine but she returned. I also meet the rich Chasid Rabbi Shimon Landau, who had also visited Eretz Yisrael and bought a parcel of land — but then returned. Then I come across Godol Czernolovski, who was a rich factory owner from Lodz; he is a Breslaver Chasid and presents me with a *Likutei Mahran* (from Rebbe Nachman Breslaver) which he himself had published just before the outbreak of the War. He tells me he has a house and plot of land in Eretz Yisrael, which my friend Meir Leichter manages for him while he is in Poland.

I find the wife of the engineer Reicher (she is the daughter

---

the Ghetto Uprising. Marcel Reich managed to save himself by jumping from the death train to Treblinka; his wife, a famous artist, was likewise saved.

of the Chasidic landlord Noson Bromberg). An agronomist, she had worked for *Toporol* (*Towarzystwo Popieraia Rolnictwa* — the Jewish Society for Promoting Agriculture). This Society utilized every empty patch of land in the Ghetto, any courtyard or ruin, to plant vegetables or flowers, trees or potatoes. Like the others, she had returned from Palestine and is now working at the factory. The teacher and Hebrew writer M. Rakovsky is here, as is the poetess Hannah Jakobovitz. She had been a clerk in the *Judenrat*, and I had put her in charge of organizing an index for the birth registry. At the start of the deportations, she vanished; now I find her here.

"What's news?" all my friends ask me. "What do they say at the *Judenrat*? What's happening with foreign passports? And what does the wide world say?" This last question in particular is on everyone's lips. Can the free world still not know yet what is going on here? What are they going to do about it? Earlier there had been strong rumors — which had been blindly accepted — about recognizing the remnants of Polish Jewry as foreign residents; of England offering her protection; of our being considered subjects of Palestine on the basis of the Balfour Declaration; of dire retribution against the Germans by the American administration; of representations to Roosevelt by Morgenthau, Bernard Baruch, and Samuel Rosenman; of pro-Jewish declarations by Roosevelt; of interventions by the Archbishop of Canterbury and Hore-Belisha; and of Churchill's stringent warnings directed at the Nazis.

Now nobody in the Ghetto speaks of such scenarios — even the die-hard optimists have fallen silent — and no one expects any help from the world outside. They have abandoned us to our fate, eyeball to eyeball with the most merciless of enemies; we have been left as prey to those bloodthirsty beasts while the world stands back to watch from a safe distance. We all experience a terrible emptiness. We feel so forlorn, totally bereft, without offers of help or support. We are left in the whole wide world alone with our despair and pain. The screams of tortured children and slaughtered adults hang suspended in the atmosphere — unanswered....

JANUARY 1943

Tuesday, January 5, 1943

Orphaned Sefarim

Like hungry and exhausted travelers braving the snow and freezing cold, we creep past abandoned apartment blocks and courtyards searching for *sefarim* from a lost civilization to transfer to the *Judenrat* archives. We enter the second story of 28 Muranowska Street where we have been told there are many *sefarim*. Indeed, large bookcases are filled to overflowing with sacred literature. I open a *Gemara* at random and read "*Shaiyach l'Rabi Yosef Albinger* — Belonging to R. Yosef Albinger." The next *sefer* has the same inscription, and I recall this is where Kehillah committee member Albinger lived.

In fact during the War, the Sochatchover Rebbe, R. Dovid Bornstein, *zt"l*, secretly stayed here, too. His grandson Nosson Bahariah, a talented young man, managed to conceal him throughout the terror, and the Rebbe merited to survive the most difficult stages of the deportations. The Rebbe died from natural causes and received a proper Jewish burial (in the Ghetto this was known as a "luxury death"). I actually took part in the Sochatchover Rebbe's *levaya*, but only a small crowd was present.

Now I find a small *sefer Torah* in the bookcase and the tables are full of Chasidic *sefarim, Gemaras*, and *Zohar* as well as rabbinical *responsa* — a classical Chasidic household. Everything has already been looted: furniture, utensils, and possessions. Only the *sefarim* remain. Apparently Albinger enjoyed other interests, too. We discover copies of the publications *Hatzefira, Hamagid, Hamelitz*, and *Hayom*. All of it is carted off to the archives.

We cross over to Nalewki Street and enter the Chevra Shass Shul at number 41. Piles of *sefarim* lie heaped on the tables and benches. Many are worn and tattered from heavy use — how much Torah has been learned here! Then we visit the Sardinar Shtiebl at 15 Nalewki Street. Here we find many *siddurim, machzorim, Tehillim*, and a few *Chumashim*.

One imagines how all these prayer books must have absorbed decades of *tefillah* — how many tear-laden sighs were uttered here! How many heartfelt *tefillas!* This *shtiebl* used to be filled with *minyanim* all day long. Where are all those many Jews now! Can I still hear their faint echo here?

After this sobering experience we walked to Nowiniarskah Street where HaRav Avraham Weinberg (also popularly known as "Reb Avrumele Stitziner") lived. He was a famous *lamdan*, renowned too for his piety, a *talmid* of the Avnei Nezer (the first Sochatchover Rebbe), and one of Poland's prominent *rabbanim*. I recollect his noble appearance, which spoke volumes of spirituality. He was fairly short, but his deep-set eyes shone with an ethereal light. He spent day and night studying or teaching *talmidim*; though he was far removed from everyday affairs, he was not a "*batlan*."

I remember when the Kehillah *shammas*, the famous "Reb Don," once attempted to deliver Reb Avrumele's stipend and reported to me that his door was locked. He surmised that he was probably working officially as a "shoemaker" at Schultz since Reb Avrumele's brother (surprisingly, not religious) was a large factory owner and a top manager at Schultz. But "Reb Don" was wrong. Rav Avraham Weinberg remained at home during the German occupation — learning diligently until he and his family were deported, after the 2nd of August. Apparently he was taken in the middle of his *shiur,* since a number of *Gemaras Bechoros* are laid out on his table, still open at the page at which they were disturbed.

In my imagination the empty room reverberates to the ancient tune "*Hoi, omar Rava, Hoi, v'omar Abaye* — O Rava said... and Abaye replied...." But the familiar cadences sound mournful and depressed. The abandoned *Gemaras* stare at us reproachfully, asking those eternal questions: Why? What for? These tomes of Talmud mount a challenge for which we have no adequate answer. I order my team to leave the *Gemaras* as they are, untouched, as if they were holy relics.

Perhaps one day, when a better world arises from the ruins of the present one, we shall gather the world leaders who now remain so silent and persuade them to file past these orphaned *Gemaras,* abandoned in the middle of a *sugya,* and see if they can answer these penetrating questions. Where were you, we shall ask them, when this pure innocent world was being destroyed? Let those who pontificate endlessly about democracy and justice give a decent reply to these tattered and well-worn *Gemaras.*

Thursday, January 7

The Revisionist Army

The Resistance Committee (popularly known as the "National Committee") commission Nochum Remba and myself to approach the Revisionist Resistance Front on their behalf. They chose Remba because of his intimate ties — his brother Izaak Remba is their leader — and I was chosen for my friendly connections with them in the past. I used to contribute to their publication, *Moment*, and was also a neighbor. Two young Beitar leaders — Asher Frankel (who ran the *Hachsharah* program at Rubishov) and Paulla Fried (who handled the distribution of the Warsaw Revisionist Underground newsheet *Af-Al-Pi-Ken*) — used to live in my apartment block in 22 Grzybowska Street. Now they have both been deported.

It was arranged that at 6 P.M., we would both arrive at the Revisionist headquarters via the neighboring house at 21 Zamenhof Street (the *Judenrat* buildings). We go up to the attic and then descend through a trapdoor into a completely closed room. All the doors and windows are bricked off and only a small skylight remains.

The Revisionists are already in session. I do not recognize all their members. I have only met about ten of them previously, and none are addressed by name for security reasons. Many masquerade under false names and I, too, am introduced as "Eisensweig."

The Revisionists were among the first in the Ghetto to speak of resistance. Though they were never recognized as a separate group (party affiliations have anyhow ceased to matter overmuch), a disproportionate number of resistance activists came from Revisionist ranks. No Revisionist would enroll as a Jewish policeman — and if they did they were automatically ejected from the movement. They were the first to issue warnings not to voluntarily go to the *Umschlagplatz* (at the beginning of deportations) when the Germans publicized the tempting offer of 3-kilo bread rations and a kilogram of jam.

What is on their present agenda? Alexander Rosenfeld, from the *Moment*, boasted, "We have organized our own combat organization (also called *Irgun Zeva Leumi*). We have members at the Praga Station Workshops near the eastbound trains where we smuggle arms." I hear that it was they who carried out the "executions" on the collaborators Jacob Leikin, the Jewish police chief, and Israel Feurst; but Szerynski, who established the Jewish police force, and Shmerling, who was in charge of the *Umschlagplatz*, were only wounded.

We suggest they should not keep their smuggled weapons and ammunition separately but should combine them with the general resistance armory. Negotiations proceed slowly since the Revisionists are suspicious. Their ideological enemies, the Bundists, have, they claim, unwisely conducted talks with Polish partisans. Admittedly these were left-wing partisans, but according to instructions from London all the partisans should be officially working together — including the antisemitic Polish Nationalists. The Revisionists are therefore afraid of betrayal.

Remba dismisses their fears. He believes that the Bundists are occupied with little more than writing reports for London. Besides, all their grandiose talk of "contacts with the Polish underground" is mere bluff and conceit. Personally, I am more than a little perturbed. From my own negotiations with the Polish underground, I saw myself what sort of attitude they all took towards Jews.

But what won't we do for peace and unity? So I allow

Remba to say his piece. However, the Revisionists are not prepared to dissolve their movement, arguing that their party is revisionist in structure and not just in membership.

They remain concerned about possible betrayal, and they warn us to be careful, too. Privately I agree with them, and I decide to quietly warn Rav Zemelman, Rav Horowitz, Kirschenbaum, and Anielwitz to be more circumspect in their dealings with the Bund.

After long and complicated negotiations it was finally agreed that Dr. Reuben Feldschuh and Dr. Wodubinski should organize and lead a common front with the main resistance. Unfortunately, since these two gentlemen are employed in factories outside the Ghetto, it is difficult to reach them. Eventually it was decided that Alexander Rosenfeld who, as well as working in the Kagan bakery, officially escorts workers and has more freedom of movement, would negotiate with these two leaders. Meanwhile Rodal, Liweh, and his brother would join sittings of the National Committee, which for the moment is overseeing the Ghetto resistance.

I take the opportunity to obtain copies of Revisionist underground literature for the archives, which I carefully conceal under my coat. These stencils have been run off on a Gestetner duplicating machine under the Latin title "Jews Condemned to Death Greet You!" and Bialik's slogan "Your Death Has as Little Purpose as Your Life!" These publications have been professionally edited. I find excerpts from Y. M. Neiman's "Hear O England" (which is as relevant today as when it was first published in *Haint*, fifteen years ago), parts of Y. Landau's poem "Massada," U. Z. Greenberg's article from *Moment*, and excerpts from Dr. Wolfgang Van Weisel's speeches in Tarnopol (which I supplied them). They also have proclamations from Rav

Eidelberg of Makov and Rav Menachem Ziemba, as well as a sharply worded article from Dr. Strikovski. Writers still alive in the Ghetto have been given pennames, but Rodal reveals to me their true identity.

Rodal also confides in me other details of their activities. Fogel (son of the Talmud Torah director in Warsaw), Moshe Melnick, Simchah Holtzberg (known as the "Chasid"), Vladka (a pseudonym), Benik Kaisar, and Shimon Kaminetzky are all busy smuggling large amounts of weapons into the Ghetto. They pay exorbitant amounts for these arms, buying them from partisans, Polish policemen, and even on occasion from German guards who are not as malevolent as the secret police.

"Where can you get all this money from?" I ask. Apparently, they have a number of sources. First of all from rich Jews, especially the workshop managers who had collected large bribes recently. Contractors and wholesalers in the vital Ghetto supplies departments have also amassed great riches now. Rodal tells me that Malowski, a wealthy businessman in groceries, gave half-unwillingly 200,000 zlotys for the cause. He shows me a list of collected "taxes" and I read the names of Fischel, Feigenbaum, N. Bornstein, Hoffenfeld, and Frankel among others.

At any rate it has been decided that the Revisionists, as an organized group, will join the general resistance movement, and its leaders will be co-opted onto the coordinating committee. We leave the Revisionist bunker well content that we have fulfilled our commission, and I remark to Remba, "Do you remember in the past how many sittings, meetings, and negotiations would have been needed to form a common front or a single electoral list?" Now it is accomplished at one sitting. This too is for the good! We will fight united — and if we fail, we will go down together.

Friday, January 8

Gestapo Agents

Surprising news today: Gansweich has reappeared in the Ghetto! The whole Gansweich saga is one of the more amazing stories in the history of the Warsaw Ghetto.

Before the war, Abraham Gansweich was a Hebrew teacher at the Tarbut Zionist school in the village of Kunin. But he was an energetic young man full of initiative who quickly became frustrated in his home village. Eventually he arrived in Lodz armed with a number of plans and ventures. He contacted various *askanim* with different proposals. Later he published a small weekly magazine, and so he became known as "an editor."

This title clung to him like a shadow since he was always careful to be known and addressed as "an editor." In 1941 he first appeared in Warsaw, again as "an editor" — and not even as a former editor — though no one could remember ever reading anything he had written. Warsaw then had about twenty past editors of large daily newspapers. Yet for none of them did the title "editor" become so firmly attached as it did to Gansweich, who needed this appellation as a cover for his more nefarious activities.

Since he had built up "good relations" with the Gestapo, he equally needed acceptance from the Jewish public. He sought to mix with Jewish authors and journalists, to be seen as their trusted colleague, and he would seek opportunities to assist any of them in need. Usually he was not successful; most journalists kept their distance.

But, as was well known in the Ghetto, he did have useful "relations." So when the situation was desperate and there was no other choice, people did turn to him for assistance. He did sometimes help, but at a price. He had "expenses" — presents, visits, bribery, and the like — which Jews had to pay for, to save lives or avoid further harassment. Gansweich did not then have any visible means of employment; he was an institution in himself. He had secretaries, deputies, underlings (and underlings of underlings), as well as "friends" and all sorts of characters who would loiter around his premises. They were all busy finding clients, brokering deals, and making recommendations. He controlled a whole division of these foot soldiers, mainly drawn from the Lodz intelligentsia: lawyers like Sharogroder or Dr. Sirota and Polish army veterans.

In the Ghetto he became a legend, and there was much talk of the large parties he would throw in his apartment, of the "favors" he could dispense or the "opportunities" he might have offered. If there was an urgent need to travel by train (which has been forbidden to Jews) one went to Gansweich. If a Jew was arrested for some reason, again Gansweich would sort it out.

Once on *Chol Hamoed* Pesach, I received a personal invitation typed out on a Hebrew typewriter from "Editor Gansweich" inviting me to a "*Chug Ivri.*" His missive also stressed the importance of inculcating the Hebrew language and literature within the Ghetto population, especially among the youth. But I ignored the invitation, thinking to myself was it not enough for Gansweich to have garnered money and power by dubious means — now he wants to win public legitimacy, too?

The first time I actually met him was on the first day of Chanukah 1941, when I went, together with my relative Yaakov Frankel from Bilitz, to ask for his assistance. A number of Crakow *rabbanim* had been deported to Auschwitz for sending a memorandum to the Archbishop, Count Sapeiha, appealing to him to do more for Jews. Among those unfortunate *rabbanim* was my relative Rav Shmelke Kornitzer, and we begged Gansweich to help. Yaakov Frankel offered him a substantial reward (and also paid a certain amount in advance). Gansweich promised his assistance. In fact, he was the only one who did anything, and he obtained travel permits for us to use the train to Crakow.

The second time I met Gansweich was on July 2, 1941, after I heard of the arrests of the Bobover Rebbe, Rav B. Z. Halberstam and the Reischer Rav (and also parliamentary senator) Rav Aaron Lewin in Lwow. Once again Gansweich promised to help, and he put forward his own plan. Since he had German "friends" in the foreign currency department, we should start a rumor that the Bobover Rebbe and the Reischer Rav had broken the currency laws, in order that they should be brought to Warsaw for questioning. Once here, Gansweich would obtain their freedom.

I contacted Lwow and they agreed to the tactics. As I later discovered, Gansweich did indeed begin to implement his plan, and the Lwow Gestapo began inquiries regarding the Bobover Rebbe's currency dealings (also arresting another Jew by the name of Halberstam). But it was all in vain. Both *rabbanim* were murdered on the day of their arrest, July 2, 1941, in the prison courtyard on Linski Street.

Gansweich could often lead one astray; he had no compunction about distorting the truth. Usually, however, he would help for a hefty fee and, extremely rarely, even for nothing. In the winter of 1941, Gansweich established (with Gestapo support, of course) the "Control Office to Combat Black Marketing and Profiteering." On the face of it, this would perform an eminently useful function. Prices in the Ghetto had soared astronomically. However this institution was in fact merely a front for an auxiliary "police force" which attracted the worst elements: drop-outs, extortionists, swindlers, and underworld dealers — and was yet another plague on the Ghetto.

The address of this evil empire, 13 Leszno Street (soon nicknamed the "*Drai Tzentle* — the Thirteenth") was enough to engender fear by itself. There was an elaborate hierarchy there, armed with their own police force and granted their own privileges. For instance, they were given charge of some eighty houses in the Ghetto, which were allocated to their proteges and provided another source of income for the "*Drai Tzentle.*" The Kehillah President Czerniakow waged a battle against the "*Drai Tzentle*," and after a long period of representations to the Ghetto Kommisar Auerswald, they agreed to the closure of the "*Drai Tzentle*" and the transfer of its files to the *Judenrat* archives.

This was when I met Gansweich for the third time, together with *Judenrat* executive members Dr. Gliksberg and Engineer Sharshavsky. We presented him with the official closure order from Kommisar Auerswald. He listened quietly but he refused to either shut his "office" or hand over his files. We did not enter into lengthy negotiations, since we realized that he was protected by the Gestapo, who were more powerful than Auerswald.

As we were about to leave, Gansweich turned to me and said, "I know you are interested in papers. Come in for a moment and I will show you something!" We entered a private room, and Gansweich pulled out a bundle of papers and handed them to me. I skimmed through them. They were copies of a weekly report which Gansweich supplied to the Gestapo. What did these contain? First of all, a weekly review of *Judenrat* activities, of the Joint and other Jewish institutions; then a chronicle of recent events and statistics of deaths, etc. It was all set out in a logical and interesting style. There were also background articles, such as "The Ghetto view regarding the situation at the front" or "Popular Ghetto opinion on military progress."

I had to admit that the last two weekly reports were well laid out; from a journalistic standpoint they were professionally produced. I asked Gansweich, "Who edits these reports?" and Gansweich mentioned the name of a German Jew previously on the staff of the *Berliner Tagblatt.* I nodded, one can recognize the touch of a professional. They contained a wealth of interesting detail and opinion. Gansweich told me that when he delivered these reports every Tuesday to Gestapo headquarters at 25 Shucha Avenue, they were waiting with bated breath. "From here," the Gestapo claimed, "we can discover what is really going on at the front or in world affairs. This is our only true source!"

Did any of these reports contain slander or *mesirah*? I skimmed through dozens of them and I saw no evidence of that. On the contrary, the reports included a number of constructive comments (professionally disguised to appear objective) to show the Germans that it was in their interests to treat the Jews more leniently. The reports also stressed the economic importance of the Ghetto.

Doubtless, however, there were on occasions indiscreet passages which, if not necessarily containing actual slander, came pretty close. Moreover, we have no particular interest that the Germans should know exactly what takes place amongst us. Besides, and this is the most important point, how does one know what is written in reports that Gansweich did not show us? But I make no judgments, I can only go by the evidence of my own eyes.

On April 14, 1942 the Gestapo posted up placards around the Ghetto proclaiming the death sentence on Abraham Gansweich, his partner Sternberg, and a third man called Zechaviasch. The Gestapo had come one night to arrest Gansweich, but he had managed to hide. So they sentenced him in absentia. At the time, this turn of events occasioned much wonder and speculation. Most concluded it resulted from the rivalry between the various gangs within the Gestapo. When the mass deportations started, the Gestapo began insisting that Gansweich was hiding out somewhere in the Ghetto, but nobody believed them. He had vanished into thin air.

Today he reappeared again. Apparently he is now living openly in the Aryan quarter — for which he has an official permit — and he intends to visit Kopeicka Street regularly, where he owns an interest in two German workshops. There are even rumors that he will soon be appointed *Judenrat* president. In the Aryan quarter he receives visitors openly at the Coffee House on Senatorska Street together with his colleague Sternberg (his partner in the death sentence). He has an office there and still employs Vladislav Lipski, the dancer Francisca Mann, and others.*

---

* His "career" was ended on November 24, 1943 by the Jewish underground. Sternberg was likewise sentenced by them and executed earlier, on May 3, 1943. Francisca Mann was deported to Maidenek and later Auschwitz. When they were leading her to the gas chamber, she grabbed a pistol from an SS guard and killed him. Obviously, she was immediately shot by another SS guard.

Sunday, January 10

Bunker with Conveniences

I made an unusual visit today, to the world beneath the ground. Two young yeshivah students, Manes Rosenstroich and Hendles, came to me this morning and informed me cryptically, "At 5 P.M., we are entering 35 Nalewki Street. Be there!" They offered no more explanation. By whom am I invited and for what?

But in the Ghetto we have learned not to ask useless questions. When you are asked to be somewhere at a certain time, you accept it as instructions to be followed implicitly. We have become used to following orders. So at 4:55 I approach the entrance to 35 Nalewki Street. A young *yeshivah bachur* dressed in the traditional headgear is already waiting for me. (Nowadays, this is the only group brave enough to retain traditional Jewish dress. Everybody else — even the religious — are too wary to be seen wearing Chasidic attire.)

As soon as he notices me he calls out "Come!" and walks away. I meekly follow him. This house was well known to me; it is the property of my old friend Senator Yaakov Trokenheim. But now I realize that there are countless routes running through it. We pass through one courtyard after another until we descend down two stories and seem to walk for ages through endless cellars. Finally we emerge at 11 Kopeicka Street and begin climbing stairs until we reach a small room.

From here a ladder leads to the attics, and now we walk from one attic to another, squeezing through narrow breaks in the party walls. Eventually we find ourselves in 38 Zamenhof Street where we begin descending again. This house is completely closed off from the outside. We enter a room which used to house a small *shtiebl* and then an adjacent room with a large fireplace. My guide climbs into this fireplace and vanishes! Puzzled, I wait outside until I receive that peremptory call again: "Come!" Gingerly, I crawl after him into the hearth and realize that a breach opened at the back leads down to the cellars. I descend via a hanging rope ladder that apparently has rungs without end.

Finally, I stand again on firm ground and look around. I am in a large, clean room lit with electricity. In the center is a large table made from rough, untreated wood and long benches are set against the walls. Then they take me into a small dark room where I am shown an electric cooker as well as a gas cooker, plus a larder full of food stocks.

"How long will your stocks last?" I ask. They tell me it all depends on the amount of people hiding in the bunker. They reckon it will be enough to feed 120 people for up to eight months. And they are confident no siege or fighting will last longer than that.

So I am now in a bunker. In the Ghetto, many words have come to take on a new meaning, and "bunker" is one of them. To the Germans a bunker meant a military strong point with gun emplacements to fire on the enemy; and a series of bunkers would have constituted a defensive line. But to us in the Ghetto a bunker was a hiding place underground, at a depth of many stories, with a cleverly concealed entrance.

This particular bunker had been built by a number of talented Jewish engineers, such as Klapfish, Oppenheim, and Zeidenbeitel, and is actually beneath a bombed-out ruin. From the outside one can only see a pile of bricks and rubble. Remnants of the previous entrance and walls are now surrounded by barbed wire, and nobody would have imagined that beneath here, deep in the bowels of the earth, people could be living.

Despite its unprepossessing surroundings, this underground shelter is well-equipped — almost, one might say, with all conveniences: electric light, gas, running water (plus water stocks and their own private well), waste disposal, and essential food stocks including flour, vegetables, syrup, dried bread, and potatoes. In case the electricity and gas is cut off, they also have stocks of charcoal, paraffin lamps, and candles.

All this has been built and prepared by enormous effort and toil through many long nights and days — and despite the great danger and urgent need for secrecy. It is a wonder of engineering, planning, and technical know-how. (I tell myself that after the War, when the Allies begin boasting of their amazing technical prowess, we should bring them down here to show them what the Jews managed to achieve under wretched and impossible conditions.)

After I finally finished admiring these technical achievements, I am introduced to the bunkers' inhabitants. Gershon Sirota, the famous *chazan*, is here (brought in by his son, a leader of the Jewish rescue corps). So is Feiwishim, the Lodz choirmaster who put on the oratorio *Hasmoneans* in the Ghetto, and the famous conductor Shimon Pulman, who had conducted the sensational Ghetto concerts. Perhaps these three musicians will together put on a concert for my benefit?

Instead of a concert, I hear the familiar tune of *Gemara* learning. I listen in astonishment. Instead of an explanation, they show me into the next room, and the amazing sight that meets me reminds me of the age-old stories of *Tannaim* learning in caves or the Marranos secretly practicing Judaism under threat of the Spanish inquisitors.

But this is not an ancient story. It is happening, here, in

front of my own eyes. About twenty *bachurim* are sitting at a long table in front of open *Gemaras*. They are learning with great *hasmadah,* with all their energy and concentration. They have arrived at page 52 of *Gemara Nedarim* and are presently studying the long commentary of the *Ran*; they are deeply absorbed by the question whether "*Ozlinon basar shem o' basar etzem*?" (Are objects considered similar or different by their essence or by the category name they go under.)

Their faces are white, and their eyes sparkle unnaturally with an unworldly fire. Indeed, they have few remaining links to this world; most are orphaned without parents or relatives. They do not really have a regular *rosh yeshivah* — though Rav Aryeh Leib Landau (the Kolobeil Rav and former *rosh yeshivah* of Chachmei Lublin) gives them a *shiur* on *Kodashim* twice a week. A pity he is not here now. His regular position is in Mila Street, where he teaches thirty *talmidim,* day and night.

I recognize a few of these *bachurim*: Hendles (son of the former *parnas* Binyamin Zev Hendles), Manes Rosenstroich (son of Eliezer Rosenstroich), Albinger (a grandson of the Lubliner Rebbe, R. Shloima Eiger), Natan Baharia (grandson of the Sochatchover Rebbe), Aaron Ziemba (son of Rav Menachem Ziemba), Leibel Alter (grandson of the Gerrer Rebbe), and Sender Frankel (the former textile manufacturer from Bilitz). Actually, Frankel is only a "guest" who comes to this underground on an occasional basis. Usually he works at the Tobbens workshop in Leszno Street. I also met two Aguda activists in *chinuch*, David Elimelech Kuper and Avraham Zakan Feldwebel.

The problem is that this yeshivah is only a "tenant" in the bunker and the rent is very high. At first their non-religious landlords (the engineers who built the bunker) looked down on these "fanatical *bachurim*" who refused to relinquish even the traditional headgear or their long *peyos*, though this made them an obvious target for the Nazis. Later they began to examine these stubborn, eccentric "characters" with curiosity — and eventually with growing admiration.

Zeidenbeitel, a well-known secularist, tells me how these *bachurim* sit and study right through the night and how they pray together "just like in a synagogue." He describes how they sing *Modzitzer zemiros* and tunes on Shabbos; he even hums to me a few *niggunim* which he has picked up in the bunker. And he repeats to me a few Chasidic insights and *vertlech* which have appealed to him. I can sense that he has respect (and even perhaps a little jealousy) for these *yeshivah bachurim*. "They at least know why they are suffering," comments Dr. Pshedworski. I reply with a *Chazal: "Ashreichah Rebbe Akiva...* You are fortunate, Rabbi Akiva, on being arrested for teaching Torah."

But Sender Frankel reminds me that I have not been invited here merely to gaze and wonder and urges me to get down to practicalities.

A tall, thin *bachur* with the face of a hermit and a deep penetrating glance begins to explain. "Yosef Scharansky, a former supporter of Chachmei Lublin, sent me a message that there is now a chance of 'legalizing' ourselves via the Herman Breuer factory at 28 Nalewki Street. We would then receive German 'numbers,' be employed at the factory, and so cease to be considered among the 'wild ones' (which is how the Germans describe those without official numbers). We shall also receive ration cards, bread, and soup; they will even set up a kosher kitchen for us. Now we have invited you to hear your opinion."

Instead of replying, I ask them, "And what is your own

view?" For a moment nobody answers, they are all deep in thought. Suddenly the young Albinger blurts out, "As for myself, I have already made my decision — I shall not go! I shall remain here. But we still have to decide the best course for everyone else."

Still I persisted. "And what are your reasons?"

"My reasons are simple enough: one should not surrender oneself into the hands of the enemy. How many different lists, orders, numbers, and changes have they made over the last three years? Somewhere around ten! But I never had myself written down even once. For I thought it was not such a simple matter to enlist under them, even for employment. What about keeping Shabbos? What about *treifus*? So I always decided not to go. True, the Germans would threaten to kill anyone who was not listed. But would they necessarily check *davka* me first? When I would hear that they had begun checking, then I would have to go and hide. In any event it is best to hide from the enemy. (In fact, no such checks were ever carried out.) So my name never appeared on all their many lists.

"Consequently, I was not conscripted for slave labor brigades, for the labor camps, or any of their murderous schemes. I have never needed recommendations from Kehillah activists, nor asked you for any favors, special privileges, or release from any restrictions. Isn't that right?" he adds triumphantly. "You have never seen me at your offices!

"On an official basis," he continues, "none of their decrees and *gezeiros* affected me, since officially I did not exist in German eyes. As for their random, unofficial swoops or other sadistic schemes, I was usually more carefully concealed than anyone else, since I would be an obvious target for the Germans and never had any of their dozen various documents, which never protected anyone in any case. *And Hakadosh Baruch Hu saved me from their hands!*

"Whenever there was an impending *shechitah*, which you prefer to call an '*aktion*' or 'deportation,' I did not run to a factory or search for work cards. I remained an illegal, a 'wild one' without an official number, and hid instead. When the SS surrounded a house and ordered all Jews to assemble in the courtyard, I was in no hurry to descend. I preferred to hide in a closed room. What did I have to lose? I would be caught and killed? Wouldn't the very same fate await me if I appeared in the courtyard without any papers?

"When that fatal decree was announced that all Jews must assemble between the roads Wolynska-Mila, again I did not go. I hid in Nalewki Street, not far from here, and I was not sucked into that terrible selection. As you can see, *Hakadosh Baruch Hu* saved me from their hands. But now that we are considering the future of a *klal*, we wait to hear your advice. You are situated at the *Judenrat* in company with *talmidei chachamim* and thinkers. What do they say to the situation? What do you say?"

But I am in no hurry to take such a weighty decision.

"If this has been your view all along," I reply, "and you did not line up for days to be inscribed on their endless lists, you did not chase after documents nor relied on them — why do you suddenly come now to ask advice? On the contrary, perhaps I should now be asking you for your advice. After all, I can see your tactics were more sensible! We all thought that you 'illegals' and 'wild ones' were the most endangered. Yet in proportion you have survived better than any legal group reliant on documents, numbers, and factory employment. Therefore, I prefer to ask your advice, it may even be *daas Torah*!"

Now the debate began in earnest. Another problem arose:

What shall we eat? Where will they acquire sufficient food stocks for a long siege? Their landlords (the owners of the bunker) made it a strict condition that the *bachurim* should have roughly equal stocks to everybody else. Otherwise the bunker's existence would be threatened. If any single person is starving it would destroy all the arrangements within the bunker. It is imperative that the food stocks are enough for everybody.

I suggest that I would forward both *shailos* (whether they should become legalized and, if not, how to obtain food stocks) to the religious *askanim* and leaders — Rav Menachem Ziemba, Rav Dovid Shapira, Rav Leib Frumer of Kozieglow, and R. A. Z. Friedman — as well as those who hold the purse strings: Avraham Gefner, Yitzchak Giterman, and David Guzik, who will certainly be generous. There is also a clandestine *Ezras Torah* committee run by R. Yosef Konigsberg, R. Dovid Shapira, R. Shimshon Stockhammer, and Senator Trokenheim who oversee the regular expenses of Torah students. They, too, will surely provide future food stocks for those in hiding.

I further agree to speak to the Resistance Committee on their behalf, since Torah study and survival in the bunkers should form part of the resistance. (Besides, I and others have argued that we should adopt a twin track approach: preparing for both resistance and survival, with priority perhaps being given to survival.) I promise them a reply within two days.

As I was about to leave the bunker, a young, black-haired *bachur* corners me. He wants to confer with me in private. We must think about obtaining weapons, too, he insists. So I should ask the Resistance Committee for sufficient pistols and ammunition. "We must be prepared! Yaakov Avinu taught us how to behave with the wicked Eisav. We tried the approach of *doron* — bribes — but it didn't work. The approach of *tefillah* — we are still engaged in prayer. But the time has now come to be prepared for *milchamah* — for war!" I promised to pass on this request, too.*

After I was brought out of this bunker though twisting passageways and narrow breaches, I looked back at the heap of rubble which concealed the bunker. Here live men who are true heroes even before any revolt breaks out. Their bravery is drawn from centuries of heroism.

Although they learn *Gemara* diligently, in depth, under impossible conditions and are immersed in the sea of Talmud, yet simultaneously they are preparing for battle — literally. Always I was fond of quoting the Talmudic epigram, "Either the sword or the book" (*Avodah Zara* 17b). Now, for the first time, I also understand the proverb, "The sword and the book descended entwined from Heaven" (*Midrash Devarim* 4:2).

Monday, January 11

Lwow's Fate

On hearing that somebody from my hometown, Lwow, had arrived in Warsaw, I rush over to find out what has transpired there.

Since August 1942 there have been a number of *aktions* and from the population of 130,000, there now remain only about 25,000 Jews. They are held at a labor camp in Yanovska

---

* The religious leaders ruled they should remain in the bunker and should be supplied with sufficient stocks. At the Uprising after April 19, *yeshivah bachurim* joined the fighting under the leadership of Rav Zemelman from Pesheitz and Rav Horowitz from Ulica. They formed a brigade together with the Revisionists and displayed great courage. This particular bunker did receive weapons and used them effectively during the Uprising.

Street or at various German workshops dotted round the town. This refugee, Mr. Klingshoffer, told me that he himself had barely escaped from the last *aktion* on January 1st. At that *aktion* no documents helped. Anybody who did not manage to hide and was caught, was taken away.

Lwow's latest *Rosh Hakahal*, Dr. Henriqs Landsberg, was hanged together with another twenty-one Jews as a reprisal after someone had shot at an SS man near the Ghetto entrance. In fact, there were four *Judenrat* presidents in Lwow within a short period. Dr. Josef Parnes, a well-known industrialist and philanthropist was arrested by the Nazis and was never heard from again; Dr. Adolf Rotfeld, previous secretary of Lwow's Federation, died from persecution; Dr. Henriqs Landsberg was hanged; and now Dr. Abenson, the lawyer, was appointed.

Harav Aaron Lewin, the Reischer Rav and senator to the Sejm, was in Lwow during the Soviet occupation. He continued his Torah studies, completing the fifth and final section of the Bible commentary *Hadrush V'haiyun* on *Devarim*. Shortly after the Germans captured Lwow on June 21, 1941, he was arrested and murdered at the same time and under similar circumstances as the Bobover Rebbe, Rav Halberstam, together with most of his family. Only a few managed to escape to Hungary.

Another prominent personality, the Husiatener Rebbe's son-in-law, Rav Nochum Friedman (who had lately settled in Lwow and whose house had become a center of *chasidus*), was dragged off to Belzec at the end of November 1942. The Boyaner Rebbe, Rav "Moshenu" Friedman, was officially a Turkish citizen and theoretically immune from deportation. But he was arrested and cruelly tortured, and the hairs of his beard were torn out. Contact with him was eventually lost and he was not heard from again. *Rabbanim* in Lwow, R. Moshe Elchanan Alter, Rav

Wolfsberg, and Rav Rappaport, were all deported among others.

The famous lawyer Dr. Leib Landau (who acted for the defense in the Steiger case) managed to find sanctuary among the Christians, but he emerged to save friends and relatives and was caught.

Those trapped in the last *aktion* include Heinrich Hershels (editor of the Polish-Jewish *Kavilla* newspaper), Moshe Hirschsprung (Agudas Israel President), Chanoch Ashkenazi, Dr. Akser (the celebrated lawyer), Shalom Wallach, and Moshe Meyer with their families.

Particularly poignant was the fate of the famous Professor Dr. Moshe Alerhand (a previous *Rosh Hakahal*), who appealed to Polish friends to save him. He had lectured at the university for many years and had taught generations of lawyers. Only two or three Poles responded to his overtures and then only for a few days each. Inevitably, when he was forced to leave his hiding place, he was caught by the Nazis and dragged off to Belzec.

Dr. Israel Osterzetzer (dean of Warsaw's Institute for Jewish Studies and son-in-law of the Zionist, Lipa Galer) was also murdered, as was recently my friend Dr. Zvi Pfeffer (previously Cracow's preacher who had come to Lwow via his hometown, Tarnopol).

My friend the learned non-Jew Dr. Tadeusz Zaretzki, who became a expert of Talmudic literature, did conceal some Jews at a village outside Lwow but later he himself was on the run from the Germans. He had sent me regards via mutual friends, Shalom Brunner and Yosef Shaul Zucker. By now they, too, have been deported.

Within twenty-four hours, I receive letters from my family in Lwow — from my brothers Moshe and Anshel, my brother-in-law Moshe Blaustein, and my sister Ruchama. They write that they are all working at the cooperative workshop Textilla, at 6 Hoffman Passage. They have all sorts of documents — but precious little hope. Every letter contains its own message of despair.

My brother informs me that our uncle, Hertzl Horowitz (well known throughout Lwow for his piety, *ahavas Yisrael*, and *mesiras nefesh* for his co-religionists), died naturally from the privations in the Ghetto and received a Jewish burial. My brother-in-law, Moshe Blaustien, wrote, "...there is no hope, our fate has been sealed. We send you our best wishes and regards from 'Aunt Nekamah.' " My brother Moshe sent me his photograph with the inscription: "Let me live until the morrow, perhaps I'll decipher the dream."

When I returned home I found another postcard from my brother Moshe in which he wrote:

> Dearest Brother, I can no longer conceal from you that on August 10, 1942, our dear father was taken away. He was caught in the street on the way to work. One of the work cards had an official stamp missing, and they held him for questioning. From the deportation railway station, he sent a note via a Jewish policeman which said: "I take my leave from my sons, daughters, and son-in-law. I ask you all for forgiveness if ever I behaved at all badly towards any of you. Yours in peace — tell Hillel."

My brother writes further that we should not give up hope; letters have arrived from people older than Father that are alive and working. Then my brother continues with more bad tidings: "Three days later our sisters Sarah and Rachel were caught. They claimed they were being taken away to work in the countryside...."

But my heart hardens into stone. Realistically, all hope is lost and yet somehow we continue to function amid unbearable pain and despair. Under normal circumstances, I would not have been capable of withstanding this tremendous tragedy. In all probability, these successive shocks would have eaten away at my soul. But now the unending routine search for food, refuge, and ultimate safety continues unabated. It is as if all natural emotion has been stifled.

Everyone secretly believes that his father, brothers, and sisters are special, even unique. But I am sure that members of my family were a cut above the ordinary strata. My father, Avraham Seidman (may Hashem avenge his blood), was well known for his exemplary *middos*, wide knowledge, Torah study, *chasidus*, and *mesiras nefesh* for *Klal Yisrael*. I have always regarded him with deep affection and enormous respect. Though the pain does hurt, it is as if my heart has turned to stone. I notice similar reactions among everyone else.

Everybody has suffered their individual trauma and loss, yet they continue their now habitual search for food and shelter; hoping to live for another day. It seems there are limits to one's endurance or capacity to absorb anguish and torment. Our emotional stamina can only function up to a certain level. The present tragedy is so overwhelming that none of us can accept or even evaluate its sheer enormity. Neither the public nor the individual are capable of understanding or defining the catastrophe.

Most survivors pay no attention at all and continue to function blindly as if nothing has happened. We seem to live in a separate existence — that which existed before the war. Those who did not personally witness the actual slaughter of their precious family (and most of us have not actually seen their murder) behave as if their relatives are still alive. Of course it signifies a retreat from the bitter truth into a world of make-believe and delusion.

For us, fantasy substitutes for reality, while reality recedes into fantasy. We exist uneasily between two conflicting worlds. Though the present cruelly encompasses us, yet we try to ignore it. Our past world has been mercilessly destroyed, yet it remains alive within our collective memory. We always prayed that the dead shall "remain bound up with the bond of life" — now the souls of the dead remain entwined with the lives of the survivors.

Monday, January 11

Resistance Committee Weighs Options

Rumors are once again rife about an impending *aktion* — scheduled for January 15. So the Resistance Committee meet to discuss their reaction. Not all of the twenty-five members are present: Menachem Kirshenbaum, Dr. Emanuel Ringelblum, Anielwicz, Rosenbaum, Tusia, Mauricy Orzech, Yosef Tennenbaum, Viktor, Nochum Remba, and Yisrael Holtskenner (Zeirei Aguda) are there. There are also two *chalutz* representatives, a representative of the Bund youth wing SKIF, and some young representatives, using pseudonyms, from Hashomer Hatzair and Hapoel Mizrachi. Later Alexander Landau arrives.

The main item on the agenda is whether to organize a resistance if the rumored *aktion* goes ahead on January 15. The SKIF representative, who had been empowered to deal directly with the Polish partisans, reports that they feel it is still too early to take any action. The partisans have not completed their preparations and cannot promise any help. They advise us to wait.

Orzech, the Bundist leader, supports this view. He has arrived from the Aryan sector (where he is protected by false Aryan documents), and he does not believe the partisans are capable of a speedy response. Their organizational structure is extremely weak.

However, all the other committee members press for immediate action — at the first opportunity. Almost inadvertently, the SKIF representative tells the meeting that one left-wing leader of the Polish underground told him that he had received fifteen million zloty on our behalf. Nobody knows where this money came from. Some speculate it had been sent from London via secret couriers; others believe the Joint must have sent it from America.

Then the meeting discusses the question of arms. Kirschenbaum says he has available 143 revolvers and four machine guns with the requisite amount of ammunition. Guns can be bought from Polish policemen or ordinary smugglers for between 3000 and 4000 zloty a revolver (while in the marketplace, revolvers cost 5000 zloty each). When the Resistance Committee begin to discuss the necessary budget, it transpires that there is no money. It is decided to levy a "tax" on the factory foremen (who earned astronomical amounts of money during the deportations by granting work cards and promising *protexias*) and to demand five million zloty from the *Judenrat*. We resolve to establish a subcommittee (not drawn from anyone present) to collect this money whether by consent or force.

After this, I deliver my own report. Due to my permit to leave the Ghetto, I had been sent as an emissary to the PPS

(Polish Socialist Party) as well as leading partisans and patriots. I had been furnished with various addresses and had fulfilled the commission to the best of my ability — the result was total and utter failure.

None of them were prepared to offer any help, using various evasions and excuses. One claimed the time was not right, another said they were waiting for "the right signal," and a third spoke openly: "We are not going to lose our popularity with the Polish masses by helping Jews for whom the Poles have no sympathy...." This was all I got for all my efforts.

True, one fellow did say, "Begin your struggle and we will immediately come to your aid!" But Orzech, who knows him well, tells us that man has no influence, and besides, he is an inveterate liar. Orzech, the Bundist leader, has less belief than all of us in any help from the partisans. "There are good reasons for this," he announces in a mysterious tone.

In general, neither the Zionists nor the religious have any faith in outside help. It is well known that the Poles routinely inform against any Jew found outside the Ghetto walls and betray them to the Germans. Many Poles have found a new source of income: threatening Jews hiding out in the Aryan sector and extorting much money from them. But the Bundist youth wing SKIF representative finds it hard to accept that one of their fundamental dogmas — "Solidarity of the Proletariat" — does not exist and never did exist. He insists we have to find the "right address" and find true and honest socialists. He claims to know a few trustworthy socialists whom he and his party are in contact with. We must not give up all hope of Polish assistance; we must continue to make approaches.

"If solidarity of the proletariat does actually exist," I point out, interrupting his peroration, "if there indeed remain any

Polish men of spirit who still regard Jews sympathetically in our overwhelming hour of need, let us at least use them for the saving of lives. There are still many Jewish children alive in the Ghetto and quite a few prominent personalities. Let us approach your Polish friends to provide sanctuary for children and a few famous personalities!

"Give me their addresses," I offer, "and I will meet them personally!" I was also sure the Joint would provide for the children's food and needs generously and probably the support for our surviving leaders as well.

"Let us not confine ourselves to resistance alone," I implored them. "Let us at least rescue some of the survivors. Can the Bund not find among all your friends in the PPS or unions anyone who is prepared to save some of us at this late stage?"

But the Bundists hesitate to reply. They cannot give us the addresses which might destroy their socialist conspiracy. Perhaps they will try something themselves, they add weakly, and it is obvious they have little faith in their own promises.

I told the meeting that I had already asked the Polish leaders I had met about concealing Jewish children or Jewish leaders, but again they all shrugged off any involvement and trotted out various excuses. (It is a sad fact that after 450,000 of Warsaw's Jews have already been exterminated, not a single Jew was saved for ideological or humanitarian considerations. Not one Pole was prepared to conceal Jews in his house. If a few hundred Jews had managed to hide outside the Ghetto, this was only by their bringing much money and paying their "rescuers" huge sums.)

We in the Ghetto have reached a defining moment. All previous trust in outside assistance, based either on doctrine or habit, now collapses in the face of the bitter reality. Even the

Bund is now forced to accept that. Yet this does not diminish our will to resist — if it is our destiny to die, let us die heroically. We discuss all manner of tactics: setting up bunkers, the supply of weapons and ammunition, food stocks, and building various fortifications. We appoint a technical committee made up from engineers and young technicians.

And we take the crucial decision. If the Germans have organized a new *aktion,* we shall set fire to a number of houses adjoining the Ghetto walls and instigate armed resistance. Thus those who are able to flee and save themselves shall have the opportunity to do so, while those who want to resist will have their chance. At least none of us will go meekly towards our total destruction.

Tuesday, January 12

"Churban Lita"

My old acquaintance Saltzwasser today arrived from Vilna and Kovno. I asked him about the general situation there, and he tells me that only a small proportion of Lithuanian Jewry still remains. The destruction has been enormous, encompassing nearly everybody — and with the willing assistance of the native Lithuanians.

The veteran Zionist activist, Dr. Vigodosky of Vilna, was tortured terribly before being shot. The same fate befell Noach Prilutzki in Minsk, Dr. Joshua Gottleib, and other authors.

Shortly after the Germans captured Vilna, they arrested the whole *Judenrat*, including Rav Yosef Shub (editor of the religious *Dos Vort*), marched them off to the Ponary Forest, and shot them all on July 15, 1941. At the same period, Harav Eiges was murdered, as was the engineer Krakovsky (son of the last

Vilna *maggid* and a well-known *askan*) and other Jewish *askanim*. Rav Bloch, *rosh yeshivah* of Telz, Rav Bakst of Shavli, and the *roshei yeshivah* of Kelm and Ponevez, were killed by the German murderers during the first few weeks of German occupation.

From the thousands of *yeshivah bachurim*, none now remain. Earlier, during the Soviet occupation, a small proportion had managed to escape to Shanghai and America. Leaving Lithuania then was extremely difficult and most did not have this opportunity. There were even *rabbanim*, *roshei yeshivah*, and *yeshivah bachurim* who had visas to America or certificates to enter Eretz Yisrael, yet they had remained stranded in Lithuania. The Soviet authorities would not let them go, and later they all fell victim to the Germans. Thus was destroyed a center for Torah and wisdom, a fount of spiritual development for all Judaism which had spread its light throughout the Jewish world.

As I understand it, all the famous *gaonim* and *roshei yeshivah* of Kovno and Slabodka have been murdered. Three days after the Germans captured Kovno from the Russians, they descended on Slabodka, a suburb of Kovno, at eight in the morning. People were dragged out and shot on the spot or marched off to execution. They entered the home of the Slabodka *rosh yeshivah*, Rav Avraham Grodzenski, where they discovered many *rabbanim* and *roshei yeshivah*.

Also present was Rav Elchanan Wasserman, the *rosh yeshivah* of Baranowitz. Revered as a great Jewish leader both in Lita and abroad, he was seen as the spiritual heir of the Chafetz Chaim. Around him had gathered all religious life in Lithuania. Shortly before the War he had been in America but had returned home. During the Soviet occupation he had been at the center of all rescue efforts. Now he was sheltering in Kovno together with his family. The SS fell upon the assembly like a pack of wild dogs. They wanted to take Rav Elchanan Wasserman and the other *rabbanim* away. Rav Elchanan Wasserman asked permission to collect his false teeth, but it was refused. Instead he picked up a *Chumash* from the table and went with them.

Apparently, the SS intended taking Rav Wasserman to the area between the Seventh and Ninth Fort in Kovno, where many had already been murdered. But on the way there, the order was given to take him aside to a nearby square, where he was summarily killed.

Later the burned body of Rav Avraham Grodzenski was discovered in a bunker where he had taken refuge.

A great light in Israel has been extinguished.

I remember Rav Wasserman in 1939 explaining to me, in that simplistic yet profound manner he adopted, why the world was in such dire economic and political straits. "Let us comprehend what exactly is missing from the world of *Hakadosh Baruch Hu*. In reality, there is no actual shortage of food. Canada is currently dumping tons of grain into the sea to artificially inflate the price. Likewise, Brazil is destroying its surplus coffee production. Nor is there a lack of money. At present the Swiss bankers complain their coffers are overflowing with gold reserves — they have no one to lend to, no worthwhile project to invest in. Yet famine reigns in various parts of the world, and everywhere economic activity is severely depressed, though no real shortage exists.

"Why are the Nations so apprehensive of war? Why are they convinced that their neighbors plan to attack them?

"The reason for both phenomena is the same: *Hakadosh Baruch Hu* is repaying us with our own coin. Because we have abandoned our *bitachon* in Hashem, He has removed our trust in our fellow man, nations distrust their neighbors — and insecurity rules. Business cannot function without mutual trust, economic activity cannot flourish without credit. Our only solution is to repent, and then Heaven will restore faith and confidence, the wheels of commerce will begin spinning again, and nations will prosper amid security."

Trial of Dr. Nossig

I was party today to a tragic episode: sitting in judgment on Dr. Alfred Nossig. This underground court has been operating for a few months now, judging Gestapo agents and informants. They have already sentenced a number of offenders (Israel Fuerst, Szerynski, Leikin, and Shmerling, who had cooperated in the mass deportations), and they mete out only one sentence — death.

Today they discuss the charges against Dr. Alfred Nossig: delivering secret reports about the Ghetto to the Gestapo, and informing and traitorous activity.

Most of those present have personally no previous knowledge of the man on whom they are sitting in judgment — never having heard of him before. They focus solely on one vital fact: Nossig is a suspected Gestapo agent. So I researched his fame and background (using history books, archive material, and the personal memoirs of Prof. Balaban, Dr. Schipper, Dr. Joshua Thun, and Dr. Heinrich Lewenhartz) and gave the meeting a fuller biography.

Dr. Nossig's career had undergone many changes of direction from his youth until today. At first he was an assimilationist who adopted Polish national dress. Then he joined the Socialist

Movement, and before the end of the last century he became a full-fledged Zionist, rising to the leadership of the Jewish National Movement in Galitzia before Hertzl. He led the Zionist's young academics in Lwow who later were Hertzl's earliest supporters.

I showed the meeting an exchange of letters between him, Hertzl, and Dr. Adolf Shtand, the Galitzian Zionist leader (these documents were from the Balaban collection in the archives). In 1894 Hertzl had approached the Zion group (of Dr. Reuven Birer in Lwow) to join the Zionist Federation which he was currently establishing. Adolf Shtand then wrote to Dr. Nossig in Vienna for advice in dealing with Hertzl, since Nossig was then considered the ideological leader of Galitzia's Zionist movement. Nossig instructed them to "...invite Hertzl, whom I don't know, to a meeting in Lwow, listen carefully, and report back to me for a decision."

Later Nossig left the Zionist movement and reverted to becoming an assimilationist. Yet whatever he joined he became a prominent leader who played a crucial role.

In addition he is unusually talented — a Renaissance Man in many aspects. He is a skilled writer, a romantic novelist, a poet, a journalist, and a dramatist — his plays were extremely successful. He also holds three doctorates in separate disciplines: in philosophy, medicine, and law.

Moreover, he is a talented musician and composer who wrote a libretto for Padwerski's operas. Lately he took up sculpture, in which again he excells. Just before the War he conceived the group sculpture entitled "Moses" and already completed most of it. When War broke out, his sculpture was crated up and transported from Berlin to Warsaw, where it was lodged in the Kehillah archives. This sculpture had been highly praised, and a group of experts has been established to prepare it for removal to Palestine.

Dr. Nossig also played an important part on the political stage. During the First World War, while in Turkey on behalf of the *Neue Freie Presse,* he also acted as the Austrian Consul there. He used his influence to persuade Turkey to join the central powers — i.e., Germany and Austria.

Here Kirshenbaum interrupted me by remarking, "See, he was already then a German agent!"

But his statecraft had a Jewish angle, and he presented Hertzl's idea of a "charter" for a Jewish political and economic presence in Palestine and received great promises from the Turks. In Dr. Gelber's book on the Balfour Declaration, there is much documentation and detail of Nossig's achievements. He made only one error, he placed all his bets on a losing horse — Turkey. Had the War turned out differently, as Dr. Schipper once remarked, Nossig would have Weitzman's prestige and position.

Almost his last political endeavor was his involvement in the Polish-Jewish Fraternity Society, which was set up in 1925 with Dr. Leon Reich and Dr. Joshua Thun representing Jewish interests, and Count Skchinski and Stanislav Gravski on behalf of the Poles. Had it succeeded as intended, Nossig would have had much to his credit.

In December 1939, immediately after Germany's capture of Poland, Nossig arrived in Warsaw. The first time I actually met him was on February 11, 1940.

Before then, the Gestapo had summoned various political activists, including the Aguda leader Rav Yitzchak Meir Lewin and myself, to 25 Shuka Avenue. After forcing us to deliver up stolen Jewish property, we were received by the Gestapo Commander Schmidt. He behaved in a friendly manner, showing great interest in Religious Jewry. But we confined ourselves to discussing Jewish emigration before the War and put forward plans to accelerate migration now, asking for Gestapo support. Schmidt listened avidly and asked for a written memorandum. We did as we were told, and I subsequently visited him a few times to receive a response.

At first the Gestapo said that the whole file had been forwarded to Berlin. Later Schmidt asked for evidence that England will co-operate, as we were mainly discussing entry into Palestine. However, we thought, let it be wherever — Madagascar or even Honolulu — as long as the Polish Jews can escape with their lives.

On February 10, the Kehillah President Adam Czerniakow told me that Dr. Nossig was also preparing plans for mass emigration from Poland and suggested we could work together. Following his suggestion I confided in Nossig what we had already done and showed him the memorandum we had already submitted. Nossig proposed we should visit the German office at 25 Shuka Avenue together to discuss our proposals. When we arrived there, I could not help noticing that he was greeted unusually warmly.

During the conversation I had an unpleasant surprise when I realized he was only discussing emigration to other destinations — mainly Madagascar. He expressed his confidence that German pressure would persuade the French to allow mass migration to Madagascar. He based himself on the previous work of the Polish captain Lipaski and Dick, the director of HIAS. I tried to raise the possibility of Palestine, but Nossig waved my intervention aside.

The situation, however, remained basically the same as before: we had to present more memoranda and plans, as well as setting up an Emigration Department at the *Judenrat*. Though this department was duly set up, nothing came from this whole affair, just as nothing much ever resulted from Nossig's activities.

Later Nossig's star with the Gestapo rose higher. He was appointed an executive in the *Judenrat*, receiving a large salary and a comfortable apartment. Besides his salary, he would regularly present bills for various expenses which Czerniakow had payed without question. Often he had held secret meetings with Czerniakow and even more frequently he would visit the Gestapo.

Some thought he was the "contact" between the *Judenrat* and the Gestapo, where he had free access. It is a fact that he wrote regular reports for the Gestapo about the Jews. What he wrote nobody knew — nor could anybody possibly know — everything around him was cloaked in secrecy. He would cut out news reports from German newspapers about Jews — and musical cabaret!

He possessed documents which protected him alone. He was never molested by the Germans; even during the mass deportations, they left him alone. Later he continued to furnish them with his reports. What exactly did he write in his reports? Did he help the Nazis in any way? Did he supply any information against the Jews? No one can tell.

Czerniakow, too, had been well aware that he provided the Gestapo with reports; in fact, he had supplied him with the necessary technical equipment (obviously under German instructions). Czerniakow, Balaban, and others regarded him with suspicion, just as they had been suspicious of anyone with close links with the Gestapo. But they did not have any firm proof that Nossig actually informed against an individual or the public.

Today he is being judged by embittered men, each with their private pain. All have lost close relatives and friends — did Nossig have any part in their loss? So they resolve to sentence him to death. Besides, we are preparing for resistance, for a struggle. We can not afford traitors, they must be removed from our midst — and that includes Nossig.

What about his famous career in the past? Or his great talents? On the contrary, this only saddles him with extra responsibility.

"A man like that ought to behave differently," declares Anielewicz, and the *chalutzah* Tusia agrees. "We are preparing for battle," adds Yisrael Holzkenner, a young Zeirei Aguda activist, "and we cannot afford any sentimentality."

I insist that Nossig is an important historical figure. Nor may we decide a matter of life and death on mere suspicion alone. Justice demands that he at least be judged by his peers — not by a court of impetuous youngsters! Perhaps we should leave his sentencing for a court of elders made up of Zionists representing the various political strands. I propose Rav Menachem Ziemba, Dr. Yitzchak Schipper, and Mauricy Orzech. At this, an argument breaks out. Time is short, if any *aktion* is truly imminent.

We must finish this disagreeable business today — we cannot tolerate traitors. Kirschenbaum presses for an immediate sentence of death, and he is supported by the *chalutzim*. Surprisingly, in the end they all agree to delay sentencing and will gather more evidence from *Judenrat* members.*

When I return from this meeting, I report back to Dr. Schipper the general thrust of the sitting. He listens carefully, and

* At the subsequent sitting of that court, Nossig was sentenced to death, and it was later carried out by armed groups of the resistance movement within the Ghetto.

when I finish, he recalls the controversial historical precedent of Josephus and utters just one word — "Flavius...."

Wednesday, January 13

In Hiding

I am no longer at my desk. It all started two days ago when my friend Rabbi Goldstein (previously the army chaplain at Lodz) came to my office to warn me that the *Judenrat* had received a list of names whom they must deliver up to the Nazis *Befehl-stelle* at the Extermination Dept. 103, Iron Street — and on that list appears my name, too!

Immediately, I raced over to the *Judenrat* secretariat to find out what was going on. Apparently it was an old list of twenty Jewish representatives who had been elected to Warsaw City Council in December 1938. Straightaway, I phoned Kolsky to explain to him that I had not actually been elected. In fact, he himself had invalidated sixteen of my votes. I beg him to remove my name from that list since that constitutes a death sentence (very few ever return alive from that *Befehl-stelle*).

After repeated conversations and pressure, he claimed that since I had received the largest number of votes after Senator Yaakov Trokenheim, I took his place when he resigned in 1934. That is as far as I can get with Kolsky.

Indeed, Trokenheim's name does not appear on this list. Actually it is quite true that Trokenheim had done me that "honor" and I had indeed been a City Council member for four weeks. But I dare not substitute Trokenheim's name, as he and his family are still alive in the Ghetto.

From that whole list, only two others besides myself remain in Warsaw: Mauricy Orzech and Galinsky. I contact

Orzech, he is already hiding out in the Aryan sector where he has many friends and — more importantly — a great deal of money. Galinsky, too, has vanished, so what can I do?

To remain at my desk within the *Judenrat* is obviously impossible. I have to go into temporary hiding. I knock on a few doors. Everybody is sympathetic and extremely willing to help — but scared. Finally, I obtain access to a cellar at 22 Franciszkanska Street.

I prepare a small stock of food, some books, notebooks, and writing materials, as well as organizing some safe contacts with the outside world (with the help of my friends Dr. Schimkovits, A. G. Friedensohn, Dr. Tulu Nussblatt, Simchah Gefen, Pinchas Levitman, and Maniah Rosenstroich).

Every so often I venture back into the *Judenrat* — usually in the evening — to find out the latest news. I have to remain incognito until the matter is forgotten. Since all Jews are anyhow condemned to death, the *Befehl-stelle* are not usually overly concerned whether these orders are carried out.

Meanwhile I delve into the Kehillah archives. I need to obtain reports and documents for my monograph on the Warsaw Kehillah during the occupation — which I feel a holy duty to record. For the last decade I had been compiling my "History of the Warsaw Kehillah," and I had already brought it up to date until 1939.* Now, apparently, it is my sad duty to record the untimely end of this glorious history. I immerse myself in the finer details and promptly forget all past or future problems. I am upset only that I am unable to sit in the large hall of the Tlomackie Street Library perusing old books and newspapers, surrounded by that vast sea of words.

How many treasures of priceless literature and

* I managed to save this work, which I have in manuscript form.

Starving women volunteering for "resettlement" for three kilos of bread and marmalade

Gestapo officers in the hall of the Warsaw Kehillah

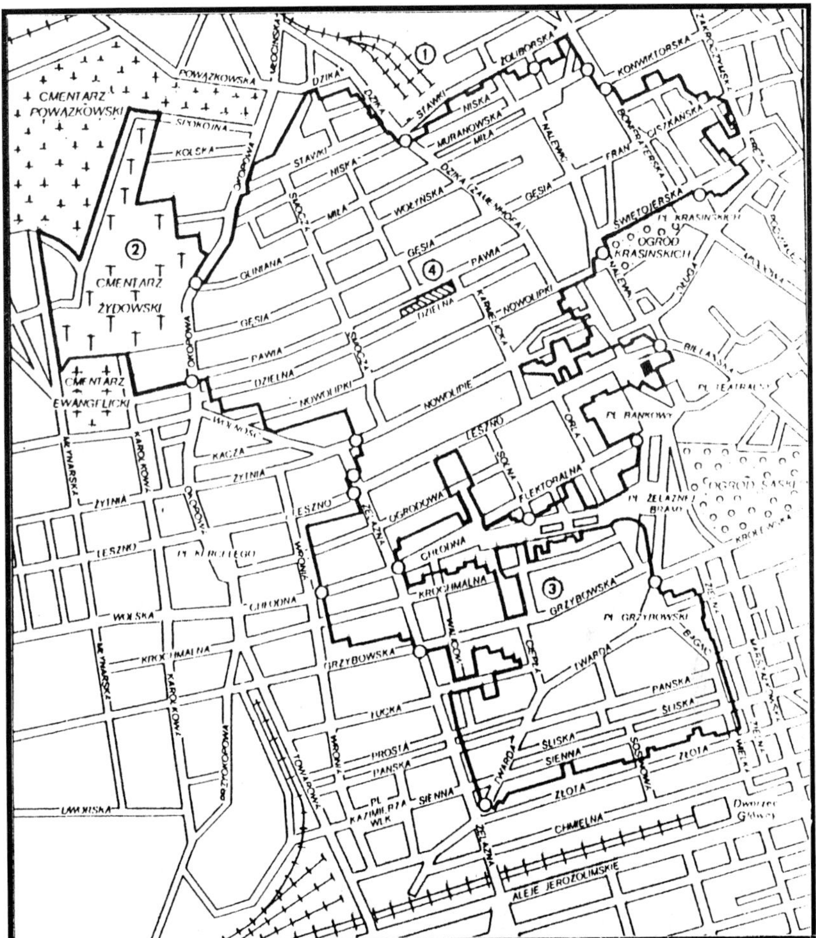

Walls and gates of the Warsaw Ghetto

Key: 1. *Umschlagplatz* (railway siding). 2. Jewish cemetery. 3. *Judenrat* building before its relocation to Zamenhof St. 4. Pawiak Prison.

Scenes from the Warsaw Ghetto

Ghetto children

The Ghetto goes up in flames after the Germans crushed the Uprising

Learning Torah in a Ghetto bunker

A gathering in a Warsaw *shul*

irreplaceable manuscripts have been stolen or destroyed by these vandals? The Tlomackie Library had already been removed in December 1939. Where to? Somebody speculates it's been taken en bloc to Munich.* Someone else claims these will be converted into recycled paper!

And what of those mounds of rabbinical literature from the many Chasidic *shtieblach* and *batei medrash*; or the private libraries of bibliophiles? But who worried for mere *sefarim* at a time when living volumes are being destroyed daily without even the benefit of a simple burial. A whole world is being extinguished despite its glorious past, its illustrious present, and its promising potential.

In my mind's eye I can see a procession of Warsaw's *parnassim*: Berke Joselovitz, the Epsteins and Natansohns, the Behrsons and Rotvands, the Posens and Eigers. And what of their rabbinical counterparts? Rav Shloma Lipshutz (the Chemdas Shloma), Rav Chaim Davidsohn, Rav Dov-Berisch Meisels (the revolutionary), Rav Yaakov Gesundheit (he of the "iron will"), up till the most recent *rabbanim*. Across the landscape of my memory flits eras of struggle and suffering, of hopes and expectations, till I come to the present day. Is this our final era?

I think of the many *askanim* who now worked and functioned within the Warsaw *Judenrat* structure. Each possessed their own particular qualities and faults. In an ideal situation all would have achieved a great deal, but in the unequal circumstances now being forced upon us, some became less than straight and others were too weak and ineffectual. All of them had wasted their time and talent on trivialities or in carrying out the cruel dictates of alien powers. But most of them at least

* When I was later in Munich during November 1945, I searched for this library but without success.

tried to serve the public, to help their brothers in their hour of need. And if a few of them were far too concerned with their own survival, who can blame them? Our role here is neither to condemn nor condone — merely to report the facts. Historians must be the final arbiter (though how can those living among the ease and security of a free society fully comprehend the unnatural, dangerous — and totally unbelievable — conditions we are now forced to work under).

I just would like to establish one important and salient fact. Very rarely throughout our long history was so much Torah and wisdom, knowledge and culture, talent and skills, energy and initiative, gathered together at one time and at one place as there had been in the Warsaw Ghetto. Much creativity was displayed in all manner of culture and spirituality, despite the constant fear of death, the horrendous situation, tragedy, and privation.

Other nations would certainly have descended down to bestial levels in similar circumstances. Yet many Jews rose to great heights of spirit and morals, displaying enormous potential in all fields of human endeavor. Their creativity and promising potential could have enriched and embellished Jewish centers around the world — a blessing for both Jews and the wider world alike.

Recently, I was present at a *Judenrat* meeting for all *Judenrat* members and directors of its various departments. The first matter on the agenda was the huge cost of the large walls which the *Judenrat* is forced to erect along the length of Gesia Street (now that the Ghetto area has been reduced down to its present size).

Then came the perennial problem — providing adequate food for the Ghetto population. However, this problem has largely been solved. We have just received fresh food stocks that are sufficient for the moment. And the Ghetto poor — the proletariat — have already been deported, which simultaneously solved the all food supply problems. Currently, the specter of hunger no longer stalks the Ghetto streets. Starvation has been removed together with the starving.

Then the *Judenrat* meeting began considering transferring some of its officials to the German workshops. At present, the *Judenrat* has too many officials for its own good. What will happen when there is a "selection" (which we expect any day now)? Many of us will be picked off. The most vocal in this discussion are the "important" members and officials, those who are closely involved in building the Ghetto walls or supplying expertise for the Germans. We, the "non-important," remain silent, too scared to draw attention to ourselves.

I look round at the gathering. I would dearly like to penetrate into their innermost recesses to discover what they are really thinking. They proudly strut about as if they are engaged in some worthwhile exercise. They stuff themselves with food and act in a grand manner.

From the beginning, two distinct types emerged in the Ghetto. There were yesterday's men who recalled their previous importance and lived on their memories. They long for the past when life was more or less normal and dream of a more pleasant future. But they have as little as possible to do with the present. Currently they are desultory in outlook and behavior and wield little influence.

Then there are the up-and-coming men of today. Though they have little past experience, they have become quickly acclimatized to the bewildering change of fortunes. Now they wield the upper hand. Apparently they are not aware how pathetic a figure they cut in the eyes of the Germans with whom they are in contact.

They are not necessarily informers. There must have been less than ten informers among the half million souls in the Warsaw Ghetto. But their main motive is to save themselves, their wives, and their children, and they believe they have discovered the solution — to surrender to the German nearly everything he demands, in order to save themselves.

These two types had always existed in the upper echelons of the Ghetto, but now the mass deportations have accentuated and sharpened the differences between yesterday's men and the men of today. It is perhaps possible to understand their attitude under unbearable circumstances and pressures, but these men have become so acclimatized to being unwitting tools of the German death machine, that they seem to forget there are limits to compliance. They have come to see nearly every situation as normal and act as if this is how matters ought to be.

They carry out their unnatural tasks not grudgingly, as if they were forced, but with energy and contentment — fulfilling their duties to the letter with far too much zeal. Generally their processes of thought and finer feeling have become stunted. Their perspective has become so contracted they cannot adequately evaluate events in the Ghetto; certainly world affairs are beyond their comprehension.

Basically their main flaw lies in assuming that our present situation is fixed and likely to last. They do not quite believe in the German's ultimate victory — there is nobody in the Ghetto who believes that — but they see the final defeat of the Germans as being so far into the distant future that it hardly colors their considerations at all.

People have changed. Those who were small-minded

before have become even more petty; those who were already evil have inevitably become worse. Many have become selfish and extremely sensitive to every possible need. They are so terrified of death that the smallest matter — even a single slice of bread — is magnified into a question of life and death.

Everyone admits that the religious Jews have withstood these tests better than most. This is not to claim that they have become enwrapped in holiness or display greater heroism. Like everyone else, they are involved in the desperate struggle to live and somehow survive, but they are different on two counts. Firstly, they did not lose their integrity or persona. They might become "shoemakers," removing nails from Nazi boots, but they still persisted with enormous *mesiras nefesh* in donning *tallis* and *tefillin* daily, in davening, learning, observing the Shabbos despite the great danger.

To quote one instance: I once heard of a group of young Chasidim who were dragged off to the *Umschlagplatz* late one Shabbos afternoon before nightfall. These included my friends Shloma Gefen, Yitzchak Eisner, Dr. Aaron Langleben (secretary of Agudas Harabbanim), Morderchai Langer (of Bilitz), Yisrael Eisenberg, and Dovid Shafran. While waiting to be taken to Treblinka, one of them produced a loaf of bread and some water. They all washed their hands and began to eat their last *seudah shlishis*. Soon they were chanting "*Askinah Seudasah*" and "*Mizmor leDavid Hashem Royi Lo Echsar,*" and all were transported to a higher spiritual plane. (I was told this episode by one of the group who later managed to escape.)

There was another vital difference about religious Jews. Though they were as eager to save themselves as everyone else, it was not entirely the same: They were not prepared to save their skins at the direct expense of others. They were always mindful of the Talmudic dictum: "How do you rate your blood as redder and more valuable than anyone else's?" So from the ranks of the religious did not come forth the kidnappers, Gestapo agents, or *Kapos*.*

The terrible destructions and mass murders did not succeed in eradicating the preeminent trait of mercy among religious Jews. While many lived by the slogan "Your life comes first," religious Jews did not forget the Biblical verse "*Vechai achicha imach* — And your brother shall live by your side."

Money for Arms

For an effective resistance, we need weapons and ammunition. And we cannot obtain these without money. Predictably, all those promises — that if we were unable to pay we will be provided with arms for nothing — have proved worthless. So we urgently need to gather money together. And a lot of it! An ordinary revolver costs between 3000 and 5000 zlotys. Where are we to find all this money?

Surprisingly, there still remain some rich men in the Ghetto. There were those who had dealt in jewelry and precious objects before the War. Then there were others who had profiteered during the occupation, making money from the German workshops. Generally these latter are greatly disliked and justifiably so. Everyone still remembers how, before the mass expulsions, people were literally starving to death in the streets while

* Even the sworn enemies of the religious Jews must admit that in the various camps at Auschwitz, Buchenwald, or Bergen Belsen, the behavior of the religious Jews was exemplary. Often they displayed enormous heroism to rescue others. The great deeds of the teachers and pupils of the Bais Yaakov girls' movement were particularly singled out for praise.

these gentlemen were living a life of luxury.

So it was decided to collect money by force. There are some people for whom it is useless trying to stress moral values or their duties towards the common good. The only language they understand is a pointed pistol! This is the only way to extract money from certain magnates, so we have been forced to resort to terror tactics. Pairs of "collectors" armed with revolvers have been organized; they even take hostages — a son or daughter — if necessary. Usually, they burst into apartments in the dead of night to demand money for the cause. Normally they receive their dues. Nor are their activities confined to wealthy individuals: institutions, too, are "taxed." The *Judenrat* President Lichtenbaum was likewise confronted by these "collectors" who demanded five million zloty from the *Judenrat* coffers. But he began to bargain them down until they agreed to three million zloty. They said he was quite amenable to this "forced levy," knowing the money was destined for a vital Jewish cause.

But many contribute willingly to the Resistance Committee's fund. The *rabbanim* impose a tax on themselves for the Committee's behalf. I saw a receipt by Rav Menachem Ziemba for 17,000 zloty which he had already sent them. R. Shimon Landau also sends a large sum, and the Joint, too, donates a sizeable sum.

Unfortunately, against this background of forced collection, deception and embezzlement also flourish. Armed gangsters still operate in the Ghetto.

They, too, visit apartments ostensibly to collect money for the resistance, but the money they steal goes into their own pockets. They burgle at night and take all the clothes first — knowing that the Ghetto Jews usually sew money and valuables into their clothes to conceal them from the Nazis. As an almost natural consequence of the external circumstance of German terror, an internal terrorism plagues the Ghetto. But the menace of gangsterism vanishes under the overwhelming pressure of ideological terror which seeks to destroy us all.

At one of our meetings we discuss the problem of money from abroad which was sent on behalf of Jews held in the camps: for resistance and for rescue. According to Polish partisans, money has been sent from London for the Ghetto. But who is empowered to receive it? The partisans now claim that the Ghetto no longer exists — it is now only a collection of German factories and workshops! They are also unsure as to what exact purpose this money was sent for.

Yechiel Reisman and Avraham Wolfovitz offer to bargain with the partisans. Perhaps they would at least agree to supply us some arms if we would agree to drop our demands for that money. The Bundists, Hoffman, and Klapfish have already tried negotiating with the partisans — to no avail.

It was impossible to even discover how much money was received, when, and from whom. On the contrary, when we approach the partisans on behalf of the Resistance Committee, they immediately begin interrogating us: How do we know anything about this money? They insist it is top secret — even for us, for whom the money was intended!

Generally, they put us off with various excuses, and it is virtually impossible to extract anything from them. Even Mauricy Orzech has tried. He lives in the Aryan sector and is both a Bundist and an experienced businessman. He has approached his Polish comrades — ostensibly all members of the same international brotherhood — to help in rescue efforts, to hide Jewish children, and to assist in armed resistance. But he, too, has had no success.

Yosef Scharansky, who is in charge of the resistance funds, remarks bitterly, "We relied on them for help during the deportations. They were meant to blow up the railway lines leading to Treblinka. We relied on them again to help in rescue efforts and hiding Jews. Then we expected arms from them. Always and throughout they have swindled and betrayed us. Now we must give up getting any money out of them — even though that money is really ours. The whole business will only depress and wear us down further. Once again we can only depend on our own meager resources!"

Thursday, January 14

We sit in the Records and Archives Department of the Kehillah — and fear gnaws at our hearts. What will the morrow bring? Are the rumors of an impending *aktion* correct? If so, how bad will it be? Will it finally provoke a resistance? Above all, will anything happen tomorrow or not? These fears and doubts are our constant companions now; we live in the shadow of death. Inevitably, deeper, underlying dilemmas surface: Why is all this happening to us?

In the Archives Department are gathered prominent *rabbanim*, intellectuals, politicians, and philosophers. Each has much to say but no one succeeds in convincing the others — perhaps they fail to convince even themselves. The questions appear overwhelming. To paraphrase the Talmud: "There is no master craftsman nor son of a master craftsman who can solve this." Neither can all agree on how to understand current events in the ghetto, whether they base their views on logic, religious belief, or metaphysics.

Dr. Edmund Stein, the former rector of the prestigious

Warsaw Institute for Judaic Studies, who was both an intellectual and a romantic, lamented the fact that he had seen little heroism. We had behaved almost like sheep going to the slaughter. But the Zionist, Dr. Schipper, vigorously retorted, "It was impossible to resist. Everyone at first thought that not all of us would be destroyed, that some might yet be saved. We all know how the Germans practice indiscriminate collective punishments. Who could have taken the tremendous responsibility of endangering the lives of possible survivors and their relatives? Resistance would have brought destruction down on everybody!"

"We still would have risked nothing," interjected Dr. Schimkovits. "We should have resisted at the beginning when we still numbered half a million."

But everyone then had hoped the *aussiedlung* decree was not directed against themselves in particular. The Nazi murderers organized our systematic extermination with satanic cunning; they encouraged every individual to falsely believe they would survive. Only now, with hindsight, can we see their special categories and criteria for the shams they really were. They had promised us that *Judenrat* employees would be spared, as well as Joint employees, factory workers, and anyone capable of work.

So we were misled into believing that the danger of "deportation" loomed over only a small proportion of the Ghetto population. This made resistance less likely, since that would have meant the immediate and total destruction of everyone....

"During the first weeks of the *aussiedlung*," I point out, "there was a plan to set fire to the Ghetto. In the resultant general confusion, many would have managed to escape. It would not have been an easy task for them to recapture and arrest half a million people. I still don't know why this plan was not carried out."

At this, Dr. Efraim Zonnenshein (now also a "clerk" in the archives) chimes in, "Well I can tell you, that plan could only work if the Polish population were on our side. Instead, the Poles actively desire our destruction so there was no *tachlis* to the whole plan."

"So what happens?" R. A. G. Friedensohn asks. "What shall we do now?"

Rav Menachem Ziemba declares, "At least we should not have gone voluntarily to the *Umschlagplatz*. We have tried to resist. But we fooled ourselves with wishful thinking. A people renowned for wisdom and intelligence lost all good sense. Throughout, we relied on 'perhaps, possibly, and maybe.' Our enemies spoke continually about our powerful brothers abroad who wielded so much influence around the world — Jews like Bernard Baruch, Morgenthau, and Hore-Belisha. Why didn't *they* remember us, their brothers and sisters threatened with extinction. So we dared to believe and hope that eventually rescue would arrive. If not for that expectation (which might have been logical in other circumstances) we might have behaved perhaps differently.

"We made the cardinal error of considering our enemies as stupid fools and thinking we would be too clever for them. *Pikchus* (cleverness) or sharpness is not the same nor as effective as wisdom. It didn't work for Korach the *pikeach*, and it hasn't worked for us. Perhaps we should have realized from the outset that the *Rasha* really did intend to destroy everything. From the beginning we should have used every opportunity and tactic to alert the conscience of the world. All we can do now is resist to the best of our abilities — we may not surrender ourselves voluntarily into enemy hands!"

I reminded everyone of Dr. W. Von Wiesel whom I met shortly before the War in Warsaw and Tarnopol. If only he was around now, he would surely know how to organize effective resistance. He had told me then with his inimitable fervor that he had only one aim left in life: he traveled from one *kehillah* to another to exhort the old and young alike: *"Yieden, lern sech shiesen!* — Jews, learn how to shoot!"

When I saw the discussion was not coming to any conclusion, I quoted the Rambam in his letter to the community of Marseilles: "...And this is what squandered our sovereignty, destroyed our Temple, prolonged our exile, and brought us to such a pass. Our ancestors, who are no longer with us, sinned after reading many books on astrology that appeared to show that this was important. They had imagined that this was a true science, a great skill with valuable benefits. Instead of learning the craft of war or capturing territory, they had thought the study of astrology would help them. So the *nevi'im* showed them how stupid and evil they were behaving...."

The Rambam clearly condemns the study of astrology — so popular then with both Jews and Arabs alike — in favor of preparing for battle. But we had always abandoned the practical for the abstract.

Eventually Rav Ziemba spoke again with great deliberation. "There are different ways to *Kiddush Hashem*. If Jews were now being forced to forsake their religion and they could save their lives by baptizing themselves — as was possible in Spain or during the Crusades — then our death alone could constitute a *Kiddush Hashem.* In fact, according to the Rambam (and that is the *halachah)* even if a Jew is killed for not denying his Jewishness, that, too, is considered a *Kiddush Hashem*. But today the only way to sanctify His Name is armed resistance!"

Everybody listens to the famous *gaon*'s words with great respect. A heavy silence surrounds the gathering; the arguing is over, the die has been cast.

Friday, January 15

"The Sefarim Collectors"

Energetically we began the task of transferring all the *sefarim* from the abandoned Jewish buildings in Nalewki Street to the archives. Early in the morning, at 6:30 A.M., I organize the work detail.

Our group of "*sefarim* collectors" has grown. It now includes R. Yehudah Leib Orlean (previously *menahel* of Bais Yaakov Seminary, Cracow), Rabbi Eliezer Gershon Friedensohn (former editor, Bais Yaakov Magazine, Lodz), Gustava Yarzkah (a famous author), Yechiel Reisman, Dr. Edmund Stein (former director of the Warsaw Institute), Dr. Rothfeld (a former lawyer and senator), Dr. Wahl (a chief hospital director), Rav Shmuel Behr, Dr. Shmuel Schimkovits, Yonah Schiffer (Lodz Kehillah secretary), Marcel Reich, Aaron Ziemba, Shalom Saltzberg, Ch. Finkelstein, Alexander Rosenfeld, and Yitzchak Rosenstroich.

All day long we trail our two wheelbarrows through the orphaned streets of Muranowska, Zamenhof, Nalewki, Franciszkanska, Kopeicka, Nowiniarska, Swietojerska, and Bonifraterska. Around us is a deathly silence. The empty buildings gaze blankly at us in utter despair; the open windows without their glass look eerily reminiscent of an eyeless corpse.

Over all those many courtyards, previously bustling with so much life and vigor, hangs this ghostly stillness. It is almost as if the rows of houses were part of a funeral cortege which has become petrified into stone. The streets of the Jewish areas have become one vast cemetery but without any visible graves. We are prevented from even pouring out our sorrow at the graveside.

Though the Jews have been totally removed from here, their souls still hover over their erstwhile homes. The fear and terror still pollutes the atmosphere.

I remember a friend, Binyamin Woolf Hendles, who had emigrated to America. Before the War he once wrote to me, "...There are days, particularly on Shabbos and Yom Tov, that I yearn to kiss the stones of Nalewki Street."

I also recall the words of Albert Londre (the French author of "The Wandering Jew," which I once translated for Warsaw's *Yiddishe Togblatt*):

> When Eliyahu Hanavi arrives to announce the redemption, where do you think he will stand to blow his shofar? Here at the corner of Gesia and Nalewki Streets! Centered around here, more than anywhere else, are the Jewish masses, the power of Jews — and Judaism. So when that fateful day finally arrives, Eliyahu Hanavi will sound the shofar of *Mashiach* at this very spot. And the crowds will stream from the streets of Franciszkanska, Walowa, Smocza, Zamenhof, and Nowolipie. Jews with beards and *peyos* as well as Jews without, Jews in modern dress and those in traditional long clothing, old and young, men and women, Chassidim and *misnagdim*, and children, children without number, their eyes round with wonder as they stare at Eliyahu Hanavi of their dreams, for whom they had waited in vain at every Pesach Seder...

So that I should not dismiss him as a hopeless dreamer he began to explain his vision with an almost mathematical simplicity. "The greatest center of Jews in the world is now in Poland. (America was not taken into account because of the dispersion of its Jews and their relatively low standard of Judaism.) And the greatest center of Polish Jews is in Warsaw. And in Warsaw, the center is at the center of Nalewki-Gesia. So it follows that here is the focal point — the center of centers — of Jewish life!"

But today we pass through these very streets and all we find is total desolation and despair. The area is completely bereft of all life and hope. Every apartment block is now an empty grave without even an inscription.

I remember one famous Chasidic Rebbe once said why the *Bais Hamikdash* was built on Mount Moriah rather than Mount Sinai. A place where a Jew had been *moser nefesh* was more important than the site where the Torah was revealed. And where else had so many Jews fallen *al kiddush Hashem* than these roads of the Warsaw Ghetto? Every street is a Mount Moriah, every stone an *akeidah*.

If, by some miracle, I survive this madness, perhaps I should bring a stone from Nalewki Street to Eretz Yisrael and place it alongside the *Kosel Maaravi*. When Jews come on pilgrimage to that sacred site, they could also weep over this stone for the loss of all their loved ones, for the destruction of a large segment of *klal Yisrael*. They will bewail the extinction of a central powerhouse in Judaism — Polish Jewry — as they mourn the *churban* of the holy Temple.

Letters from Abroad

Sensation in the enclosed Ghetto — letters have arrived; letters from abroad, from the free, wide world. A flicker of hope lightens the darkness of our dismal lives. Somebody remembers us, perhaps we are not entirely forgotten. The few postal officials in the Ghetto tackle their task with gusto. If they can show their importance, that they are essential workers, then perhaps they will be spared during the impending deportations.

Besides, just handling these letters is a welcome diversion. It is pleasant for people imprisoned behind sealed barriers to enjoy some contact with the free world. I visited the Jewish mail office and watched the young Rivka Lewin (a relative of R. Yitzchak Meir Lewin) sorting through the letters.

Most of the addresses are no longer relevant, the streets to which they were destined have long been "evacuated" — some as early as August 10th. Any Jew who appears there now would be shot on sight. It may be extremely difficult to journey from Zamenhof Street to Eretz Yisrael, but neither is travel from Zamenhof to Grzybowska an easy matter.

So they decide to contact the addressees via the various workshops and factories. Typed lists of names are distributed to the factories, and another list is displayed at the Kehillah building. But the results are soon evident: very few people turn up to claim their mail, the majority have already been "eliminated."

What should they do with all the unclaimed letters? Well, apparently there is one address in the Ghetto for all unwanted goods — mine, Hillel Seidman, director of the Kehillah Archives. No doubt he will happily store the surplus mail in his archives. Late at night, my door opens and two mailmen enter (one of them my friend Michelsohn, son of Rav Michelsohn) with sackfuls of letters for the "*genizah*," as the ancient stores of sacred Hebrew literature were called.

All my instincts would not allow me to deposit this mail just like that, without at least first reading the orphaned letters — since they cannot now reach their intended destination. I open a sack and a flood of postcards and letters cascade out, most of them on the Red Cross format.

All contain only a few laconic words (on the International Red Cross form one can only write twenty-five words including the address). But though each word is counted, they all display so much heart, longing, dedication, worry, and pain. And they come from all corners of the globe, most from Palestine and America but also from England, France, New Zealand, Johannesburg, Shanghai, Harbin, Japan, Antwerp, and Trieste.

From every letter, those still at liberty cry out to their father and mother, to their brothers and sisters, to friends and relatives.

"Tell us how you are. Why don't we hear from you? Why are you silent?"

"I got married," writes a *chalutzah* from Hertzlia. "My husband is also from Warsaw (from a respectable family in Praga). I'd be happy if only I'd hear from you."

"I'm earning well and have a wonderful boy. But how are you?" writes a son from New York.

"Why doesn't Moshe write? Has something happened? Please tell me the truth!" pleads a letter from Baltimore.

"Why have you stopped writing since July?" asks a postcard from Brussels. "What has happened?"

"Everybody here in Tel Aviv is well, *baruch Hashem.* We have jobs with good salaries. But how are you?"

"If Daddy could only see how my boy learns *Chumash*, he

would have great *nachas*," writes a son from Brooklyn.

"We sent certificates via Istanbul. Did you receive them?" they ask in Haifa.

"We have got stuck here in Shanghai, en route to America. It's not too bad, there is *parnassah* and Jews — we daven with a *minyan*."

"I've tried every way to get some news of you. I'm sick with worry — is Mother well?" comes a postcard from Toronto. I glance at the address — Zelazna Street — it has been made *Judenrein* and "Mother" is, alas, no longer.

"Together with this letter I am sending parcels via Lisbon. Why don't you write via the Red Cross?"

This last question is repeated a thousand times over "Why?" or "What has happened?" shrieks out from every postcard. Every line is heaving with longing and unspoken fear; every letter is wet with tears wept during sleepless nights of worry. They betray the pain of those who stand helplessly by as their family and friends are destroyed. Every letter is a strangled sob, every message a cry of despair.

It is late at night but I sit riveted in the archives, unable to tear my eyes away from this huge mound of mail. It is already three in the morning and outside I can hear the arrogant tread of the German guards, but I continue reading and reading. I try to imagine those distant lands where these Jews — sons of Warsaw — live normally, in freedom. They stretch out their helping hands to us, their relatives condemned to death. Do they already know what is really taking place here? Surely they do.

Jewish hearts are like seismographs. When it quakes in one part of the Jewish world it immediately registers with other Jews across the globe. Surely they will not remain silent. But will their protests be as loud as our pain and destruction? Can they possibly save us? Surely our brothers will not rest, will scale every obstacle, will storm the heavens, to rescue us.

I continue to skim through the mail, seeking solace and hope. Some of the names are familiar, famous from the past; others are totally unknown to me. But all are now close to my heart. Shortly before daybreak, I collect the post together carefully, as if I am handling holy "*sheimos*." I place them among the most important and precious documents and manuscripts of the Warsaw Kehillah since they must have been written with the purest of motives.*

Sunday, January 17

Broadcasting News

Once again "good news" spreads through the Ghetto. Actually, there is nothing new in these reports, only now apparently it is "official." The British government is alleged to have announced in Parliament that, on the basis of the Balfour Declaration, Churchill is prepared to recognize all Polish Jews as citizens of the British Empire and under British protection. Others add that Churchill and Roosevelt have pressed Germany via the Swiss Consular Service (which now represents English and American interests) that Jews should possess the rights afforded to enemy aliens under the Geneva Convention.

This latest "news" spreads like wildfire. People previously sunk in despair and despondency begin to brighten with hope. Jews now believe this information with perfect faith — the

* Later, on April 28, 1943 when the Nazis torched the Warsaw Kehillah, these letters were burnt together with thousands of important *sefarim* and hundreds of priceless historical documents. But the emotions and fear contained within those letters still haunt the ruins of the largest *kehillah* in Europe.

awful truth itself is far too horrible to contemplate. They take refuge in dreams and flights of imagination which eventually appear to them more real than the actual reality. As always there are sceptics, though they are now in the minority.

For instance my relative Yetty Turkel-Frankel tells me she does not want to hear any more news from the front or on the political situation. All she wants to know is: Are they still here or have they already left yet? Others, when hearing of battles around Stalingrad or El-Alamein want to pin these events down to their own immediate concerns and ask, "How far are these battlefields from Sochatchov?"

Actually, I number myself among the sceptics but I keep my doubts to myself since I have no real way of knowing whether any of these "news items" might not in fact be true. Besides, the stories are not usually completely untrue, though perhaps they anticipate events, they might be a year or two too early. Moreover, these "reports," whether true or not, play a vital role in the Ghetto by injecting hope and newfound optimism into faint hearts; they strengthen the will to survive.

This is no minor matter. Many have perished simply by succumbing to despair. Once they accepted their fate was sealed, that there was no chance of rescue, they lost all will to resist. So the spread of even false reports has a positive function. Often these rumors begin with a grain of truth, but the hearer either does not listen or understand properly and passes on an imperfect version. Others further down the news chain amplify the item and add tidbits of their own until the resultant misinterpretations, distortion, and exaggeration acquire a momentum of their own.

With everybody continually hoping and praying for salvation, the Ghetto provides a fertile breeding ground for the "news broadcasts." So it was with today's news. When I first heard it, though I remained sceptical, I commented, "The great British statesman Gladstone* once declared that behind every British citizen stood the might of the British Empire on land and sea!" By the time I heard that "news" again later in the evening, it had acquired an extra dimension — Churchill also apparently announced that behind every Jew stands all the might of the British armed forces on land, sea, and air! (Of course in Gladstone's time, Britain had no air force, so that last cliche could only have been said in the name of Churchill.) So are rumors created.

People remain hungry for news. Whoever they meet, they ask, "*Vos herts zech?* — What's new?" and not merely as a matter of habit. They genuinely want to know of any developments — particularly good news. One Jew even pleaded, "Let it be untrue, but let it at least be good!" In response to the constant, insatiable demand for news, there has sprung up in the Ghetto a whole distribution network — manufacturers, wholesalers, and retailers — of news stories. There are those who listen to the BBC on clandestine radios or hear reports from non-Jewish acquaintances. Some have become adept at reading between the lines, while others have authoritative sources.

But Ghetto cynics retell a story of one inveterate supplier of news stories who was feeling a bit low. When asked the inevitable "*Vos herts zech*," he replied angrily, "I can't be bothered, make up some story yourself!"

Every report from the battlefront is invariably analyzed for the best possible gloss. Whenever Germany stages a strategic retreat, by the time this news reaches the Ghetto the significance has been magnified tenfold. Even when the *Wehrmacht*

---

* Translator's note: Palmerston actually said this.

scores a victory, it is reinterpreted for the best — the Germans were actually advancing towards their inevitable debacle.

Sometimes to the ordinary man in the Ghetto, the identities, of the victor and vanquished were confused so that Allied defeats were converted into German defeats — with those defeats greatly exaggerated and the numbers of German casualties usually had some zeros added for good measure. Stories abounded of Hitler's committing suicide, purging his generals, arresting Göring, or the Nazis suing for peace.

Nearly everyday, however, my friend Papower would meet me, carefully close the door, unroll a scrap of paper, and read to me the British reports from the front. These were always accurate, but they were not always "good news."

Yet there remain those who are busy spreading their brand of news to all and sundry. All day long they patrol the Ghetto, questioning passersby, "*Vos herts zech, vos is neues.*" As soon as they hear something — anything — they begin to trade tidbits of information. News is their elixir, they can never have enough of it. How can they resist retailing their tales to friends, chance acquaintances, or anyone who will listen. As long as there is a grain of hard news, they will embroider and embellish it from their fertile imagination. For them a phrase, a word, a hint is enough, and they will supply the rest. After repeating the resultant story a number of times, they begin to implicitly believe it themselves.

When the battle of El-Alamein took place, many in the Ghetto became confident that this was the beginning of the end. Why? Obviously, since the War was moving closer to Eretz Yisrael, it must end with the cataclysmic conflict between Gog and Magog. Tales were told of sea serpents moving up the Nile Delta to cut off the German advance, how the British were firing at the Germans from the pyramids, how the natives were emerging from the African deserts to shoot poisoned arrows at the *Wehrmacht*.

"Whatever happens, it must signal the end of this latter day Haman. Attacking Eretz Yisrael — with the bombing of Haifa — must bring about his demise."

Other Jewish "sources," based on a mystical tradition, emerged, since the reality in the Ghetto was no less unreal: Biblical prophecies and visions, hints contained within holy tomes, traditions from *tzadikim, gematrias,* signs, various excerpts from the *Zohar,* and even dreams. A number of "Ends of Exile" were predicted, and by the time allotted for one hypothetical *keitz* had expired, the Ghetto inmates were already eagerly awaiting a new predicted *keitz.*

While news stories from the radio constituted our daily diet, these can only reflect a fleeting moment in time. Mystical pronouncements, however, leave a lasting impression. Anxious to escape the horror of the present, we sought relief in the safer worlds of the past or future. Here at least, there is justice and retribution and ultimately everything will end happily ever after.

Everyone wrestles with his Maker, so to speak, trying to fathom the reasons why we have been brought to such a pass. We puzzle over the eternal riddle: How can the wicked thrive while the righteous suffer? Now this riddle has taken on worldwide dimensions. What pen can portray the cries of men unto Heaven when they reach the depths of despair, when they experience the seven furnaces of Hell, the unanswered cry of thousands drowning in their lifeblood, the groans of the dying.

I shall never forget that night I spent in Mila Street during that terrible "selection" when hundreds of thousands of

Warsaw's Jews were dragged away to their death. An acquaintance of mine, a religious Jew, had arrived in the cordon with his wife and three children. They were all forcibly taken away from him. He had wanted to accompany them, but he had been forced back as the SS rained murderous blows down on him. Dripping blood and pain, he had crawled to the dark cellar where I was hiding. All night long he gave me no rest, endlessly repeating, between his bitter tears, the question "Tell me, Hillel, why and what for?"

A typical Iyov of our generation, but with us in that gloomy cellar, surrounded by the bloodthirsty fiends, there was no Elifaz, Bildad, or Tzofar to comfort him. I could only repeat Iyov's refrain, "Today reigns a darkness in which God Above shows no interest nor throws any light over.... This night will remain forever in darkness." Throughout that frightful night of slaughter and destruction, I recited verses from Iyov and felt as if they were now being written for the first time. They seemed more relevant in the Ghetto than they had ever done before. How could the trials and tribulations of Iyov possibly compare with what the Jews of Warsaw were undergoing?

On the other hand, every Jew who still lived had usually survived by such a unique and complicated — almost unbelievable — chain of events that these could not possibly be dismissed as mere coincidence. One could feel the touch of a Divine Hand guiding from Above. Each individual survival defied all rational logic, it could only be adequately described as a *nes*, a miracle. This was the springboard for belief in the paranormal, in imminent salvation and solace, in accepting a different scale of "reality."

When I studied *Koheles*, I hit upon a new interpretation for the penultimate verse: "*Sof davar hakol nishmah* — as the chain of events comes to an end, everything will become clear, all questions will be solved, all doubts will be clarified."

Meanwhile we float on a sea of suffering. The nation's lifeblood is ebbing away but the inner kernel must survive. As in his dealing with Iyov, surely now, too, the Satan of Destruction must have been instructed to spare our soul — or so everyone believes.

Monday, January 18

The First Resistance

As dawn broke today, from 5:00 A.M., the Ghetto has been surrounded by Latvian and Ukrainian auxiliaries under SS command — this is known ambiguously as an "*aktion.*"

First, the SS swoop on the Kehillah Building at 19 Zamenhof Street, arresting anybody they find. Now for the first time they also take away members of the *Judenrat*, including Izaak-Ber Ackerman, Hurvitz, and Josef Yaschunski. Then they march off to Mila Street and surround apartments where railroad workers of the *Ostbahn* live together with the "wild ones." Once again, whoever they find is dragged away to the *Umschlagplatz.*

Simultaneously they blockade Niska Street where Jews employed in the *Werterfassung* (the German agency which deals with confiscated Jewish goods) live. This agency is really nothing more than the organized looting of any Jewish valuables or property left over after the "resettlements" and forcible deportations — which are then packed off to Germany. Many of the over three thousand Jews who are employed in the processing and sorting of these goods have only recently arrived in Warsaw from the surrounding towns. Most had hoped to be safer here under the common assumption that Warsaw would be one of the few Ghettos likely to remain in the "General gouvernement" (as the Germans describe that part of annexed Poland closest to Germany). Now they, too, have been caught.

The SS, with their fiendish underlings from Latvia and Ukraine, also descend on the factories and workshops to carry out "selections": taking away any Jew who does not meet their fancy. These selections now take place at the Schultz factory at Nowolipie Street, where they also drag away Rav Avraham Alter from Pavianitz and Rav Z. Gur-Arye. A terrible "selection" is carried out among the brush workers in Swietojerska Street and at the factories of Von Sneh and Schaniawski in Kopeicka Street, and Herman Breuer at 18–28 Nalewki Street.

A wild panic breaks out in the Ghetto. Nobody puts any trust in German documents and permits. Instead they stow away anywhere they can — in lofts, bunkers, and hiding places.

The simple construction of a typical refuge goes somewhat like this. The door is sealed and bricked up, and a new cavity is opened up in the ceiling. From above, the trap door is well concealed by furniture such as an old sofa and tables. All day long they sit in their hiding places with bated breath; the slightest noise could give them away. At night they emerge via ladders to cook small amounts of foods, obtain more stocks, and discover the latest "developments."

The so-called illegal "wild ones," who are not registered at any of the German authorized workshops and have no official papers or "numbers," immediately vanish into hiding and survive practically unscathed. By contrast, most of those now caught by the Germans are "legitimate" workers who carry all the correct documents and work cards.

The SS also descend on the Jewish orphanage on Stawki Street. This had been established by the *Judenrat* with the official sanction of the Gestapo. The chief of the murderers, Brandt, even delivered a speech for the occasion in which he called upon the Kehillah to take good care of the children, since they were "the future of your nation." Apparently there are no limits to the barbaric German's duplicity and barefaced impudence. Today they take all these children away to be killed at the Treblinka gas chambers.

The Nazi fiends race through the Ghetto streets like wild beasts searching apartments, workshops, and *Judenrat* offices. But most *Judenrat* officials are not at work, since few trust all their many cards and permits purported to protect them. Those who are at their desks, carrying out their allotted tasks, are dragged away for deportation without discrimination.

However, in Wolynska Street there are the first signs of armed resistance. A unit of ZOB (*Zydowska Organizacja Bojowa* — the Jewish Resistance Organization) lives at 7 Wolynska Street. When the Latvians and Ukrainians approach the building, a few hand grenades are thrown at them from the windows.

A number of them are killed, including their SS officer. They immediately panic and run blindly in all directions. An eerie silence descends on the street.

Yet all know this cannot last, the Germans won't give up so easily. The Resistance instructs all Jews to leave the street immediately, and everybody evacuates the area.

As darkness falls, a few SS arrive. They proceed down the street holding electric pocket torches, which they shine at every apartment entrance as they pass. At the gate to 21 Wolynska Street, they discover Yitzchak Giterman (director of the Polish Joint and president of Yivo) who was out together with Dr.

Nachman Kovleski (a young mathematician and academic, a son of the Wlutzlanker Rabbi, Senator Y. L. Kovleski). The SS order them to halt before shooting them both on the spot. Similar outrages take place on other streets; the SS torment and shoot whomever they find.

In the "small Ghetto," however, the German *aktion* continues as planned. Workers are dragged away from the German workshops — Tobbens, Wilhelm Dehring and Ziegmund — and marched off to the *Umschlagplatz*. Chance plays the central role in these "selections." Anybody who for any reason does not find favor in their eyes is removed by the SS. Occasionally, pleas for mercy by factory owners or managers are successful in retrieving some workers, but this is unusual. Generally nothing can suffice once the SS have made their decision — there are no appeals. Six thousand from the already greatly depleted population in the Ghetto have fallen prey in this latest *aktion*.

Moreover, the survivors have now lost all hope. From October 1942 until today (January 18) there had been a relative calm without any mass slaughter. True, every so often a Gestapo officer would appear and shoot a number of passersby at random. But that was no longer taken into account — it has come to be regarded as almost normal under German rule! People spoke of the situation stabilizing and thought those who had survived would be allowed to remain.

In the Ghetto, people began to rebuild their shattered lives. In fact, the food rations even improved. More stocks were allowed into the Ghetto, and those working at factories outside also brought in food. Many dared to hope and believe that this situation would continue. And now this awful calamity has befallen us — another *aktion*. This clearly shows that we can not take anything for granted. Who knows what tomorrow will bring?

As the Torah forewarned, "Your life shall hang uneasily in front of you" (*Devarim* 28:66). There is no hope, no escape, nowhere to hide. And the merciless enemy seeks to destroy everything.

APRIL 1943

The Warsaw Ghetto Uprising

Before this diary begins recording the Ghetto Uprising, I must make a few points clear to the reader. Though I was in Warsaw as these events began unfolding, I did not personally witness them.

I was already incarcerated in the Pawiak Prison (as explained in the Foreword). Subsequently, I was transferred to France. Nonetheless, I remained in close contact with many of those who had either taken part in planning the revolt (as I had myself), those who were in the ranks of fighters, or those who happened to be then in Warsaw when it all took place. I only wrote down exactly what was said by sources I could trust. I ignored all legendary exploits which sprang from too fertile imaginations — often by those who claimed to have been the hero of the hour at each and every battle.

Since I was intimately acquainted with the Warsaw Ghetto: its geography and organization, its populace and leaders — I was well placed to sieve the chaff from the kernel of the truth. I apologize in advance if my diary appears too dry and unemotional, but these reports are, at the very least, true. (Indeed, considering the circumstances under which it was written, I was not striving for literary effect throughout my diary.) Furthermore, the fighters in the Ghetto during their desperate struggle had more immediate concerns. They spared little thought to appear as heroes; neither were they seeking adulation or a place in history.

Those who supplied me with information came from varying backgrounds and different strata in society. Some expired later under oppression or were murdered in the death camps, while others survived until the liberation. These are their names: Yitzchak Katzenelsohn (the Hebrew poet) and his son Zvi; Simchah, Yaakov, and Aaron Rapaport (originally from Bilitz); Alexander Landau (Resistance Committee member); Nachman Goldstein; Mendel Frankel; and Yitzchak Mintz and Aaronsohn from Zagraz (all of these were later deported from France to Auschwitz). Moshe Kravitz Heiman; Rav Yitzchak and Avraham Ziemba (nephews of Rav Menachem Ziemba); Stephen Reisner; Rivka Lewin; Moshe Zilberberg (a Revisionist activist); Berisch Ehrlich (son of the famous lamdan Rav Nosson Ehrlich, president of Kollel Rav Meir Baal Haness, Warsaw); Ruchama Rotstein; Ruchama Frank; N. Gelbaum; M. Kossover; Prof. Sachs (member of Poland's Central Jewish Committee); Zvi Altuski; and Leibel Pinkesevitch.

Tuesday, April 13

The factory owners of Tobbens and Schultz, their Jewish managers, as well as *Judenrat* President Mark Lichtenbaum, published posters requesting workers to volunteer for the labor camps of Poniatowa and Trawniki near Lublin. The large factories of Tobbens and Schultz will now also relocate there, and volunteers are promised workplaces and better conditions. In any event, Warsaw must now become "free" of Jews. All Jews will have to leave Warsaw.

Those who do not evacuate voluntarily will be compelled

to go by force, and their fate will be worse. In that case, no one can know where people will be deported to — these posters end with scarcely veiled threats.

In response, the ZKN (*Zydowski Komilet Narodowy* — the Jewish National Committee) held a meeting and decided that nobody should volunteer.

Printed placards were distributed to the workers and hung up in the streets, workshops, and *Judenrat* offices:

> Jews! Do not fall for these false promises. We have been misled too often. For far too long we have been cheated by Gestapo agents, factory managers — all these Schultzs and Tobbens. Are 50,000 deaths not enough? We must not leave our places. We know only too well what "Nach Osten" really means — death in halls of gas! "Poniatowa" and "Trawniki" are nothing more than Treblinka.
>
> Jews! Let no one leave Warsaw. Here we shall stay; the last remnant may not disperse. We shall remain here together, united in our pain and suffering — and in our battle.
>
> Our strength lies in our numbers. All dispersions, every desertion weakens our resistance and betrays both the memory of the martyred and the survivors.
>
> We shall not leave our place. Whatever is destined to happen, should happen here on our home ground. Let us remain together, united both in adversity and struggles.

These placards were signed by the "Jewish National Agency," which was really the Resistance masquerading under another name. The placards made a tremendous impression. On the day they appeared, not a man volunteered to leave Warsaw — nor for the next few days either. The *rabbanim* advised the many individuals who consulted them to stay in Warsaw, neither did any of the *rabbanim* themselves volunteer for the Lublin labor camps.

The *rabbanim* met formally to consider the practical problems after the German-inspired campaign was intensified to get the Jews to evacuate voluntarily. This was directed primarily at those who were starving — and did not have the resources to conceal themselves in bunkers. The meeting was held at Kopeicka Street where Rav Menachem Ziemba resided (in Yitzchak Ziemba's, his nephew's, apartment). Among those present were the *rabbanim* R. Goldschlag, R. Dovid Shapira, R. Shimshon Stockhammer, R. Arieh Frumer (Kozieglow), R. Eliezer Yitzchak Meisels (Lodz), R. Dovid Halberstam (Sosonovitch), R. Sender (Posen), R. Reuvain Horowitz, R. Zemelman (Pesheitz), R. Dr. Efraim Sonnenschein (Bidgoschz), and R. Dr. Glitzenschein (Turn). Also present were Senator R. Yaakov Trokenheim, R. Yosef Konigsberg, and Menachem Kirshenbaum. Once again the *rabbanim* decided to continue advising Warsaw's Jews not to travel to Poniatowa and Trawniki.

This formal decision emboldened Resistance activists to take further action. In addition to their previous public defiance of the German "resettlement" plans, they now began to sabotage the movement of workers to the labor camps. Tires of the workers' buses were slashed and their engines damaged. Germans holding workers in transit were attacked and the Jews released.

Often this resulted in clashes — shots were fired and casualties inflicted. These bold actions, too, encouraged Jews not to volunteer for evacuation. The *Judenrat* continued to appeal for volunteers but it was transparently obvious that it did so without enthusiasm or conviction — merely carrying out German orders about which it had no choice. In fact, they were happy to see their propaganda exposed as a sham. *Judenrat* officials were in no way convinced of the truth of the German assurances, especially after having been betrayed so many times in the past.

A delegation in the "small Ghetto" comprising Dr. Tulu Nussblatt, Yechiel Reisman, Nochum Remba, Gur Arye Orenstein, and Shmuel Orenstein, visited factories in Nowolipie Street (Schultz and Schilling) and Leszno Street (Tobbens) and persuaded Jewish workers not to be tempted — and not to volunteer. This ploy was successful and no Jews traveled voluntarily.

Only a minority who were literally starving were prepared to go. The Resistance in conjunction with the *rabbanim* appealed to the *Judenrat*, to the Ghetto's Jewish Supply Department, and to Jewish magnates to support the poor and help them withstand the pressure. A special fund was established for this purpose, and the Resistance Committee allocated some of the funds it had forcibly expropriated from rich Jews (particularly those who had profited during the occupation). Now they saw the support of the poor as an integral part of the resistance.

Much effort was then invested into the building of bunkers. Everyone fully realized that the mass refusal to volunteer for the Lublin labor camps would inevitably result in more repression — probably more *aktions*. Nobody still put credence in German documents or trusted to their protection. So the only practical step still available was the construction of bunkers. That is in what everyone then invested all their energy and whatever money they still had left.

Building a bunker and making it habitable demands combined skills; no one person can do it by himself. A great deal of money is needed to fund building and repair work and also for laying down large stocks of food. One needs to call on various expert skills: architects, engineers, builders, technicians, electricians, plumbers, etc. Alongside the Resistance, a technical committee was set up, comprising many members of the *Judenrat* Building Department, whose official duties were the building and repair of the large wall surrounding the Ghetto. Furthermore, these technicians possessed various tools, machine parts, and electrical and plumbing equipment, which had originally been supplied by the Germans. Every factory and workshop has established its own clandestine committee for this purpose — even in the small Ghetto.

These bunkers were built at night, since everything had to be accomplished with great secrecy; only a select few were in the know. All unauthorized movement of bricks and cement was extremely dangerous. So it was carried out late at night, after midnight. I had earlier visited some of these bunkers, and it was impossible for an outsider to enter or even guess of their existence. They were hidden behind tens of secret entrances, passageways, and hideaways. Inside, they had electricity, kitchens, fresh water supply, showers, and toilets. This was the latest development in the Ghetto.

Experts confirmed to me that people in these bunkers could, in theory, survive for a year or perhaps even a year and a half. It all depended on the food stocks available. That was the central concern in the bunkers. If some in the bunker had enough food while the others did not, it could descend into anarchy. So it was essential to ensure there were sufficient food stocks for all, in equal measure. We are no longer talking of mutual tolerance, political idealism, or concern for the proletariat, merely the strong instinct for survival. All were now equal under the threat of extermination. So everyone had to share in an equitable chance at survival.

Those who had a lot of money sought acquaintances in the Aryan sector of Warsaw who could provide hiding places. Some obtained Aryan identity papers and escaped to the provincial cities. Other Jews with an Aryan (i.e., non-Jewish) appearance applied for Aryan documents and volunteered for work in Germany, where they believed their chances of survival were better than in the Warsaw Ghetto. All the previous delusions had collapsed. Now nobody allowed himself to hope or dream; everyone could see the end directly ahead.

Those who had contacts abroad, especially in Switzerland, tried to get South American passports. Owners of these passports were sent to Vittel in France where, according to reports, conditions were good and they lived in peace. Desperate letters were sent via the Aryan sector to Switzerland, pleading for help. "Aunty Sakanah sends her wishes"; "Your sister Hatzalah sends food parcels"; "Your brother Ezra begs you to write to him."

Meanwhile, they prepared for war. More arms were obtained — weapons had become the greatest need. In Mila Street, where the black market flourished, people bought bread, kilos of potatoes, shirts — and revolvers.

Monday, *erev* Pesach, April 19

The Fight Begins

At 5 A.M., the news spread like lightning —*Aktion*! An *aktion* to end all *aktions*. Now, they realized, there will surely be no escape, no exceptions, and no selections. Finally, these murderers plan to make Warsaw *Judenrein*. This information passed from one workshop to another, from each apartment block to its neighbor, and all the bunkers were informed. The internal Ghetto news service functioned perfectly and their response was unequivocal — armed resistance!

The High Command of the armed groups passed the order: Be prepared to fire! There were feverish, last-minute preparations. Everyone enlisted for the coming battle. Some of the armed groups (including Bar Kochba, Biryonim, Akiva, Beitar, and Botwin) had for some time been on a continual high alert.

The "Party" (which is how the Resistance Committee was popularly known) passed their commands along their line of control, one by one: "Don't look out of windows," "To the bunkers," "On guard," and then "Fire."

At 5:30 A.M., while it was still dark, the "small Ghetto" was surrounded by German SS troops and Latvians. The German army battalions meanwhile appeared at Wolynska and Mila Streets. They approached from both ends — from Nalewki and Stawki — and lined up in ranks to block Muranowska Street off at the corner of Zamenhof. But the Party was ensconced at 31 Zamenhof Street, and they fired the first shots through the windows.

This was so unexpected, that as some German SS and *Wehrmacht* were hit and fell, the rest panicked. Meanwhile, the hail of bullets from the roofs and windows intensified. By now, the Germans were trapped in an ambush and were simultaneously being fired at from Zamenhof and Muranowska. The first to flee were the Latvians and Ukrainians, who sought shelter behind the apartment block entrances. Then the Germans ordered them to fire back. They shot at the doors and windows but could not summon up the courage to storm any of the apartments or smash down the sealed doors.

Knowing that a bullet might await each of them behind any gate, their customary swaggering bravado disappeared. The firing from the windows increased, with the Jews shooting with revolvers, rifles, and even machine guns. The Germans issued conflicting orders. Confusion reigned, until they ordered a retreat.

But it was not that simple for them to withdraw. Shots were fired at them from windows, from hidden apertures, from apparent ruins and clandestine bunkers. The Germans fled towards Dluga Street. But at the crossroads of Nalewki-Swietojerska, firing broke out again. The Party had a powerful battalion drawn from the brush workers stationed there. They were well equipped with a number of machine guns and hand grenades.

The Germans were unable to proceed and their retreat was blocked. So now they ran back down towards Muranowska. In the meantime, however, the Party had been reinforced with fresh battalions. The heat of battle grew ever stronger. Some Germans shot blindly at no particular target, while others fled in confusion. A number of Germans sought shelter among the ruins or at apartment block entrances. Meanwhile, they had sustained many casualties and their morale was broken.

For the first time, a Party battalion ventured onto the street — dressed in stolen German uniforms. They shot down the fleeing Germans and Latvians without mercy. This battle lasted until 11:30 A.M.

Then silence fell: complete and utter silence, the still, eerie silence of a graveyard. No German now dared show himself in the Ghetto, nor did any Jews appear on the streets. Instead, they sat waiting in their bunkers. The Resistance battalions realized only too well that this was the lull before the storm. Hours passed amid this deathly hush. Not a whisper, not a footfall. The Ghetto was becalmed in a deep silence. It was as if everyone had gone to sleep.

In reality, of course, all were wide awake — and on guard. All the senses were alert, tense in watchful anticipation. Everyone's nerves were tightly stretched. Hearts, however, began to falter. What would happen now?

Meanwhile the long day moved towards evening — and it was still *erev* Pesach. In only two hours, the festival of liberation would begin. This only increased the tension. They searched the bunkers and food stocks for the few matzos which the *Judenrat* had baked (this was to be its last public service) and sat down to conduct the Seder.

As the hours passed in quiet and inaction, people gathered for the Seder in bunkers and cellars, like the Marranos in Spain. Yet the dramatic situation here was even more tragic. Though they followed the standard ritual — asking the *Mah Nishtanah,* replying with *Avadim Hayinu,* and decrying the *Shefoch Chamascha*: *"Pour out Your wrath on the heathens that do not know You...for they have destroyed Yaakov and laid their dwellings waste"* — they could palpably sense that this was their very last Pesach in this world. Later that fateful night people surreptitiously flitted from one bunker to another to exchange "news," to size up the situation, to plan for tomorrow, and to join *sedarim*.

At 21 Zamenhof Street, opposite Kopeicka, at the Party headquarters, a Pesach Seder was also in progress. Among those present there was Rav Reuvain Horowitz (a Mizrachi activist and Rabbi of Ulica), R. Zemelman (a Zeirei Aguda member and Rabbi of Pesheitz), the Rodal brothers, R. Yosef Konigsberg and his son-in-law Simchah, Menachem Kirschenbaum and his daughter (who was the secret courier to the Schultz and Schilling factories) as well as his son-in-law Birnbaum (who had the Resistance pseudonym "Stask" and helped organize the January 18 resistance), A. Ziemba (son of R. Yitzchak Meir Ziemba), Zvi Zilberstein (from Lublin), Yosef Tennenbaum, Fogel, Finkelkraut, Anielewicz, and "Tusia." The *rabbanim* did not deliver lengthy sermons; instead, they coined slogans urging steadfastness and prowess.

A number of *rabbanim* joined R. Menachem Ziemba for the Seder at 7 Kopeicka Street, including Rav Behr (from Zednoska Welle), Rav Goldschlag, Rav Eliezer Yitzchak Meisels (from Lodz), A. G. Friedensohn, Senator Yaakov Trokenheim, and Yosef Scharanski.

The Seders passed off in the darkness of uncertainty; the fear of death was blended with the emotions of Pesach and liberation, Yom Tov and struggle.

Suddenly, after midnight, shots were heard. The Germans had returned to attack the Ghetto again. Strong battalions of *Wehrmacht* simultaneously marched down Dluga Street and Stawki Street, and the sounds of explosions were also heard.

Quickly everyone descended to their bunkers. Again the Party orders — "Fire!" Shots from all the windows, attics, roofs, ruins, and bunkers are directed at the Germans.

The Germans returned fire and now they also tossed hand grenades into the houses. A bitter fight erupted in the Ghetto.

Thursday, April 22

Alone in Battle

At night one did not see Germans. The Germans were afraid to venture into the Ghetto in the darkness; an ambush could have awaited them behind every doorway.

So at night people felt safe enough to leave their bunkers and take a breath of fresh air or search for food among the abandoned apartments. It was the safest time to establish contact with other bunkers, as well as to visit friends and relatives. Darkness was when people gathered to hear the latest "news" or to plan ahead. Yet one could hardly hear a sound, as ghostly shadows slipped silently between the ruined buildings. Everyone was on the alert, since one could not know who might have been hiding behind the next house.

The nights were also utilized for washing clothes and minimal cooking (i.e., boiling potatoes, baking and frying vegetables) and stocking up for all eventualities. Food and cleanliness had now become crucial to their ongoing struggle to survive underground. Life in the Ghetto only began at nightfall; all day long they waited in their bunkers for the battles to begin.

On Second Day Pesach — which was the third day of the revolt — a set battle broke out. An SS battalion armed with rifles, machine guns, and grenades approached the Ghetto from Dluga Street and turned towards the Ghetto wall, which ran down the center of the streets Franciszkanska and Gesia. A hand grenade was thrown at them from the ruins of 29 Nalewki Street (where it crosses Gesia), and a number of Germans were killed and wounded. At the same time another grenade was dropped onto them from 33 Nalewki Street.

The SS troop formations collapsed in panic. Some tried to

retreat, while others fired blindly to the left and right without aiming at any target. By contrast, the resistance fighters did have a specific objective: to defend the Ghetto wall at the center of Gesia-Franciszkanska and prevent the Germans from approaching it.

Shots were fired at the SS from the windows of 31 Franciszkanska and 18 Gesia where the Party had powerful resistance groups stationed. At that time they were commanded by Kirschenbaum, the Rodal brothers, Zvi Zilberberg, Dovid Zeitlin (grandson of Hillel Zeitlin), Yisrael Holtzkenner, Anielewicz, and the Landau girl from the *chalutzim* group of Grochov. This battle lasted a few hours before the Germans finally retreated. It was already getting dark and the Germans were afraid of the Ghetto at night. But the Jewish fighters remained at their posts on full alert.

Resistance reinforcements were sent up from Muranowska where the "northern command" was stationed and from the "southern command" in Swietojerska Street. The "north" was led by R. Reuvain Horowitz, R. Zemelman, Eichenbaum (a revisionist who escaped from Majdenek to Warsaw), and the *chalutzim*, including Meir Teitelbaum and Yitzchak Schrabati. The "south" was commanded by Yosef Tennenbaum (son of the late Mizrachi *Parnas* Eliyahu Tennenbaum), Binyamin Kaminer (son of the *parnas* Meshulam Kaminer), and Birnbaum and his wife (the daughter and son-in-law of Kirschenbaum). But that night passed off peacefully.

This time was used to reorganize the potential battlefield. All the civilian non-combatant population were cleared from the houses alongside that Ghetto wall (i.e., the even numbers in Gesia and the odd numbers in Franciszkanska). It was a logical assumption that these apartments would bear the full brunt and ferocity of the German revenge. The inhabitants — elderly, women, and children — crossed over to the relative safety of 35–49 Nalewki Street, as well as Kopeicka Street which was accessible via 39 Nalewki Street. This evacuation took place in the middle of the night, at 1 A.M., in total silence.

Meanwhile, the Resistance Committee (which had by now become the central command) met to distribute weapons and ammunition as well as to station fighters at strategic flashpoints. They, too, concluded that the present tactic must be to defend that Ghetto wall.

The coming confrontation would no longer be an inconclusive skirmish. It had now resolved itself into one strategic aim: to prevent the Germans gaining access to that section of the Ghetto wall. For the moment at least, they could not conceive any long-term military objective. The enemy was overwhelmingly powerful — and the armies of both the Russians and Americans were still at a great distance.

And what of their so-called close allies — the Polish partisans? Dr. Ringelblum and Kirschenbaum had asked this question of the Bundist members of the Resistance. In the past, these had often assured us that even if the partisans did not give us the go-ahead to begin the armed struggle, nonetheless, once the revolt began, the Polish partisans would not hold back.

Well, the time had finally arrived for them to show their oft declared "solidarity with the proletariat." Surely the Polish partisans — particularly those on the left wing — would not watch our life and death struggle indifferently without providing the least assistance? The Bundists had already decided to send two emissaries to their leader Mauricy Orzech, who was hiding out in the Aryan sector (not, incidentally, with socialist colleagues who were assisting him for ideological reasons, but in the care of a Polish household who were simply helping for a large financial reward).

Next to 7–9 Muranowska Street there was a break in the town sewer which lead to Bonifrarterska and even Zeliborska. In the past, this sewer had been used for smuggling arms into the Ghetto. Now these two Bundist emissaries, Lebartovski and Mullman, used this route to alert the Socialist partisans via Orzech to the Jews' struggle and obtain their help. But these couriers were never seen again; they vanished without a trace.

Nevertheless, by now the Polish partisans knew full well that the revolt had begun — it was not a secret. Yet they watched the unequal struggle between David and Goliath without lifting a finger to help.

Some allege that certain Socialist partisan leaders, Witolt and Ulschinski, had previously declared that if the revolt broke out, they should give the signal and help would arrive. The agreed signal was to fly the red flag and a blue and white flag on a house at the corner of Muranowska and Bonifrarterska Streets. Indeed, for the last two days these two flags had been hoisted to the roof of 2 Muranowska Street, yet no assistance was forthcoming.

Schrabati recalls that, at the last meeting with the Socialist partisans, one of the Poles revealed that they had received several million zloty for the Ghetto resistance from a Jewish committee in London. Since the Resistance Committee had received nothing and could not even track down the whereabouts of this money, Dr. Ringelblum and Schrabati agreed in desperation to "surrender" this money to the partisans in exchange for arms.

A solemn deal was struck and a detailed list of weapons and ammunition (at exorbitant prices) was reluctantly agreed upon and signed. Now the delivery date for those expensive arms had also passed but again nothing arrived. Three days ago a courier had been despatched to the Aryan sector to demand these weapons — if not now then when? — and today this courier, Shnitberg, returned empty-handed.

If, in the past, anybody deceived themselves with hopes of outside help, certainly nobody does so now. Our generation, too, have drunk the bitter dregs of that prophetic curse, "I called to my friends, but they betrayed me" (*Eichah* 1:19). The only military prowess they could rely on is that which they managed to garner themselves.

The whole wide world remained silent — and their close neighbors watched idly, with arms folded — the unequal and bloody struggle between the tiny, ill-equipped remnant and a most powerful enemy.

This sad realization depressed the Resistance leaders but these latest betrayals also strengthened their resolve, as well as increasing their bitterness. Despite the setbacks, they had no real alternative to continuing the battle even without outside assistance. That doleful night passed peacefully, which surely meant that tomorrow's struggle would erupt with even greater ferocity.

Friday, April 23

The Ghetto in Flames

The fourth day of the revolt coincided with the first day of *Chol Hamoed*. At 5 in the morning the bunkers were visited by the Rodal brothers, Dovid Zeitlin, and Shnitberg, who warn the inhabitants to be prepared — "something" is due to happen.

Since the previous afternoon, the Germans had not initiated any action. In fact, they had even ceased sniping into the

Ghetto. From experience, all knew that every lull was an ominous sign. It was not promising if the situation appeared "too good." So everyone sat waiting for trouble.

Nerves were again stretched to breaking point, minds were weighed down with morbid foreboding. Some of the more energetic youngsters used the time to initiate action of their own. Armed with axes and crowbars, they smashed open more breaches — bolt holes for emergencies. They built new bunkers among the ruins, in case the existing bunkers were attacked. The Resistance fighters stood on guard with loaded revolvers and machine guns. By now, they had an efficient news service, employing special signs and code words, to link the bunkers and command posts.

No sooner did a German appear anywhere in Nowolipki, Pawia, Niska, or Stawki Streets, than this information was immediately flashed to all the commands along Zamenhof, Muranowska and Swietojerska Streets, and they prepared for an ambush. The Germans were allowed to get a little closer before a hail of bullets was loosed off from a number of directions. Their skill and coordination had been honed by experience.

The Ghetto was enlarged by the fighters breaking down the Ghetto walls and taking up positions in the adjacent houses that were officially *Judenrein*. They took over the even-numbered blocks along Gesia, Franciszkanska, and Bonifrarterska Streets. Until now, these apartments had been "neutral": Jews were forbidden to live there, but so were the Poles. They had been left empty, and the Germans had not expected machine gun emplacements to be concealed among these ghost houses.

But the Jewish Resistance fighters particularly chose these buildings. Battles around these abandoned apartments posed no threat to the Jewish non-combatant population sheltering in the bunkers of the Ghetto proper. There was also the element of surprise. Since that area had been devoid of all life for many months, the Germans would not dream of attacks from there.

Yet the day slowly passed in an uneasy calm; expectations of a ferocious battle so far unfulfilled. As night fell, not a shot had been fired, not a German had been seen. A fearful darkness muffled the Ghetto and morbid thoughts stalked the bunkers; everybody was extremely tired and tense. Suddenly, after midnight, a shot shattered the stillness, followed by a second, then a third shot. Minutes passed in uneasy anticipation which stretched into a full half-hour.

Then, suddenly, the darkness of the Ghetto was disturbed by bright lights. Fierce flames shot up at the center of Zamenhof Street and illuminated the neighboring houses — the Kehillah building was burning!

The Germans had torched the *Judenrat* headquarters at 19 Zamenhof Street. It contained many documents. All the files of the various departments and offices were lodged there. A huge amount of material was also stored in the archives, including the files from many Jewish institutions, thousands of *sefarim* painfully collected in the Ghetto over the last six months, and nearly five hundred *sifrei Torah*. The flames spread and began to lick at the next house, 21 Zamenhof Street, where the Party had a command post, and they quickly evacuated this position.

There was a commotion in the bunkers as everyone voiced those eternal questions: "What will happen now? What will the future bring?"

Even at this late stage there remained optimists who insisted that the Germans would be content with the *Judenrat* burning down and any other houses which happened to catch fire. But the pessimists believed that the Germans would burn down the whole Ghetto. They sent lookouts who watched developments from windows and returned with the information that only the Kehillah building and the nearby house on Gesia Street were actually burning.

At 2 A.M. they heard a series of bangs and explosions as reports came in of the Germans tossing bombs into the cellars and houses along Zamenhof Street. The sounds of explosions continued. After each blast, house walls collapsed; this allowed the fire to spread further, and it surrounded numerous apartment blocks. From 21 Zamenhof Street, the flames reached across to numbers 1 and 3 Wolynska Street. Dovid Zeitlin* was sent to check on the situation.

After about half an hour, he reported back that 25 Zamenhof Street was already on fire. He saw two people, a man and a woman, trying to escape to the apartments of 27 Zamenhof Street next door, which was not yet alight. Gripping onto the window grills they were edging their way along the moulding on the outside of the burning building at the third story. They wore no shoes and hardly any clothes, and these were still smouldering.

German snipers, apparently concealed nearby, noticed them and took aim. It looked as if only the man was hit, and they vanished through a window.

Meanwhile, the Germans continued lobbing grenades into cellars. A group of German sappers with mines were seen

* Dovid was an active fighter in the resistance movement and also edited material for the underground press. He died a few weeks after the liberation, on Rosh Chodesh Tammuz 1945, and was buried in the Jewish section of the cemetery near Munich. I visited his grave in November 1945 and arranged for a headstone and a memorial for his father, Elchanan, and his grandfather, Hillel Zeitlin.

blowing up the house in Swietojerska Street. Every so often they exchanged shots with the Jewish fighters.

The Party's central command retreated to 21 Mila Street, including Kirschenbaum with his daughter and son-in-law, Alexander Landau with his daughter,* R. Zemelman, R. Reuvain Horowitz, Yisrael Holtzkenner, the Rodal brothers, Nochum Remba and his wife, Tusia, Aneilevitz, Frankel, Zvi Zilberberg, A. Ziemba (son of R. Yitzchak Meir Ziemba), Binyamin Kaminer, Broder (a relative of R. Yitzchak Meir Lewin), and the daughter and son-in-law of Dr. Yitzchak Schipper (Schipper himself was with his wife and young daughter at 16 Kopeicka Street).

They were in control of the battleground around Zamenhof, Muranowska, and Kopeicka Streets. But they could already hear the sounds of explosions and the crackling flames getting closer — the smell of smoke was pervasive. Their position rapidly became unbearable. But what could they do? Where could they run to?

The raging fire reached 17 Mila Street which housed a bunker and an underground yeshivah with over thirty armed *yeshivah bachurim*. Yosef Tennenbaum and one of the Rodals went to check. They were gone so long — over two hours — the command post became increasingly concerned. At 4 A.M. they returned to report that the *yeshivah bachurim* had managed to escape intact from the burning house with their grenades and molotov cocktails. They were joined by Rav Zemelman and Rav Reuvain Horowitz, and they all ran towards Zamenhof-Kopeicka. On the way, they came across a group of SS troops and sappers who were methodically torching all the houses. These *bachurim*, mostly from the Gerrer *minyan* at 19 Nalewki

* I heard she later fell throwing explosives at a German officer.

Street, took shelter at the block entrance to 44 Zamenhof Street and began lobbing hand grenades and molotov cocktails at the Germans. The Germans retaliated with grenades.

What happened after that, they could not say since it had already become too risky for Tennenbaum and Rodal to watch this skirmish any longer. This was the last ever heard of R. Zemelman and R. Horowitz or that group of *bachurim*.*

Sunday, April 25

The Fight Continues

They heard the news. A German tank was positioned on Mila Street between Zamenhof and Nalewki Streets. That was a visible and relatively easy target which posed no problems for the Ghetto fighters. Everything available was thrown at the tank, from all overlooking windows. A molotov cocktail hit its target, then a hand grenade, followed by another, until the tank caught fire.

Germans fled from their tank, haphazardly firing their revolvers in all directions as they ran. Then they vanished from sight and silence again descended on Mila Street — the lull before the storm.

A Report from the Bunkers

We took refuge in a hiding place which was not actually below

---

* This report was written down at the time by Alexander Landau who was present in the command headquarters at 14 Mila Street. He was later arrested and transported to the relative safety of the Vittel Camp in France — before being deported to Auschwitz in April 1944. Other Ghetto survivors, including Berish Ehrlich and Rav Yitzchak Meir Ziemba, were also eyewitnesses to this episode.

ground, but on the second story of 42 Muranowska Street. There were more than forty of us there, including Dr. Tulu Nussblatt, Dr. Samuel Schimkovits, and Edmund Minovitz. Our room had a disguised entrance. The door was sealed up and completely papered over, so nobody would suspect that the apartment had an extra room. Entry and exit was now by way of a trapdoor in the ceiling which was carefully concealed from above. (Many similar concealed rooms now exist throughout the Ghetto.)

Through the window, we could see that all the neighboring buildings were burning fiercely, and one did not need much foresight to guess that the same fate soon awaited our own block. But we still did not move out — where else should we go? Leaving our sanctuary would most probably result in our falling into German hands — and that meant death. So we waited in fear for three whole days.

On the fourth day, we suddenly sensed a strong smell of smoke, which became stronger by the minute. This smoke was no longer wafting across from the neighboring blocks, it was billowing up from the lower floors. So finally our building was also on fire, there can be no question about it — the flames were below us. Reluctantly, we decided to leave our hiding place.

It was already midnight, which was the safest time in the Ghetto, when the least Germans were about. We collected food and belongings, packed these into backpacks, and left. We did not have any particular plan or destination; our fate would be in the Hands of Heaven.

But when we reached the lobby, we found the staircase was already on fire. There was no time to lose. Covering ourselves with old worn pillows and quilts, we raced down the burning stairs. The smoke was unbearable, blinding our eyes and choking our lungs; burning feathers floated around us but we all escaped unscathed. As we reached the outer courtyard we met another obstacle — the block entrance itself was fiercely burning, it would be impossible to cross that wall of flames. We had little choice but to wait there in the courtyard.

As we stood around, sparks from from the burning roof and timbers rained down on us. Suddenly Dr. Nussblatt cried out excitedly, "*Vaart noch*!" The porch entrance will soon burn down and then we can pass through!"

To speed things up a few of the men found metal staves and attacked the wooden beams to make them burn faster. In the meantime we were surrounded by a roaring sea of flames as the walls of our building caught alight. Yet how could we escape? One of the men, a heroic "Nachshan," leapt through the burning entranceway and emerged safely on the other side. He called on us to follow his example. One by one, we raced through the fiery porchway. Some of the women's hair and summer dresses caught fire but these were quickly put out.

In the street we met an unbelievable sight: the whole of Muranowska Street, until Nalewki, is one long avenue of bright, hot flames. The massive conflagration illuminated the Ghetto like the sun at midday. We ran towards the Kehillah Building. The front of the building at 19 Zamenhof Street was completely destroyed. Even the next courtyard contained only a mass of ruins. But in the third courtyard, we discovered that a complete cellar still remained.

On entering, we found about twelve people already sheltering there. These "veterans" were rather angry at our breathless arrival and suspected we were being closely chased by the Germans. With some difficulty, we settled down in our new sanctuary and prepared to wait. In the distance we could hear the wild yells of the Germans and the shrieks of those being burnt alive, screams sufficient to freeze the blood in our veins.

With grim foreboding, we expected the same fate to eventually befall us there. Certainly we could not stay there too long. The flames were all around — and above — us. The heat was so oppressive, we had to lie in our underclothes. Even the brick walls in the cellar were baking hot. The air was so humid it was almost impossible to breathe.

Another threat now was the prevalence of forced informers. When the Germans caught any Ghetto Jews, they generally threatened to shoot them unless they led them to a bunker or hiding place. Most Jews allowed themselves to be shot rather than betray other Jews. But there were a few who were unable to withstand the pressure and became informers — albeit under duress.

Moreover we managed to bring very little food supply with us, barely enough for a week.

And we lasted a week. A miserable existence in a dark cellar, hovering between fear and panic. Because of the unbearable heat, we were unable to sleep. Yet we were so overwhelmed by exhaustion that we were never fully awake. The long days and nights passed without hope or prospects as we stumbled about in the darkness of the unlit cellar. It was weeks since we last saw daylight.

On May 6, we suddenly heard loud voices in the courtyard. Everyone held their breath. Eventually we realized it was somebody addressing us in Polish: "These are fellow Jews speaking. Leave your hiding places and the Germans promise you that you will be sent to work. Nothing will happen to you if you leave now. Otherwise they will pump gas into your cellar!"

We consulted among ourselves in whispers, and a clear split emerged. Some were for surrendering, while others were reluctant. Meanwhile, nobody made a move. Yet the Germans hesitated to enter our cellar in case any of us were armed. For some time they stood guard outside — while we waited inside.

The stalemate was broken by shots and screams. Suddenly, we began to smell gas in the cellar and breathing became more difficult. Two men ventured out of the cellar but returned immediately with the news that the barrel of a machine gun was poked through the outside entrance. So they were too scared to go any further. But what should we do about the gas?

For the moment we could still withstand the gas but this was only a question of time — a matter of between ten and twenty minutes. Yet we still put off taking any decisions. Who knew what would happen in the meantime? Perhaps we might be saved miraculously at the last moment. Maybe the Red Army would finally arrive.

Slowly but surely, we began to suffocate. Simultaneously, we experienced a strong thirst. We drank water but it only made it worse. It accelerated our absorbtion of the gas. Some of us began to faint, mainly children and the elderly. Ironically, it was the weak and women who held out best against the gas. Whereas the young, healthier men had difficulty breathing.

We tried to light our darkness with a candle but it went out immediately — there was not enough oxygen. We stumbled to a window but it was covered with a sheet of metal. Panic stricken, we tried to break the iron sheet with our bare hands. The rusty metal cut our fingers. But though our blood ran freely, we desperately continued tugging with our remaining strength. As many more collapsed from suffocation, the rest of us rushed at that metal sheet as our last resort, to no avail.

We had no other option but to try the cellar's main entrance again. When we ventured out there afresh, the machine gun had been withdrawn. Neither could we see any Germans nor could we hear their raucous yells. They had already left, relying on the gas to do its deadly work.

In fear and trepidation, we carefully came out into the open. But the sunlight blinded us. It must have been some three weeks since we last saw daylight (until now we had only left our previous hiding place at night and we had lost nearly all track of time). We stood bewildered in the third courtyard of the Kehillah building, staring aimlessly about us. As far as the eye could see were burnt-out ruins. Stark skeletons of what were previously apartment blocks were all that remained of the Warsaw Ghetto.

Simultaneously, our senses were assailed by the smell of spring. Unbelievably, a tree was budding in that desolate courtyard and weeds sprouted forth along the ground. When we first went into hiding, it was still cold and wintry, now spring had arrived. The seasonal cycle continued as if nothing was amiss, only our world had gone dark before our eyes.

But we had no time for philosophical speculation. We had more immediate concerns, such as where on earth do we go from here?

Despite all we had just lived through, our survival instinct remained stronger than ever. We wanted to see the end and taste the sweetness of revenge! Would we merit at least that? We walked down Wolynska Street — or rather where Wolynska Street previously used to be.

We had only gone a few yards when, in front of us, four Germans suddenly materialized out of nowhere and yelled, "*Hande Hoch!*" Wearily, we raised our hands, and they approached us warily to search us for weapons. Though they found no arms they stole everything they found — money, valuables, etc. — before ordering us to the *Umschlagplatz*.

One woman burst out sobbing and the Germans attempted to calm her, "You are going to Lublin — to work."

And so began the journey to the *Umschlagplatz*, to Majdanek, to Auschwitz, a long route of travail and misery. This is how the resistance in the Warsaw Ghetto ended for us.

REFLECTIONS AFTER THE REVOLT

REFLECTIONS AFTER THE REVOLT

When the resistance collapsed, there was no longer a Warsaw Ghetto to speak of. It was the final act, following three years of intense persecution and annihilation, of the hundred-year-old Kehillah.

Survivors surveying the ruins of their once glorious community are bound to repeat those eternal questions which plagued us through the cruel occupation: How could such a calamity occur? Why were the Jews led to the slaughter offering little resistance? Why was the revolt delayed until everyone had already been debilitated by years of starvation and privation? Why did they wait till the Ghetto population had already been drastically diminished? Would we not have stood a better chance when we still numbered over half a million? And why did we ever allow ourselves to be enclosed in a Ghetto in the first place — an obvious prelude to mass slaughter?

These searching questions can only be answered cooly, logically, and unemotionally. Clear evidence still does not exist that the Nazis always intended from the very beginning to wipe out the Jewish race in its entirety. Nor was that yet obvious when they established ghettos in 1940.

Personally, I had carefully observed the Nazis and their machinations throughout their existence and still cannot say for sure whether this had always been their sole objective. Certainly, not all Nazis were of one mind, they had various different approaches to the "Jewish Question."

Of course there were many sadists in SS ranks — wild, ravenous beasts in human form, pathological murderers capable of every crime and outrage. Their main motive was murder and destruction — but even then not completely and not en masse. This was not because they were incapable of genocide or had met resistance from other Germans (none of the Germans had much morality, conscience, or compassion), but simply because of the many benefits they stood to lose.

The SS exploited the Jews, their wealth, their slave labor, and their ingenuity. Even they were not so bestial as to easily imagine annihilating a whole nation — elderly, sick, women, and children. Some were also wary of world opinion and feared the fury of the free world. They hesitated to blatantly display their ruthless cruelty, which would probably increase dislike and hatred of the Germans and produce a violent reaction. (Apparently they erred in rating world opinion more highly than it deserved.) All these were important reasons militating against genocide.

Perhaps when Hitler and his close clique spoke of *Entfernung* ("removal" of European Jewry) they meant it literally, but which Jew could comprehend such barbaric depravity? To literally kill and annihilate?

We thought they merely meant the daily occurrences of German rule: starvation rations, torture, persecution, arbitrary oppression, periodic pogroms — but not the total elimination of an entire people.

We also relied on our *galus* experiences through the centuries — "*Shelo echod bilvad...* more than one oppressor arose to destroy us, but *Hakodesh Baruch Hu* always saved us from their hands." So we never took Hitler's threats in their literal sense. Jews' eternal optimism and *bitachon*, coupled with our inability to comprehend their inhuman plans, products of sick minds, was what led us to our not taking their threats at face value.

Not only the *chareidim*, even the non-religious, believed in the eternity of the Jewish nation. Inevitably, this colored our thinking and dispelled all pessimism as to the fate of the community. We realized that not every individual might live through till the end, but at first we were all firmly convinced that the *klal* would somehow survive. If necessary, we were prepared to submit and suffer.

We gritted our teeth and absorbed everything they threw at us. We did not sink into depression, lost neither our *bitachon* nor our belief in the eventual German debacle. (Even during the blackest periods, nobody in the Ghetto, even the pessimist, doubted that Germany would lose.) We were sure the core of our people would survive to see another day even if it were weakened and diminished by many thousands.

Our irrepressible optimism fueled our cultural and economic endeavors. Large enterprises sprang up in the Ghetto, firms which produced goods and constituted a force to be reckoned with. The German *transferstelle* on 43 Krolewska Street (which acted as the Ghetto customs post and also monitored industrial production within the Ghetto) had vested interests in our economic activity; they supported Ghetto manufacture, which owed so much to Jewish inventiveness and industry.

Every so often, they eased certain restrictions and allowed limited cultural activity: schools, kindergartens, concerts, and laboratory research. Was this (as those not closely involved later claimed) merely fostering deception to pave the way for their extermination program? I, for one, cannot believe that.

True our illusions allowed more conducive conditions for total extermination. But how would matters have turned out otherwise if we had not fallen prey to delusion? Would our chances of escape have been any rosier?

All those many Jews who fled to the Aryan sector when the deportations began, to hide there under the guise of being non-Jewish, quickly returned at the earliest opportunity, as soon as there was a lull in those deportations. Hiding among non-Jews cost a great deal of money. Even those few individuals who could afford it found their money quickly ran out. Moreover, they had no respite from the fear of death there. Polish informers continually stalked every Jew.

Throughout the "Resettlement Program" nearly everyone wrongly assumed that they were not personally at risk. The original *Aussiedlung* decree of July 22 listed so many exemptions that most thought they would be spared. Either they were among the 10,000 *Judenrat* employees, or they were employed in one of the many factories both inside and outside the Ghetto. In theory, the "Resettlement" only applied to a very small percentage of the Ghetto population. Most assumed that holders of identity cards and work cards — issued by the Germans — or passports, would be spared.

They were convinced the Germans did not intend to kill everybody — why otherwise did they indulge in so many "selections" or set up German workshops? And everyone individually felt sure that they would ultimately be among the minority which came through. Was there any rational alternative to their beliefs, their hopes, their dreams?

The Jews also pinned their faith on public opinion. Surely, as soon as the outside world finally discovered what was truly going on — and despite the secrecy and restrictions, some news must eventually reach the free world — public opinion would be shocked, horrified, and stampeded into action. Could anybody with a spark of humanity remain silent after hearing of these atrocities? Surely then the world would put a stop to it.

As to how "the world" would actually prevent further outrages? Nobody in the Ghetto was particularly preoccupied with the practicalities. The wider world was talented enough, rich enough, powerful enough to employ the right levers to stop the slaughter: threatening punishment for the Germans, offering us protection under neutral flags, the Red Cross, the Pope, granting Jews foreign citizenships with foreign passports. Why should the prisoners of the Ghettos have to devise solutions for the world to act upon?

Were there not abroad enough Jewish organizations, activists, jurists, diplomats, and statesmen with the stature of Morgenthau, Baruch, Roseman, and Hore-Belisha (for whose alleged misdeeds the Nazis saddled us with responsibility)? These were intelligent and capable enough to act on their own initiative.

With all these arguments in mind, would it have been reasonable to endanger the lives of our relatives, children, parents, brothers, and sisters to engage in a suicidal battle? How could we defeat the most powerful nation in Europe which had not yet been beaten by any other army?

Should we of all people — starved, persecuted, and untrained — take up the fight, risking brutal reprisals against our own wives, children, elderly, and sick?

Incidentally, the Germans also set up mass killing camps

for Russian prisoners of war. Did those ex-soldiers manage to organize a revolt or resistance?

Every resistance movement needs the tacit support of the civilian population. If we could have at least relied on the Poles to come to our aid, our tactics and reactions might have been different. But only the naive socialists and Bundists, blinded by their own rhetoric and out of touch with reality, could blithely speak about Polish assistance. Their party leaders, in closer contact with the Polish fraternity, had no such illusions.

Everything combined against any willingness to fight: our continuing hopes of rescue, the paucity of available weapons, the lack of assistance from abroad, betrayal by the Poles, and the near certainty of defeat.

It was only when our loved ones had already been deported to death, when we finally accepted how hopeless our situation really was, that more desperate measures were widely contemplated. Life itself had by then lost all value, we were half-dead ourselves with despair and grief. It was only when all hope and self-delusion had dissipated and we were united in our desire for revenge that the Warsaw uprising finally erupted in blood and fire.

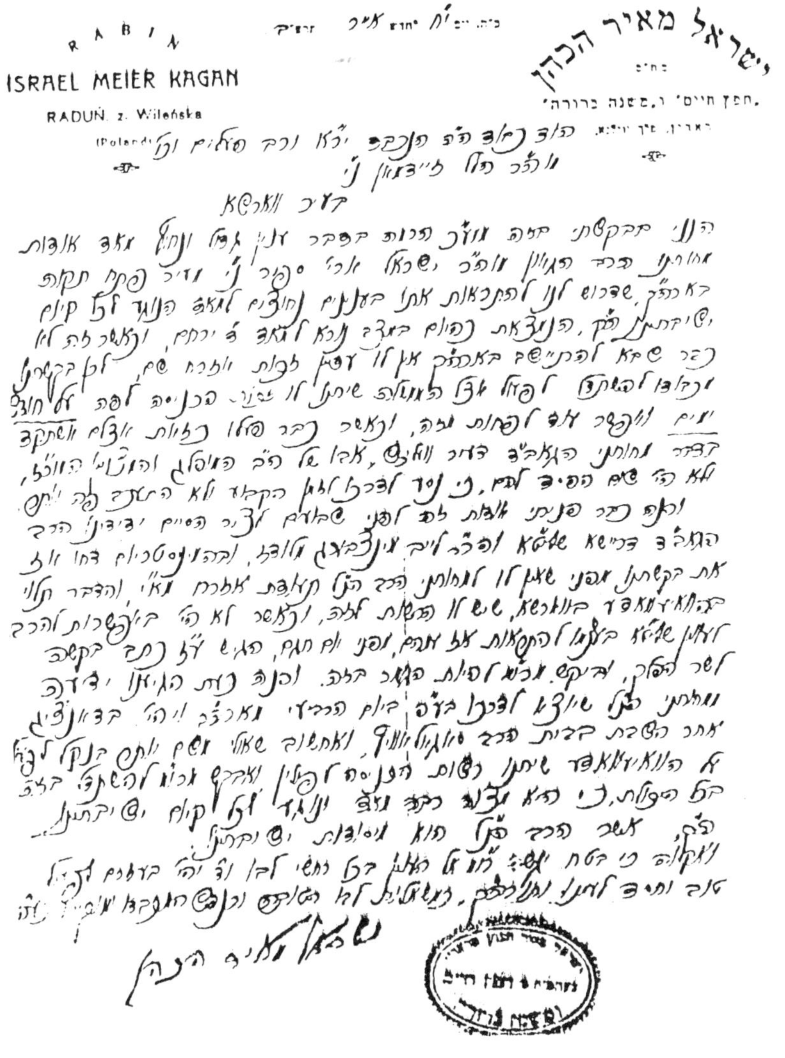

RABIN

ISRAEL MEIER KAGAN

RADUŃ z. Wileńska

(Poland)

ישראל מאיר הכהן

בעהמ״ס

חפץ חיים׳ ו״משנה ברורה׳

ראדין

Letter from Rabbi Israel Meir Kagan (Chofetz Chaim) to Dr. Seidman, 1932

RADIN

ISRAEL MEIER KAGAN

RADUŃ, z. Wileńska

ישראל מאיר הכהן

בעל

״חפץ חיים״ ו״משנה ברורה״

ראדין, פלך ווילנא

מכתב רבי ישראל מאיר הכהן ה׳חפץ חיים׳ זצ״ל

מכתב האדמו״ר מגור רבי אברהם מרדכי אלטר זצ״ל

Letter from the Chofetz Chaim and Gerer Rebbe to Dr. Seidman

RADIN

ISRAEL MEIER KAGAN

RADUŃ, z. Wileńska

(Poland).

ישראל מאיר הכהן

בח"ס

"חפץ חיים" ו"משנה ברורה"

ראדין, פלך ווילנא.

ב"ה. יום ט' לחדש אדר תרצ"ג

כבוד הנכבד המופלג רב פעלים לתורה ולתעודה

הדוקטור ד"ר ה. זיידמאן נ"י בעיר ווארשא.

הנני לפנות בבקשה לבוא להשתתף בדבר הנוגע לפיקוח נפש [illegible]

[illegible]

[illegible]

[illegible]

[illegible]

[illegible]

[illegible]

[illegible]

[illegible]

[illegible]

ישראל מאיר הכהן

Letter from Rabbi Israel Meir Kagan (Chofetz Chaim) to Dr. Seidman, 1933

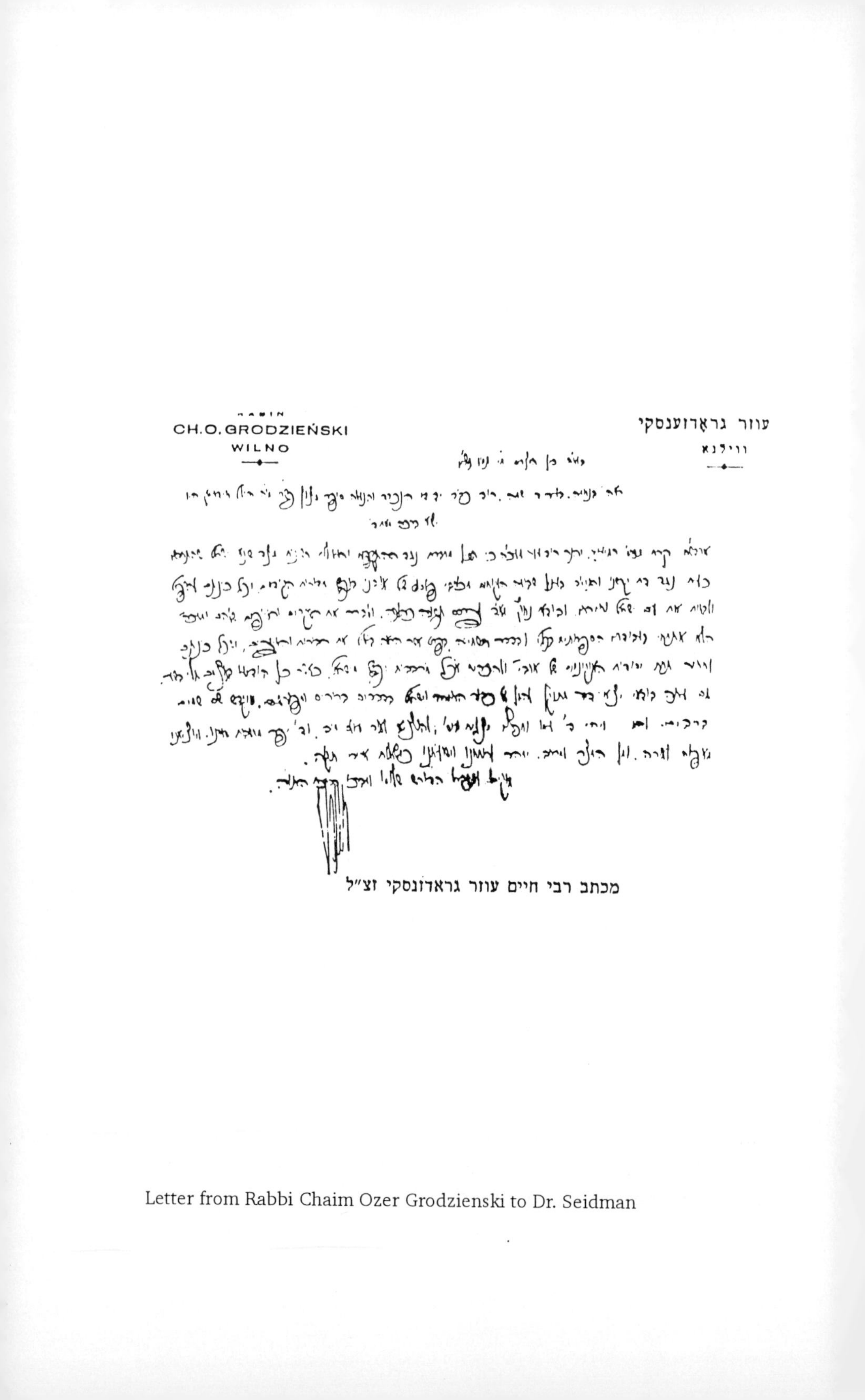

RABIN
CH.O. GRODZIEŃSKI
WILNO

עוזר גראָדזענסקי
ווילנא

מכתב רבי חיים עוזר גראדזנסקי זצ"ל

Letter from Rabbi Chaim Ozer Grodzienski to Dr. Seidman

1.3.43

Geliebter Freund! Es wundert uns sehr von Ihnen bis nun keine Antwort bekommen zu haben, obwohl die Angelegenheit unserer Freunde von erstrangiger Wichtigkeit ist u. Eile hat ist. Ich habe Sie nämlich ersucht den Herren Lipie Frydman, L. Orlean, Jacob Trockenheim, Mr. Lamba u.A. Pakete zu senden. Sie sind krank und brauchen sie dringend. Botschko wird Ihnen näheres mitteilen können. Auch wegen der Art dieser Paketen, die er an den Seinigen gesandt hatte. – Wir befinden uns hier G.s. wohl. Wohnung, Behandlung gut. Auch die Ernährung nicht schlecht. Wir brauchen nur Osterbrot für etwa 150 Person. Sie können dieses durch den Roten Kreuz-Service besorgen. Wir bitten rechtzeitig dies zu erledigen. –

Ich glaube, dass Sie u. Ihre Freunde ihrer Pflicht gegenüber Frydagan L. G. sich bewusst sind u. Sie werden ihr genügen. – Es wäre direkt ein unverzeihlicher Fehler wenn Ihr diese heilige Pflicht gegenüber unseren Besten nicht erfüllet. – Bitte mir Grüsse zu übermitteln von Jacob Morgenroth, [illegible] u. Alter. – Ich erwarte Ihre umgehende telegrafische Antwort. Auch Seidman ist [illegible] grüsse. Ihr

[illegible]

Detacher le long du pointillé!

Hier abtrennen!

Letter written by Dr. Seidman (one out of at least 72 letters) from detention camp in Vittel, France to Switzerland requesting aid from the free world (Mr. Eiss returned these letters after the War.)

Dr. H. Seidman with his father, Avraham Meir Seidman הי"ד, and grandfather, Yisroel הי"ד, c. 1930s

Dr. H. Seidman with Mathieu Muller (left) and priest (center) who smuggled the Muller family with five daughters from France to Switzerland (1945)

Dr. H. Seidman with Pierre Mendès, later Prime Minister of France

Dr. H. Seidman with Rabbi Binyamin Mintz (leader of Poalei Agudath Israel) visiting refugee children's home in France, c. 1945

Dr. H. Seidman with former Sephardic Chief Rabbi of Israel Ovadiah Yosef

Dr. H. Seidman with late President Zalman Shazar and Rabbi J. B. Soloveichik of Yeshiva University

Dr. H. Seidman receiving honorary degree at Yeshiva University, N.Y.C.

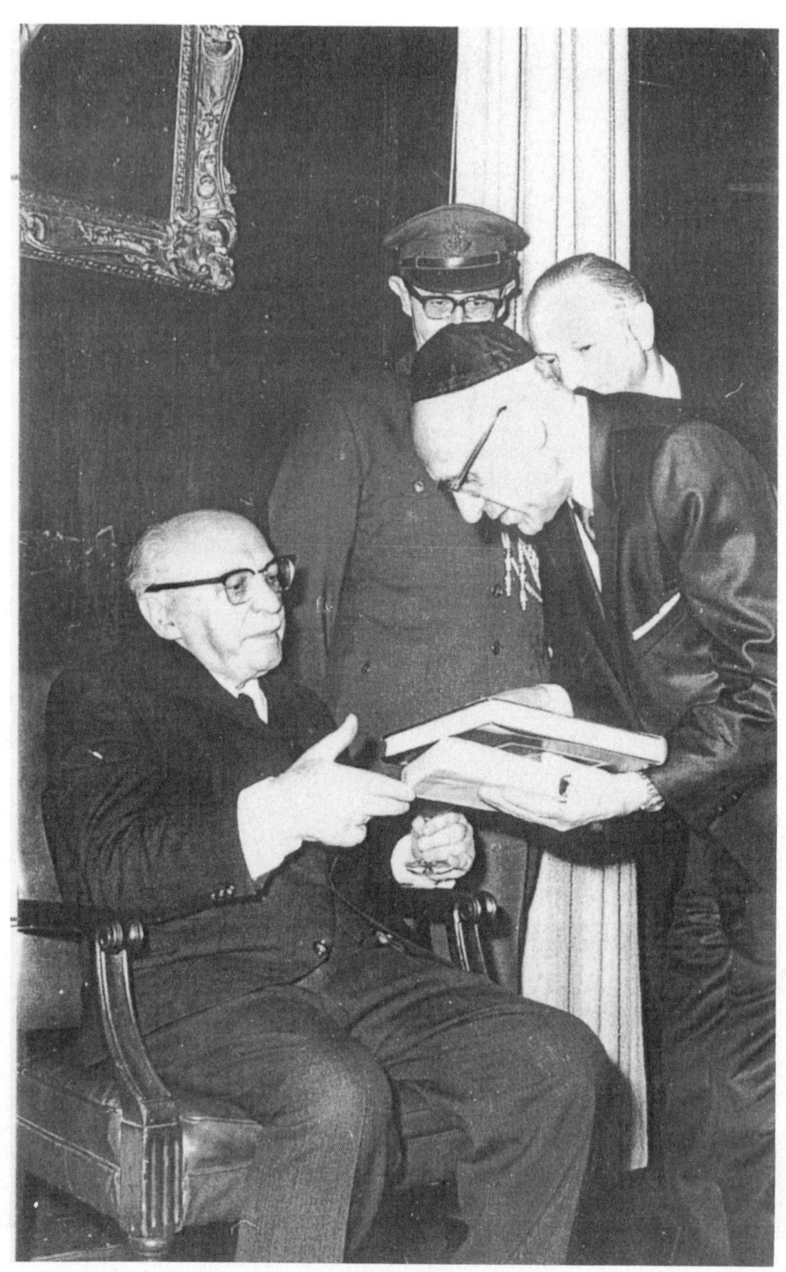

Late President Zalman Shazar of Israel with Dr. Seidman

Dr. Seidman addressing the Poalei Agudah Convention, 1954

Israeli ambassador to the United Nations Abba Eban with Dr. H. Seidman

Late Prime Minister of Israel Menachem Begin with Dr. H. Seidman

Rabbi Elbaz, founder of Ohr HaChaim Institutions, addressing rally, with Chief Rabbi Ovadiah Yosef and Dr. H. Seidman, Israel, 1979

Former United States Secretary of State Henry Kissinger with Dr. H. Seidman

Dr. Seidman receiving the Jabotinsky Centennial Medal for "distinguished service to the State of Israel and the Jewish people," from Menachem Begin, N.Y.C., 1980

Dr. H. Seidman at home with New York Senator Daniel Patrick Moynihan and Dr. Josef Kaminetsky, of Torah U'Mesorah

THE WARSAW GHETTO JUDENRAT

THE WARSAW GHETTO JUDENRAT

An Overview

When first hearing the news, on January 14, 1943, that they finally intended liquidating the Kehillah, I was quite prepared to accept the story as probably accurate. In the past, I had not lent much credence to similar news items, but this time it made sense. What further use was the Kehillah to the Germans?

By then, each factory or workshop was reduced to individual entities functioning on their own. All physical contact with the *Judenrat* had been virtually severed. Blocks of empty streets, totally devoid of Jews — Pawia, Leszno, Karmelicka, Dzielna, even Swietojerska with its brushworks — lay between the factories and the Kehillah offices. It was impossible for factory workers to approach the *Judenrat* in Zamenhof Street.

So why should the Kehillah structure, with its three thousand officials, have been allowed to continue? What useful function did it still provide? Our imminent destruction was eminently logical and feasible. Who cared for its worthy employees — intellectuals, lawyers, doctors, or spiritual leaders? Even its architects and engineers no longer played a productive role in the overall war effort. Thus had our fate been summarily decided!

Within the Kehillah Records and Archives Office that I directed, a debate raged. As usual there were optimists and pessimists, but eventually all agreed that their best course was in dispatching me to question Lichtenbaum, the *Judenrat* president. Perhaps I could extract some nuggets of information from him. Officially, Mark Lichtenbaum told me, he knew nothing. And unofficially? "Certainly," he replied, "it would be worthwhile for the *Judenrat* officials to seek sanctuary at the workshops.... "

Was this, then, the end of the Kehillah? Should I apply to Avraham Hendel, in order to join his work force? So many of my relatives had previously perished there — the families of Feivel Turkel, Yaakov Frankel, Perel Kornitzer, and countless others. As I sat forlornly in my office pondering my fate, my officials quietly left. Most were racked with despair and despondency, though a few made desperate plans for the future. I remained alone in my office, filled with gloomy foreboding.

Many years of my life had been devoted to my dissertation on the "History of the Warsaw Kehillah"; now had come the time to write the final chapter. Since the great historian, Professor Balaban, was no longer among the living, this task fell to me: to record a partial testimonial for this Holy congregation, its life sacrificed *al kiddush Hashem.* There was no shortage of historic material. During the last three years, papers upon papers had accumulated. The Kehillah files had been carefully rescued by the extraordinary tenacity of Professor Balaban and transferred from Grzybowska Street. Should the outside world not learn how we lived, suffered, hoped — and were ultimately destroyed?

Memories sprang up unsummoned before my eyes, memories recent and memories distant. Also countless Warsaw personalities, a few still alive but functioning in the baleful shadow of the Angel of Death. Some stood at the helm of the Kehillah in its most tragic period. Not all fulfilled their role honorably, but their task was not simple by any criteria. None of us have the right to sit in facile judgment over them; so I attempted to record some of their activities without malice or exaggeration. Within the Ghetto, the *Judenrat*'s role was severely censured — indeed any Kehillah receives its share of criticism. Undoubtedly some of this censure was valid; it made a number of mistakes by force of circumstances. While it was not my duty to defend its record, I did not hasten to castigate either, particularly since most of its members had already perished. They were all *kedoshim* laboring under the worst conditions imaginable. Let their actions be judged at the bar of history.

On October 3, 1939, shortly after the Germans captured Warsaw, the United Citizens Committee met and concluded that the Jews lacked representation of their own and should not be left leaderless, without protection. Since Mauricy Meisels, the Kehillah president, had fled the fighting, a list of Kehillah activists was presented to Stefan Stajinski, Warsaw's town mayor. The Germans further stipulated that the list should contain twenty-four names and we should no longer be known as the Jewish Kehillah Administration but as the *Judische Altestenrate* (Council of Jewish Elders — periodically this title was arbitrarily changed to *Judenrat*, Jewish Ghetto Council, or similar variations).

Judenrat members were drawn from non-politicals, nationalists, assimilationists, Yivo, business leaders, Bundists, Zionists, Mizrachi (Dr. Avraham Weiss), and Agudas Yisrael (I. M.

Lewin, M. Kaminer, and I. B. Ackerman), as well as representatives from the Warsaw Rabbinate (R. Shimshon Stockhammer and R. Dovid Shapira). By March 1940 some *Judenrat* delegates had escaped to America, England, or Eretz Yisrael (including I. M. Lewin). Others were shot by the Germans, and Meshulam Kaminer died on Simchas Torah 1941. On July 25, 1942, following *Judenrat* President Czerniakow's suicide, Mark Lichtenbaum was chosen to replace him.

During the three years of occupation, the position and departments of the Kehillah grew in importance and scope. From one perspective, the Germans used it as their instrument both in subjecting the Jews to their overall strategy and in facilitating their persecution. On the opposite side of the spectrum, the Jews utilized this self-same organization to cushion the German blows raining down on them and alleviate their precarious plight. Constantly, these two conflicting strategies fought a bitter war, with the Kehillah infrastructure the undeclared battlefield. Albeit the Nazi decrees were softened as they filtered down the *Judenrat* command, nonetheless it remained a German tool harnessed to their relentless campaign against the Jews.

Inside the Kehillah, they had their own view of the situation. Czerniakow saw his position as a higher calling, convinced that history would judge him favorably, recognizing him as a heroic figure who sought to save his people. Our situation would have been intolerable, he felt, without the intervention of the Kehillah acting as a buffer, absorbing the vicious edicts directed against the Jews. Eventually these decrees did strike home, but by then their cruelty was somewhat mitigated, their effect a little modified.

Critics of the Kehillah, however, did not perceive the cruel hand behind their suffering — they saw only the whip as it struck them. They claimed that without the *Judenrat*'s existence, the Germans would have failed to inflict their evil plans and would have been incapable of registering Warsaw's Jewish population. Later, they would have been unable to find their way around the Ghetto. The *Judenrat* was, they believed, no more than a German agency: the Nazis decreed and the *Judenrat* obeyed.

Additionally, individual members of the *Judenrat* executive came in for specific criticism by behaving callously. In particular, it was the newcomers — who under normal circumstances would never have been elected onto the Kehillah executive — that received the most distrust and disdain. They were variously accused of misusing their position to further their own private concerns, and of abusing their power when granting influence and *protexia*. Also there were dark rumors of bribery and corruption. Admittedly, there was substance to these complaints, but equal weight must be given to the tragic circumstances and the individual interplay between some personalities among the Kehillah leadership and members of the Ghetto population.

The *Judenrat* had a number of important departments and was involved in various activities, usually outside the scope of an ordinary Kehillah.

Labor Office

The Labor Office was presided over by the quiet but hardworking M. Rosen and run by Goldfile, a young lawyer (son of the Burial Department director who perished during the intense aerial bombardment of September 1939). This office had an invidious task — daily supplying a designated number of Jews for forced labor either within Warsaw or outside. Providing workers to the labor camps was an impossible job. The conditions there were horrendous and everyone did everything possible to avoid them. Yet the Germans compelled the Ghetto to supply able-bodied laborers. This office would try to negotiate, bargain, plead, or somehow postpone the evil decree. However, a certain number had to be yielded. Regrettably, the Jewish police would mount night raids to forcibly conscript workers. If the Germans themselves had undertaken to requisition the workers, the consequences would have been even worse. Reports from those labor camps were hair-raising — the crushing workload, the hunger, the vicious beatings. The death rate there was colossal — at times up to 60 percent! The Kehillah did help a little: despatching food parcels, clothing, and sanitary assistance, but not all got through and these could mitigate only minimally the cruelty of the barbaric guards.

The Labor Office grew into a large organization. Originally housed within the Religious Department of the Kehillah, it moved into its own five-story building (previously the *Collegium* High School at 80 Leszno Street). Four hundred and twenty officials processed identity cards and permits, prepared lists, cards, and notices, or despatched requests and demands. Many intellectuals worked here — mainly former lawyers — it was easier to order others into slave labor than enlist themselves. Supervising all these lawyers was a German called Ziegler. The building was always crowded: thousands entering or leaving after paying a designated amount to be freed from the threat of forced labor. The money accumulated this way was soon calculated in the millions.

On *erev* Sukkos, September 1942, the Labor Office was

suddenly liquidated. All its officials were deported to Treblinka except for a minority who escaped to Aryan Warsaw outside the Ghetto or to the Zamenhof, Nalewki, and Franciszkanska Streets inside the Ghetto. Rosen, its president, was shot in the Ghetto on September 29, 1942.

Due to *Judenrat* involvement, this decree to supply workers for the slave labor camps during 1940 and 1941, until June 1942, was less severe than it might otherwise have been. First of all, the number of Kehillah employees rose from sixty-eight before the War to tens of thousands in 1942, thereby providing them some sort of wage and relative safety from slave labor — which very often meant death. Also the Kehillah circumvented the rules and manipulated the figures. Thousands, perhaps hundreds of thousands, evaded this terrible imposition with Kehillah connivance. One typical example was the list of *rabbanim*.

It all started in the winter of 1939–40. Under German instructions, the *Judenrat* sent out humiliating demands to many Jews ordering them to clear the heavy snow from the streets. Some of these demands were even received by elderly *rabbanim*, including Rav Yaakov Silberstein of Praga, Rav Yaakov Zamchik, Rav Patman, Rav Stockhammer, and Rav Shapira. In desperation, they turned to me as head of the Kehillah's Religious Department. In addition, Rabbi Shloma David Kahana (who later escaped to Eretz Yisrael) summoned me and insisted that I take this matter into my own hands.

I approached Czerniakow and he suggested I compile a list of *rabbanim* who ought to be relieved from onerous work. When I drew up this list I included not only the twenty-one rabbis officially recognized by the Kehillah, but also those "non-official" rabbis who answered halachic *shailos* in their respective districts. I thought to myself: was it not bad enough that the Kehillah did not pay them for their services, they should also conscript them for degrading work? Subsequently, I showed Czerniakow the rule in *Shulchan Aruch* (*Hilchos Talmud Torah*) that Talmudic scholars are exempted from conscription into the "King's service," and Czerniakow acquiesced.

Then Rav Y. M. Kanal demanded to know why his son-in-law, R. Heiman, was requisitioned for this forced labor, and Rav Menachem Ziemba similarly complained on behalf of his sons-in-law R. Shmuel Leib Behr and R. Aaron Seidenfeld as well as his son Aaron. Inevitably, the *rabbanim* list grew until it comprised ninety-five names. Subsequently included were provincial rabbis, *yeshivah bachurim*, students from the Jewish Studies Institute, religious teachers, Hebrew writers, and religious activists. By June 1942, the numbers totalled eighteen hundred and this list had to be renewed every month. At each renewal, their work cards had to be stamped afresh by the German-controlled Labor Office. To assist me, I eventually had to organize a whole group of *yeshivah bachurim*, and this extra work took up all my time and energy. Often I had to withstand various complaints and maneuvers from non-Orthodox Jews who could not stomach this mass "desertion."

In fact, this particular community was the most discriminated against in the Ghetto. Lawyers, engineers, doctors, and anyone with a diploma had little trouble finding positions within the *Judenrat*, Joint, or other organizations. These afforded them some protection and also generated an income. However, *talmidei chachamim* and the religious were not generally accepted to these posts. This *rabbanim* list was their only salvation in that living hell. *Judenrat* President Czerniakow not only permitted me to spend most of my time on these extraneous affairs — rather than on my official position in the archives — he also actively helped me overcome obstacles raised by the Jewish "new leadership" in the Labor Department.

Should the Germans have imposed their decrees directly, without the intervention of the *Judenrat*, it would have been impossible to protect the *rabbanim* with my list — or to save other intellectuals by inventing fictitious positions for them in the *Judenrat* or the Joint.

Kehillah Rabbanim

When the *Judenrat* revived the various Kehillah functions during the winter of 1939–40, the Warsaw Rabbinate remained closed. The *rabbanim* were neither recognized as Kehillah employees nor received wages. Nonetheless, each Rav continued to serve his particular area and remained central to spiritual activities — perhaps more than ever — being called upon for help, encouragement, and advice, and their homes became centers of Judaism. During 1940, many provincial *rabbanim* arrived with the refugees; thus Warsaw became their new sphere of activity, part of their Kehillah duties. Most notable and most influential among them was the Kalisher Rav, Rabbi Mendel Alter, president of the Polish Agudas Harabbanim. Only at the end of 1940 did a small degree of rabbinical infrastructure begin to develop, when members of the Rabbinate were officially recognized for registering births, marriages, and deaths within their respective districts.

In January 1941, this was put onto a formal footing. The Ghetto was divided into areas and individual rabbis became responsible for a few streets, finally receiving a wage from the Kehillah. At that time the Warsaw Rabbinate included world famous *rabbanim*: R. Yaakov Meir Biderman, R. Menachem Ziemba, R. Avraham Weinberg, R. Yaakov Silberstein, R. Noach Rogosnitzky, R. Shloma Marker, R. Yitzchak Meir Kanal, R. Zvi Yecheskel Michelson, R. Dovid Shapira, R. Shimshon Stockhammer, R. Yaakov Zamtschik, R. Eliyahu Patman, R. Meir Warsawiak, R. Aharon Naftali Zablodover, R. Efraim Maimon, and R. Shloma Platow.

Between 1940 and 1942, Rabbis Y. M. Biderman, M. Warsawiak, Y. Silberstein, and S. Platow died and were replaced by Rabbis N. Huberband, Leib Biderman, and Pinchas Warsawiak. The Reform ministers Dr. M. Tauber and Prof. M. Balaban succeeded Dr. M. Schorr following his death in Russia. Notwithstanding the *rabbanim*'s non-recognition as an organized group, they would often gather to take decisions on various spiritual dilemmas. Despite their own personal suffering from persecution and privation, they organized assistance for provincial *rabbanim* and *talmidei chachamim* who had sought refuge in Warsaw and had no viable livelihood. A special committee, "*Ezras Harabbanim*," was established under Rav Mendel Alter (Kalisher Rav), Rabbi Dr. Yechiel Weinberg (director of Hildersheimer's Rabbinical Seminary in Berlin and author of the *Seridei Aish*), Rav Yechiel Meir Blumenfeld (of Tachkemoni), Rav Edelberg (from Makow), Rav Behr (of Zadonska Welle), Rav Elberg (of Blashki). Three Warsaw *rabbanim*, R. Ziemba, R. Shapira, and R. Stockhammer, were exceptionally active on this committee.

At the end of 1941, R. Shapira and R. Stockhammer were co-opted onto the *Judenrat*, where they represented the religious Jews and were particularly concerned to rescue *rabbanim* and *yeshivah bachurim* from labor camps (in reality death camps). *Rabbanim* were also active members of the Kehillah's

Religious Committee — especially R. Zisha Friedman and R. Shloma Mazur.

Until the beginning of the mass deportations, the *rabbanim* were an important religious force in the Ghetto and also took an active part in various social welfare organizations. During the deportations they were officials in the *Judenrat*'s Archives and Records Department, but this did not protect them and most were deported during August and September 1942. Only three *rabbanim* survived — R. Ziemba, R. Shapira, and R. Stockhammer — who were classified not as *rabbanim* but as *Judenrat* officials. Later Rav Menachem Ziemba was shot on the third day of *Chol Hamoed* Pesach 1943 and buried at 7 Kupieca Street. Rav Shimshon Stockhammer was deported to Majdanek and from there to Flosenberg. When that camp was liquidated in January 1944 he was fatally injured in an explosion. Rav Dovid Shapira survived the concentration camps and was later Rav of Fuerth, Germany. Out of Warsaw's many *rabbanim*, he was the only one to survive the War.

Housing Department

The *Judenrat* maintained a Real Estate Department headed by the lawyer Rosenthal — a non-political with assimilationist tendencies. This administered all Jewish property within the Ghetto while Jewish property in the Aryan half of Warsaw was controlled by Polish commissions. All those rents (both from inside and outside the Ghetto) went to a German-controlled escrow account, managed by a Breslau lawyer, and the true Jewish owners usually derived no income from their properties. Only if they produced certification of poverty would they receive paltry sums, up to a maximum of three hundred zloty a month. Often the real owners were reduced to total starvation.

The *Judenrat*'s Housing Department levied rents and appointed apartment directors, caretakers, and commissionaires. When the previous Polish commissionaires were ordered to relinquish their posts from within the Ghetto, thousands of the Jewish intelligentsia descended, flourishing all manner of recommendations and *protexia*, fighting to obtain these positions which guaranteed them an apartment and a small income. Almost always, when one rang at an apartment entrance at night, the gate was opened by a bespectacled gentleman with an intellectual appearance, and one could be fairly sure this man had a university degree. This department was headed by a Dr. A. Rosenkrancz (formerly a government director in the Polish Finance Unit and author of countless books on economics), who died in the Ghetto in July 1941. The Housing Department was one of those in the Ghetto that grew into a powerful institution dominating our lives. As usual, these were controlled by newcomers who swam through the muddy Ghetto tide to prominence.

Due to the continual contraction of the Ghetto, many Jews were regularly on the move — the majority of the Ghetto population were unsettled, almost as if they were living in a railway station, waiting with their suitcases packed to discover their next destination. Every few days, a new decree would be published: certain streets were to be cleared of their inhabitants and the frantic residents rushed to the Housing Department for alternative accommodation. Always they lost in the haggling — exchanging reasonable homes for an inadequate one, an inferior apartment for something even more wretched — since the crush was impossible. Officials of the Housing Department were constantly surrounded by thousands of people clamoring for an apartment or even part of an apartment using all means — money, recommendations, or pleading. The writers, intellectuals, *rabbanim*, and ordinary religious Jews were always dispossessed, they found no favor in the eyes of our new masters. To the newcomers who ran the Housing Department, most of the world famous personalities in the Ghetto were unknown and worthless. The intellectual elite had to make do with the worst apartments.

Tenement Committees

Faced with overwhelming terror and persecution, the Ghetto Jews instinctively felt the need to band together and resist the enemy. All the pre-War organizations — political parties, craft associations, and synagogue communities — were unsuited to the new situation. Contact between districts had become extraordinarily difficult; even crossing over from one street to another was fraught with danger. After dark, the overnight curfew prevented us going out altogether.

Even before the War, Warsaw's tenements housed a large number of tenants; during the occupation the residents could be counted in their thousands. After the curfew descended (at 6 P.M. in winter and 8 P.M. in summer) the tenement gates were closed, so at night each tenement was confined to an isolated village of its own. Often the number of Jews crammed into a single large tenement amounted to more than a small, provincial Kehillah. The overall stress and shared experiences united each apartment block into a single collective. Neighbors who had lived side by side for years, hardly exchanging a word, now found much in common. The proverb "Better a close neighbor than a distant relative" *(Mishle* 27:10) never seemed more appropriate. In the evenings, they would gather together to hear the latest news, reports from the battlefront, speeches of Roosevelt or Churchill.

The *Vaad Habayis*, or tenement committee, became central to their lives and replaced the pre-War organizations in importance. Drawn from the most respectable and energetic of residents, these democratically elected committees represented their respective tenements at the *Judenrat*, distributed the plethora of German decrees that descended daily, and protected their tenants from unfair taxes and similar problems. Additionally, tenement committees provided mutual assistance for those in need. Erstwhile businessmen had gone bankrupt, professionals had lost their jobs, intellectuals were starving, and ill health flourished in the Ghetto. The tenement committees organized charity collections among their residents and sought help from the Joint to alleviate starvation and suffering. The committees were fully aware of who among them had made money and could persuade them to support those less fortunate.

Within the Ghetto, these social units were a positive phenomenon. People no longer felt totally alone and vulnerable in the face of the enemy; they had an address to turn to when in trouble. The network of tenement committees was a striking example of how the Jews united closely together under duress to help one another. Some committees maintained soup kitchens and kindergartens, others established lectures and study groups before the schools were reopened.

Children constituted one of the greatest challenges in the Ghetto. From the onset of the German occupation, Jewish children were deprived of any education, and nothing was officially available for the next two years. The only option was to operate a clandestine schooling system. Most of the various pre-War educational networks or children's groups that had been dismantled by the Germans eventually began to function underground. Teachers were gathered, premises organized, and lessons restarted. In time, the American-based Joint and the ZSS *(Zydowska Samopomoc Spoleczno* — Jewish Communal Self-Help) financed the secret schools.

Covert classes were carefully hidden behind fictitious, permitted activities. Generally they masqueraded as "Children's Centers," usually maintained by tenement committees where children — officially under age — received extra nourishment: soup plus slices of bread and jam. Actually most of the children were already of school age and the cooks and caregivers were really teachers. Such schools were administered by either TOZ (*Towarzystwo Ochrony Zdrowia* — the pre-War Society for Preservation of Health) or CENTOS (*Centralia Towarzystwa nad Sierotami* — the pre-War National Society for Care of Orphans) but the educational context was left in the hands of the individual school networks. Most widespread was the religious school system. Immediately after Sukkos 1939, Yesodey Hatorah boys' schools opened throughout Warsaw and later Beis Yaakov girls' schools, and lecture courses secretly began during that winter. Yavne, the school network under Mizrachi auspices, also reopened, as did eventually the Zionist Tarbut schools, and finally the Yiddishists opened theirs. (Only the assimilationists and the moderate Yiddishists did not revive their schools and were mostly absorbed by the other streams. Private tuition existed for their children — as well as generally for extra subjects.)

Additionally a number of yeshivos, *bachurim* study circles, and *shiurim* operated totally underground, making no attempt to hide behind subterfuge. They were completely concealed from the Germans and usually relied on an alert watcher posted outside their tenement entrance to warn them of the imminent approach of Nazis. Tens of these groups learned Torah day and night and were under the control of Rav Menachem Ziemba, Rav Yehuda Arye Frumer (Rav of Kozielglow and previously *rosh yeshivah* of Lublin), Rav Avraham Weinberg, and other *rabbanim*. A few of the Chasidic *shtiebls* also learned together in secret. According to outside estimates, a total of over three thousand learned in the various clandestine yeshivos and *shiurim*. Their *mesiras nefesh* was unimaginable — being completely outlawed by the German regulations, they endured endless persecution and privation.

Continuing the traditions of the Cracow Beis Yaakov Girls' Seminary, R. Alexander Zishe Friedman and R. Yehudah Leib Orlean covertly delivered teachers' training lectures. Later, when the *Judenrat* officially reopened a number of schools, all the various educational streams reported on their previous underground activities. The Agudas Yisrael report revealed that in 1940 it had employed 114 teachers plus another twelve lady teachers trained at the Beis Yaakov Seminary. Their yeshivos were supervised by sixteen *rabbanim* and the total intake amounted to 2,250 children. In 1941, this had expanded to forty-six boys' *chadarim* under Yesodey Hatorah employing 132 teachers and four Beis Yaakov classes employing sixteen teachers. Moreover, they also had six *yeshivos ketanos* and two *yeshivos gadolos*. Their total intake in 1941 reached 3,500.

A new chapter in the history of the Ghetto schools began on January 2, 1942, when the *Judenrat* finally obtained German permission to officially open schools for up to five thousand children. Czerniakow had petitioned for this permit since the establishment of the Ghetto, and, on receiving permission, he summoned representatives of all the pre-War school networks to a meeting at the *Judenrat*. R. A. Z. Friedman and I were present on behalf of the religious movement Horev, R. Shloma Mazur and Yehudah Yefes on behalf of Yavne, and R. Yehudah Leib Orlean and Reb Avraham Mordechai Rogovy represented *Beis Yaakov*.

Czerniakow bridled at the suggestion that the various schools be allowed to function independently of the *Judenrat*. "When it comes to fulfilling German decrees, then you leave it to the *Judenrat*," he argued, "but when it's a question of providing something positive, you want the Kehillah out of the picture?" As a compromise it was agreed the Kehillah would become responsible for wages, funding, and premises (via its Housing Department) but internal management would be left with individual educational streams. The Kehillah's Educational Department, run by Samuel Horenstein and Dr. Meir Tauber, helped in administration and certifying the teachers. Since many schools were already functioning, albeit covertly, a rapid reopening of the schools was planned and each school network provided the *Judenrat* with reports of their activities.

The schools actually began operating openly and officially during April 1942. Finally, thousands of children were permitted the opportunity to study from an organized curriculum, the constant fear and trepidation of teachers who had taught clandestinely was removed, and many intellectuals achieved employment and status in the Ghetto. Since the schools provided extra nutrition, they proved very attractive, but there were insufficient school places to cope with the demand. The Germans did not interfere with the content of the lessons, besides forbidding the teaching of the German language — a restriction the Jews were happy to comply with.

Naturally the reopening of the schools boosted Ghetto morale and stamina. Also worthy of mention were the kindergartens and playgrounds established by Czerniakow in April 1942. Utilizing bombed-out sites in the Ghetto, Jewish architects and engineers landscaped them over, converting piles of rubble into artificial hills and valleys planted with trees and flowers. The two most striking new "parks" were at 21 Grzybowska Street (on the site of the destroyed Mizrachi seminary Tachkemoni) and in the large courtyard at the corner of Nalewki Franciszkanska Streets. Thousands of children exercised there during the spring and summer of 1942, coached by teachers with diplomas; and thousands of young children marched through these large sports grounds during May 1942. Czerniakow also established university standard lectures on Judaism and the Natural Sciences — though officially they were only teacher training courses.

Despite the schools' official recognition, the yeshivos and Talmud study groups remained underground and continued to operate under conditions of hunger and fear. During the mass deportations, when the schools were again closed down, the yeshivos maintained their covert existence in the bunkers and other hiding places — until the Uprising erupted on April 19, 1943, forcing everybody out onto the streets to fight for their survival.

Sanitary Department

Theoretically, the Sanitary Department had a crucial role in the Ghetto, where typhus was endemic and a public campaign against this scourge was urgently required. Obviously, the ideal solution would have been to provide better nutrition and less crowded housing conditions. However, the German doctors ostensibly in charge of sanitary conditions in the Ghetto contented themselves by establishing (with monetary support extracted from the *Judenrat*) the bureaucratic machinery to circularize hygiene advice, despatch orders, and organize "cleansing" routines.

These so-called cleansing operations were a chastening punishment all of their own. They would descend on an apartment block, seal it off, round up all its inhabitants, and march them off to the public baths. Hygiene and cleanliness at these places were extremely substandard. Many would catch a chill there and return home ill. More often than not, typhus itself was spread at those cleansing sessions. Furthermore, clothing was usually damaged in the process or vanished altogether. As a result most people preferred to bribe their way out of this ordeal. Soon the Sanitary Department amassed a substantial income, becoming in effect a prime source of bribery and corruption — and yet another of the many plagues inflicted upon the Ghetto population.

Business Activity

Officially, business activity was organized on "national" lines; in reality, only a caricature of a national administration existed in the Ghetto. According to the German *Transferstelle*, the Customs Office, staffed by extortionists and swindlers, the Ghetto was meant to be self-supporting. How they expected the Ghetto population of half-a-million, completely cut off from the outside world and restricted to a tiny area without raw materials or natural resources, to support themselves is beyond comprehension. Yet this was their basic premise, from which no logical argument could sway them. All contact with the outside was strictly forbidden except via the *Transferstelle*, which carefully limited all contacts and made these as awkward as possible.

Large numbers survived on their pre-War possessions (apart from those who succumbed to hunger and disease). After expending their savings, they sold their jewelry, ornaments, clothes, and underclothes. Finally, they were forced to sell off their furniture, kitchen utensils — anything that could be converted into a few zloty. A number of brokers were stationed at an empty plot of land in Gesia Street, not far from the Jewish cemetery, and most of the Ghetto business was conducted there. Most of these second-hand goods were smuggled across from here to the Aryan quarter. However, some were processed by Jewish firms who had obtained certain privileges from the *Judenrat*'s Business Department.

After being registered with the *Transferstelle*, these firms received permission to export their goods into the *Generalgouvernement* (German administered southwest Poland, stretching from Warsaw to Rumania). The firms produced shirts from sheets, clothes from old rags, or else manufactured torches, toys, and other small wares. They specialized in producing substitute items (such as paper-based shoes with wooden soles), and these goods were exported throughout Poland. Some Jews profited greatly, others only enough to feed themselves.

Raw materials were also smuggled in from the Aryan side, yet they were processed openly in the Ghetto. The *Transferstelle* never questioned the source of the raw materials — to the warped Nazi ideology, the answer was obvious: did not the Jews control everything? Other businessmen on the outside were amazed how the enclosed and starving Ghetto managed to supply manufactured goods throughout Poland. It reminded them of the situation before the First World War when the small workshops along Nalewki Street supplied goods even to the far-flung Siberian wastelands. The Jews displayed initiative, inventiveness, flair, and strenuous exertion.

At least the *Judenrat* officials who were the middlemen between the *Transferstelle* and Ghetto businesses did not interfere overmuch and usually did not burden the businessmen with onerous German regulations and red tape. They allowed private enterprise to develop in any way it saw fit. Every so often the *Judenrat* obtained minor concessions. For instance, the Jews were officially forbidden to own more than 3000 zloty in available cash — though most Jews ignored this decree — and in the winter of 1941–42 this regulation was officially withdrawn in Warsaw. Occasionally the *Judenrat* obtained various relaxations in the export restrictions.

In time, new products and skills were developed: processing tin and rubber, and producing perfumes and chemical products. Factory owners who had escaped from Bilitz experimented with manufacturing bales of recycled textiles from old rags. Each of these newfledged enterprises served a double purpose. Not only did they provide a livelihood for thousands of starving residents, they also underpinned the industrial importance of the Ghetto and should have guaranteed its survival. Ultimately, however, the Germans paid scant notice. Positive economic ventures may have slightly slowed the pace of extermination, but plans for the "final solution" were never shelved.

Vocational Education

Josef Jashunski, one of the most active and reliable communal leaders, headed the Vocational Education Department that established and administered scores of technical schools specializing in electricity, mechanics, metalworking, carpentry, graphics, and related subjects. All the skills previously taught by ORT now became the responsibility of this department, which discovered fresh talents in the Ghetto. These schools achieved quite a standard and earned high praise from experts whenever they mounted an exhibition. Czerniakow — a past lecturer of Kehillah vocational courses — took a special interest in this department, and a number of Ghetto vocational schools were later housed in the Kehillah campus.

These courses trained adolescents and adults, including lawyers and intellectuals, in skills useful in Eretz Yisrael; *aliyah* became the prime objective of both students and faculty. Inevitably much of Jashunski's work was now tinged with Zionism, though he had a Bundist background. Amidst the slave labor, hunger, cold, and fear, the students and lecturers warmed themselves in the glow of a better future in a liberated Palestine. Many of them openly told me: Here we will not remain; if we are destined to survive, we will emigrate to Eretz Yisrael. At a small celebration commemorating Jashunski's seventieth birthday, I found many activists from all circles — Zionists (Kirshenbaum and Bloch), Mizrachi (Yehudah Yefes and Shloma Mazur), and also Aguda (A. G. Friedenson and A. M. Krongrad) — but hardly any Bundists. In my speech, I wished him a sweet revenge: that he should live to meet his students in the Jezreel Valley. (He was visibly touched and later told me this sentiment had made a deeper impression than all the other speeches.) Jashunski also was in charge of the Statistical Department, which he took very seriously. In all, he earned the respect of all his political contemporaries — though perhaps least of all from his fellow Bundists.

Supplies Department

Throughout the Ghetto's existence, Abraham Stoltsman took charge of the Supplies Department, allocating food rations against our ration cards. Unfortunately, this food had to be purchased outside the Ghetto and imported via the German controlled *Transferstelle* (officially nothing was allowed in or out of the Ghetto without their approval), and they skimmed off between 15 and 30 percent of all food brought in for the Jews. Stoltsman was in constant contact with German officials who wielded crucial power over the Ghetto. Permits were grudgingly given for pitifully small portions of food — twelve dekagrams of bread per head of Ghetto population. Every so often, small amounts of jam, syrup (produced in the Ghetto), or sugar were also made available.

Fortunately, these starvation rations were augmented by smuggling, otherwise the famine raging in the Ghetto would have been even worse. Stoltsman was joined by activists and other businessmen, and their whole department was presided over by Abraham Gefner. Obviously the Supplies Department could not possibly satisfy the overwhelming needs of the Ghetto. Yet it was heavily criticized for failing even in the minor role it could have played, due to incompetence and corruption. During the deportations, Stoltsman made little impact and had no opportunity to do so.

Before the War, Stoltsman was the deputy director of the Central Businessmen's Union in Senatorska Street and was previously known as an energetic activist. As from July 25, 1942, he was also a *Judenrat* vice president, together with Dr. Gustav Wlikovski, a well-known advocate before the War, who concentrated on providing social assistance and presided over the

Jewish Communal Self-Help organization in Warsaw. Later, after joining the *Judenrat*, Wlikovski headed its Social Welfare Department and liaised with the independent Jewish Communal Self-Help organization which received its funding from the Joint. The Joint itself was headed by Neustadt, Yitzchak Gitterman, and David Guzik and operated by borrowing large sums from rich magnates to be repaid by the Joint's head offices in America after the War. Many rich Jews lent money on that basis.

Mail Service

Since the Ghetto was entirely cut off from the rest of Warsaw, it had to have its own mail service to deliver and accept letters. Like every postal service, it had facilities for parcels and money orders — but could not accept telegrams. All letters going abroad had to undergo an internal censor (besides the German censor). Many intellectuals were employed in the Ghetto mail service — particularly writers and teachers, and a few were even employed as mailmen.

From 1941 to 1942, many food parcels arrived from the provinces, which greatly alleviated famine in the Ghetto. Even Soviet administered Poland (after the Nazi-Russian partition) sent food parcels up till June 1941, which were likewise a great help. However, the Germans could not stomach this and suddenly swooped on the Jewish mail service to confiscate all the parcels. Later this became their routine practice, and the food parcels stopped coming. Smaller food parcels were also received from Portugal. Generally mailed by the Histradrut or individuals for prominent personages in the Ghetto, these arrived infrequently and contained very little: a quarter kilo of dried figs, a tin of sardines, and ten dekagrams of the worst quality tea that was almost impossible to use. This mail service lasted for two years — January 1941 to January 1943.

The Palestine Register

On March 27, 1942, the Germans ordered the *Judenrat* to list all Jews in the Warsaw Ghetto who: (a) possessed visas for Palestine, (b) were Palestinian citizens, (c) had close relatives in Palestine, or (d) owned property in Palestine.

Hardly had this proclamation been posted up in the Ghetto when the news spread like wildfire. (The internal "news service" worked brilliantly — half a million Jews confined to a tiny area, each constantly asking, "What news?" When something did occur, all eagerly told their friends, neighbors, relatives, and sundry passersby.) This "Eretz Yisrael list" engendered much interest and speculation. From past experience we knew that behind every bland announcement usually lurked a hidden motive.

As usual, there were pessimists and optimists. The pessimists roundly declared, "This is undoubtedly not planned for our benefit. Everybody who registers will become a public enemy number one, liable to be deported to who-knows-where. *Challilah!* Nobody should register. Just don't do it — *chas veshalom!*"

However the optimists argued, "The Gestapo simply want to exchange us with German citizens now resident in Palestine, America, or wherever. All they want to know is how many Jews are involved. Perhaps this will lead to our salvation — who knows?"

Within the Ghetto, our imagination was fired, dreams took shape, hope sprang eternal; rescue from our inferno to the sanctuary of Eretz Yisrael, from bitter darkness to scintillating light. It became the central topic of conversation in the evenings; everybody desperately wanted to believe. Their innate optimism dispelled all thought of danger.

The *Judenrat* prepared forms to be completed by potential emigrants detailing the degree of kinship and the land registry particulars of real estate they owned in Eretz Yisrael. Thousands of Jews lined up at their offices at 26–28 Grzybowska Street, the line stretching all the way back to Ciepla Street. Those desperate enough employed personal recommendations or money to avoid the long lines. Many wanted to know how close a kinship was needed: A cousin? An uncle? A step brother? A brother-in-law? The *Judenrat*'s Legal Sub-Committee dealing with the registration judged all queries leniently. They were broad-minded — any relation was sufficient to be registered. The paper mountain grew: forms upon filled forms and long lists of those hoping to emigrate to Palestine.

Officially, according to the German instructions, everyone had to turn up personally to register. Yet there remained in the Ghetto a number of Chasidic Rebbes and prominent *rabbanim* who were too apprehensive to appear outside in the street. With their distinctive Chasidic attire, they were an obvious target and in greater danger from the Nazis than anyone else. After a personal request from the Sochatchover Rebbe, R. Dovid Bornstein, I undertook to overcome their predicament. Accompanied by two of the *Judenrat* officials in charge of the register, Asher Frankel and Mrs. Movshovitz, we visited all the prominent rabbinical personages at home.

I remember when we met the Stoliner Rebbe, R. Perlow (at 7–9 Muranowska Street), how grateful he was; he just could not imagine how else he would have registered. We also visited the

Sochatchover Rebbe, the Radomsker Rebbe (who lived with his Chasid, the well-known and learned Nosson Ehrlich at 30 Nowolipie Street), Rav Mendel Alter of Kalish, the Grodzisker Rebbe, the Kozmirer Rebbe, the Kotzker Rebbe (at 38 Zamenhof Street), Rebbe Moshe Betzalel Alter and Rebbe Meir Alter of Gur, the famous *rosh yeshivah* Rav Nosson Spiegelglass (at 15 Elektornalna Street), and R. Shimon Landau, with his son-in-law, R. Moshe Leib Ingleman, previously president of the Otvosk Kehillah. In all we visited all the famous *rabbanim* and Rebbes in Warsaw, and everywhere we went we were met with words of encouragement regarding Eretz Yisrael.

The registration process took two days. While we waited for further developments, various rumors circulated in the Ghetto, both good and bad. Apparently, one family who had Palestinian documents (nobody is quite sure what type of documentation — British entry certificates, citizenship, or merely visas) were suddenly picked up one night and transported directly to Lisbon en route to be exchanged in Eretz Yisrael. A postcard has already been received from them in Lisbon. However others report that registration also took place in other towns: Cracow, Lemberg, Kielce, Radom, etc. — and in Opatow, a number of Jews who had registered for Eretz Yisrael were summarily shot. Both hope and fear were heightened by the conflicting reports.

Soon I was approached for my help. Those who had previously hesitated to register out of fear (or had no relatives in Palestine) now wanted to join the list by any means possible. They did not want to miss what might be their last chance. Others who had registered now regretted their haste and wanted assistance in removing their names from the list. Weeks dragged by and those forms and lists, so painstakingly numbered and sorted in alphabetical order, languished untouched and unread. Had the Germans forgotten the whole episode? Was it all just a passing whim? Sources in the Kehillah tell me the instructions had originated with the Gestapo's Foreign Affairs Bureau.

Finally in early May 1942, the Gestapo ordered the *Judenrat* to hand over these lists and forms to their foreign department under Kommissar Niklaus. Not a word more was heard about the affair, though speculation was rife regarding negotiations with the British Mandate authorities in Palestine. Until today it has never been clarified what the registration was really all about; it merely served to bestow yet another disappointment on the beleaguered Ghetto.

The Judenrat's Role

Would the Jews have been better off without the *Judenrat*? In other countries with no previous Kehillah structure — France for example — the Germans established *Judenrate* with which to entrap the Jews. In those areas, it might have been possible and perhaps preferable not to cooperate with their ersatz *kehillah*. However, that was not the case in Poland. Here a sophisticated Jewish communal structure already existed. To dismantle it against German *diktat* was almost impossible. Nor, according to all the Jewish organizations, would that have been particularly desirable. At that perilous time, after the German capture of Poland, the Jews wanted unity at all costs to enable them to face the common enemy — and the Kehillah was a unifying factor. The Germans may have treated it as their *Judenrat*, but for the Jews it remained the Kehillah.

During our lengthy *galus*, it was not the first time that foreign rulers imposed umbrella organizations over their Jewish subjects for their own private motives, yet the Jews utilized these to benefit Jewish objectives. For instance, the "Council of Four Lands" (*Vaad Arba Aratzos*) was set up merely to facilitate tax collecting from the Jews, but with Jewish input it soon became their major institution. Similarly in the Ghetto, they originally believed the *Judenrat* would evolve into a positive development. If not for the mass slaughter, that nobody could have foreseen or ever imagined, the *Judenrat* would have filled a useful function. Until the *aktions*, the *Judenrat* softened the German decrees and minimized the bloodshed.

Obviously, those who acted as intermediaries between the Jews and Germans were not from the most refined class. Those of a genteel character were unwilling and totally unsuited to bargain with murderers and sadists. Nonetheless, there remained among the *Judenrat* men of consequence who displayed extraordinary heroism and accomplished a great deal. The *Judenrat* also contained people of spirit who never forgot their duty to the public for a second — men such as Adam Czerniakow, Abraham Gefner, and Meshulam Kaminer. There were many others who at least fulfilled their allotted role with integrity, though they did nothing beyond the strict call of duty. As such, it is unfair to saddle the *Judenrat* with collective guilt. In common with most organizations it had both good and bad elements, men of strong as well as weak characters, and not all were able to withstand the pressure.

Testing times came frequently. The Germans deliberately manipulated our situation to increase the pressure, sow internal discord, corrupt the Jews, and ensure that no one survived except at the direct or indirect expense of someone else. Invariably, every *galus* compromises virtue and creates unwelcome behavioral traits, but the German ordeal was the most sordid and degrading *galus* Jews ever had to contend with.

In sharp contrast to the *Judenrat*, experienced activists within the Ghetto sought to emphasize the communal spirit of the ZSS, the Jewish Self-Help organization. Indeed the ZSS was entirely concerned with assisting Jews while the *Judenrat* primarily had to carry out German instructions — particularly in supplying workers for forced labor — necessitating daily contact with the German overseers. It was an unpleasant task but somebody, in this case the *Judenrat*, had to do it. Moreover the ZSS employed many activists who had become famous before the war, many well-known journalists, pedagogues, actors, and political leaders, while the *Judenrat* was mainly staffed by newcomers with little previous experience, nationally or locally.

However, concomitant with the *Judenrat*'s unpalatable role, it sometimes obtained extra supplies of food that the ZSS could then distribute. Officially, as far as the Germans were concerned, Czerniakow as *Judenrat* president was also the titular head of the ZSS. Besides, ZSS regularly received substantial support from the *Judenrat*. As previously stated, the Kehillah employed — and therefore protected — more than 10,000 officials, many from the intellectual elite.

When the future historians come to evaluate the *Judenrat*'s ambiguous role, the central question they must answer is: Did the *Judenrat* ease the entrapment of Poland's Jews and pave the way for their annihilation?

It was not so much the *Judenrat* that facilitated the extermination program, but the establishment of Ghettos. Many Jews survived in France where *Judenrat*e existed but no Ghettos. On the contrary, in Poland, particularly in the latter half of 1942, there were Ghettos without *Judenrat*, yet the liquidation was total. Enclosing the Jews into Ghettos and the hostile attitude of the Polish population ensured the complete seizure of Poland's Jews and the subsequent slaughter, unequaled in history.

The fairest period to judge the *Judenrat*e and their activities is up till the summer of 1942. Then everybody still believed we would somehow survive, despite everything, and witness the ultimate victory over the regime of evil.

PERSONALITIES I KNEW IN THE GHETTO

PERSONALITIES I KNEW IN THE GHETTO

The Judenrat Presidents

Even when fulfilling anti-Jewish decrees of the Nazis, *Judenrat* President Adam Czerniakow saw his role in a positive light and he willingly sacrificed himself to this chosen calling. He told me how he came to the Kehillah building in 1905, when it was attacked by revolutionaries, and found the Kehillah president, the aged Berson, sitting forlornly amidst a ruin of shattered glass, broken chairs, and smashed desks. He tried to help the old man out of the building but Berson proudly declared, "I remain at my post!" Czerniakow consciously modeled himself on that image. He bitterly decried those who now fled Warsaw and could not forgive them.

"They stayed only while seeking the mandate of the Jewish masses!" he complained to me. "But now we are in trouble, they are quick to abandon us!" Czerniakow suffered personally for remaining at his post. Daily he had to come face to face with the Nazi overseers. More than once he was incarcerated and severely beaten. Each time his life hung by a thread but on surviving, he returned to his dangerous position. Czerniakow was responsible and methodical, working hard all day yet taking home more files to plough through at night. He headed a large bureaucratic administration that oversaw twenty-five separate departments. Besides the conventional Kehillah functions — including education, burial, welfare, statistics, and communal taxes — in the Ghetto it was now likewise responsible for housing, police, utilities, food, health, sanitation, and employment.

Principally, there were two complaints against Czerniakow. He was too soft, tolerating unworthy people or activities. Moreover, he encouraged assimilationists and renegades. Yet all had to admit that no one else of his calibre was available to replace him in the Ghetto. His integrity was unquestioned. Perhaps I am not totally objective about Czerniakow since he supported me in my position as chief archivist, even before the War. Later, under the occupation, in all my machinations to rescue Torah scholars, writers, and intellectuals, he was particularly helpful. Nonetheless, I can unreservedly bear witness that he wholeheartedly served his people with pride, honor, and honesty. He accepted the Nazi beatings and continued to serve at his post, fulfilling his duty both in life and death.

Mark Lichtenbaum, his successor as *Judenrat* president (following Czerniakow's suicide on July 23, 1942) was swept along with the tide. He watched passively, with minimal assertiveness and little hope — his credo: "Let everyone save their own skin." Trained as an engineer, he headed the *Judenrat*'s Business Department in addition to being a non-elected vice-president. Although permanently short tempered, he retained a respect for spiritual matters, anything holy to Judaism. He tried to resurrect synagogues destroyed in the aerial bombardment and became a member of the religious committee established in the winter of 1941–42. Likewise, he supported the Zionist *Hachshara* programme at Grochov. Lacking social graces, callous and often rude, he voiced his opinion whenever he could. Officially his duties lay in fulfilling the Nazi's technical demands — an extremely difficult task.

Unfortunately, he obeyed the German orders far too precisely. As an architect he built the high walls surrounding the Ghetto scrupulously, with the zeal and care he had previously lavished on pre-War communal projects. In his professional enthusiasm, he often forgot what was being built and for whom. His two sons, both engineers and architects, whom he had enrolled in his department, had no tradition of communal service. They showed him little respect and were too obedient to the Germans. They did not understand how to maintain a proper distance.

Throughout the deportations, he functioned unthinkingly, almost as a robot, passively carrying out the German orders, fooling himself that something could be saved. Even after the mass deportations began, he still believed a remnant would survive and might be resurrected. Yet he helped wherever he could. He had various plans and was receptive to practical suggestions such as establishing courses, schools, or orphanages. Perhaps, under normal circumstances he might have been a respectable leader, fulfilling his role with honor. In the face of our unique catastrophe, he was a totally colorless figure, though he helped within his limited capacity.

Occasionally, as when I implored him to save certain individuals from the deportations — for example Agudas Harabbanim president Rav Mendel Alter, the Mizrachi leader Rav Yitzchak Nissenbaum, R. Yaakov Frankel, Gershon Sirota, R.

Shimon Landau, and R. Shloma Mazur — he gave orders for their removal from the death march. He was effective only in saving Rav Nissenbaum but his underlings did not exert themselves to carry out his instructions regarding the others. Often I approached him for assistance on behalf of individuals — for instance, the widow of Eliyahu Kirshenbraun and her sister-in-law, the widow of Elchanan Zeitlin — and he willingly helped. Likewise, he assisted in the collection of *sifrei Torah* and other holy books after the first stage of the deportations.

He was shot at the Warsaw *Umschlagplatz* on April 29, 1943.

ABRAHAM GEFNER

Abraham Gefner, who presided over the Business and Distribution Departments, was another significant personality in the Kehillah. He was a most active *parnas,* yet he always found the time to greet everyone with a smile and good cheer, with open arms and an open heart. He would help to the best of his ability, particularly encouraging men of religion — *rabbanim* and religious activists. His relationship with children was heartwarming. Swarms of starving street children in the Ghetto would beg at doors or importune passersby. Gefner would not content himself merely by offering a donation. He would stop for a small chat, investigating these children's individual circumstances with both heart and humor.

Once I remember accompanying him out of the Kehillah, when we met a ten-year-old boy — thin, his white face pinched with hunger. This young boy leaned up against a wall and sang to us in a beautiful, ringing voice. He was quite famous in the Ghetto, who nicknamed him "*Moreinu*" after his favorite song.

Gefner waited patiently until the song was completed before he began questioning the boy as to where he lived and what his parents did. He soon discovered that there were no parents — both had died in the famine. Gently, he took the child by the hand and led him to the orphanage in Dzielna Street that he had founded.

This orphanage was a story in itself; perhaps one of the most poignant in the Ghetto. Gefner invested all his substantial energy — and every zloty he obtained from communal institutions, rich businessmen, and his own resources. It was run in an exemplary manner, providing nourishing food for the children and a satisfactory education. (Indeed, some complained this was currently an unnecessary luxury and unfair to the other Ghetto children.) All of Gefner's zeal was lavished on his favorite institution and it gave him much pleasure.

In 1942, I was invited there to the first night Pesach Seder. The tables were set "as usual" with matzos, eggs, and a portion of meat for every child — the best the Ghetto could provide. Gefner, his wife, Dr. Pinkert, the director Herschaft, and others had surpassed themselves. By then, eggs in the Ghetto were unheard of and meat was unattainable — a distant memory. The children were dressed in festival finery and there was a holiday atmosphere. The children's eyes shone in anticipation.

Abraham Gefner himself led the Seder, reciting the Haggadah and explaining the story of the Exodus. The children understood and believed him when he predicted that their liberation must eventually arrive. After the meal, Gefner invited one of the children to sing. I recognized the boy — it was "*Moreinu.*" His face had filled out a little and had gained a little color. He stared at Gefner in surprise, as Gefner had strictly forbidden him to sing in public. Now he had Gefner's permission, and the large, lighted hall was treated to an exquisite rendering of the Hebrew song "*Al Yam Kinneret*" ("By the Sea of Galilee"). We are transported to a different planet — a world of light, hope, and freedom. The boy sang and the audience wept.... That was our last Passover Seder in the Warsaw Ghetto. Where is the young singer "*Moreinu*" and those two hundred young children now? *Ribono Shel Olam,* what great sins did we commit that these innocent young souls were destroyed?

Gefner could have easily escaped from Warsaw at the beginning of hostilities. He was a very rich man with contacts abroad. Yet he forbore to do so — and he had his reasons. I still have a small note he wrote Gitta Eisensweig, who acted as his secretary and assistant in his endeavors for his orphans. This was a farewell note, since Miss Eisensweig was then in Pawiak Prison, in transit, with a permit to leave Poland as a foreign resident. He wrote:

> *Warsaw, January 1, 1943*
>
> *I wish you all success but I do not regret my staying here. From all my decisions in my long life (I have just reached seventy), I now see that my cleverest move was to remain in Warsaw with my brethren. If I have shed any tears, let these be my reward.*
>
> *Go in peace,*
>
> *Abraham Gefner*

Together with a number of other *Judenrat* personnel, Gefner was shot dead at the *Umschlagplatz* on April 21, 1943. He once told me he had a married daughter in America and asked me to send regards, but I forgot her name and lost the address. If these words ever reach her, she may be assured that her father lived a life of righteousness and died as a hero in the Warsaw Ghetto.

REB MESHULAM KAMINER

Who in the Polish Jewish metropolis did not know R. Meshulam Kaminer? No burden was too heavy for his wide shoulders; no job for Agudas Yisrael considered beneath his dignity. If something had to be done, R. Meshulam would gird his loins and do it. His first venture was in the field of publishing. When the Aguda was first founded in Poland under the name of *Shlome Emune Yisrael* in 1919, it needed a program. R. Meshulam was then a young Gerrer Chasid from the Nalewki Street *shtiebl* with no experience in writing. Yet he sat down and wrote a short pamphlet in Yiddish, "*What does Shlome Emune Yisrael want?*" Published in thousands of copies and distributed throughout Poland, it laid the foundation of each branch.

Once again when the new party realized it needed a newspaper, it was R. Meshulam who shouldered the heavy burden. On November 7, 1919, he founded the first Aguda newspaper, *Der Yid*, in Yiddish, originally as a weekly and later as a daily. The Polish Aguda did not yet possess talented writers and most newspaper employees were irreligious, necessitating constant checking to ensure nothing untoward would be published in the Aguda newspaper. Kaminer had to edit and censor their work; eventually he began to write his own articles. In common with most party funded newspapers, it suffered from a continual deficit, and occasionally writers and print workers walked out on strike. In response, R. Meshulam Kaminer would prepare himself a large pot of tea and sit down to write incessantly for twelve to fourteen hours. He composed the editorial, publicity, reports, and news, as well as compiling the advertisements — single-handedly completing the weekend edition (the largest issue) so that the religious readership should not be deprived.

After the Polish government demanded that the *chadarim* should include secular knowledge on the curriculum, R. Meshulam Kaminer was among the founders of the Yesodey Hatorah schools network with a balance of secular and religious subjects. When concern was raised that history books might contain views and conclusions contrary to Judaism, R. Meshulam again sat down to write. While various committees were still discussing and arguing about what history textbook might be admitted to the Yesodey Hatorah network, R. Meshulam's "*Der Yiddishe Geschichte Loit der Torah*" (Jewish History Conforming to the Torah — Warsaw, 1924) appeared in seven thick volumes. Even those liable to criticize and dismiss others' work had to admit that R. Meshulam's book was remarkably useful, filled a void, and gladly accepted by teachers and pupils alike.

When the newly founded seminary for religious teachers in 6 Twarda Street had no lecturers, R. Meshulam stepped into the breach, and his lectures earned him much praise from religious circles. During the elections to the Polish parliament and senate, R. Meshulam strode from one meeting to another delivering rousing speeches. Nor was that all — manifestos were needed, so R. Meshulam was the writer, editor, and proofreader working day and night. After all the workers had left at night, he alone would remain in his office working until morning, bundling together all the notices, parcelling them up, and dispatching them to the mail office. No job was too small or beneath his dignity. Whenever Agudas Yisrael went through a crisis, financial or otherwise, it was R. Meshulam who strengthened himself to save his party.

He was on the Kehillah executive since 1926, and was elected onto the ruling council of the Warsaw Kehillah in 1930, when Aguda won a majority in the democratic elections. R. Meshulam Kaminer worked tirelessly and successfully in the fields of education, religion, social assistance — and also the Burial Department. Unlike other delegates, he put the interest of the Kehillah paramount, above all party interests (even occasionally his own party). During his thirteen years in office, from 1926–39, he was unusually successful in the religious field, and pioneered summer camps for poor pupils in villages outside Warsaw. Later the Kehillah assumed responsibility for this project and expanded it.

Born in Warsaw in 1891, R. Meshulam inherited an apartment block that generated a healthy income. Although he was from a Gerrer family closely related to the Sefas Emes, he was receptive to the views of other Chasidic Rebbes, Lithuanian scholars, and German intellectuals. Unlike members of the German Aguda, R. Meshulam had no interest in ideology — he could get that from the Torah — he was more interested in practical solutions for religious Jewry.

During the German invasion, R. Meshulam received an *esrog* from Eretz Yisrael, before Sukkcos, 1939. Since it was extremely dangerous for crowds to gather, the existence of this *esrog* should have remained secret; but word got out and religious Jews from all over Warsaw began to stream towards R. Meshulam's apartment at 11 Pawia Street. Very few *esrogim* were available then in Warsaw. One had arrived for Rav Shloma David Kahana and was in the possession of Rav Yitzchak Zev Soloveitchik (the Brisker Rav, then temporarily in Warsaw), but not many heard of that *esrog*. However, despite the danger from German patrols, Pawia Street was full of religious Jews anxious to perform the mitzvah. Nor did R. Meshulam take fright, and he bravely helped Jews handle his precious *esrog*.

As part of the Kehillah executive, R. Meshulam became a *Judenrat* official in the Ghetto and was most concerned for the fate of religious Jews, whom he felt were deprived and discriminated against in employment and assistance. His office in the Kehillah and his apartment were crowded with thousands of religious Jews asking for help, advice, support, protection, or recommendations. With enormous devotion, R. Meshulam worked together with Rav Dovid Shapira, Rav Shimshon Stockhammer, and R. Isaak Ber Ackerman, to help his brethren and lighten their burden. Likewise, he was exceedingly active in freeing *rabbanim* and *yeshivah bachurim* from forced labor. In 1942, R. Meshulam, together with Manes Rosenstroich, the religious activist, established a soup kitchen in Gesia Street where a few hundred Talmudic students received hot soup. Surprisingly, R. Meshulam retained some sympathy for artists, writers, and even sculptors (with whom he had cooperated as Burial Department director), who were now deprived and seen as "yesterday's men" by the new masters in the *Judenrat*. Although many of them were far removed from his own religious standpoint and some, especially the writers, had earlier attacked him during pre-War elections, R. Meshulam never bore a grudge and always tried to assist them.

Even in the Ghetto, R. Meshulam was involved with literary endeavors. Sensing that Polish Jewry lacked a Yiddish translation of *Tanach,* he began two textbooks simultanously: on *Chumash* and *Tehillim.* While he spent most of the day in the *Judenrat* trying to help people, he devoted the nights to his Yiddish anthology of the traditional commentaries. External experts, including the Oztrovzer Rebbe, Rav Menachem Ziemba, and Rav Yitzchak Nissenbaum, praised his work.

His writings also had a practical significance — sustaining religious employees of the Kehillah who were not given any obvious work in the *Judenrat.* Each morning, R. Meshulam would appear with large foolscap pages filled with his tiny handwriting, the work of many hours. A team of religious workers (erstwhile writers and *b'nei Torah*) would sit before a bank of Hebrew typewriters in the Archives and Records Office, slowly tap-tapping their way through his script. (The slow typing was not merely due to inexperience — if they finished the task too quickly the Germans might notice they had no work to do and that could be fatal.) Dr. Mordechai Rosner, the writer and scholar, proofread and edited R. Meshulam's work. Within a short time he had completed *Bereishis* and two volumes of *Tehillim.* Unfortunately, the manuscripts were lost with the destruction of the Ghetto.

On *erev* Sukkos 1941, he fell victim to the typhus epidemic and took ill. He passed away at midday, Simchas Torah. News of his demise spread like wildfire through the Ghetto, and though death was by then a frequent visitor in Warsaw, tens of thousands came to his funeral. It became almost a public demonstration on behalf of Religious Jewry and Agudas Yisrael. The cortège included *rabbanim,* Chasidic Rebbes, *yeshivah bachurim,* and pupils of Yesodey Hatorah, and also writers, journalists, and activists from all circles.

In the crowd assembled before his apartment at 11 Pawia

Street, I noticed R. Nechemia Alter (brother of the Gerrer Rebbe), Rav Mendel Alter (of Kalish), the Kozmirer Rebbe (Rav Taub), the Stoliner Rebbe (Rav Perlow), the Novominsker Rebbe (Rav Perlow), and nearly all of Warsaw's *rabbanim*. Eulogies were delivered by *Judenrat* President Adam Czerniakow, Rav Yitzchak Meir Kanal, and R. Alexander Zisha Friedman (on behalf of Agudas Yisrael). Czerniakow was so impressed by R. Friedman's eulogy that he immediately suggested that he assume Kaminer's place in the *Judenrat*, but R. Zisha refused. This memorial service was the last mass funeral in Jewish Warsaw.

RABBI ALEXANDER ZISHA FRIEDMAN

As General Secretary of the Polish Aguda, R. Zisha had a symbiotic relationship with Agudas Yisrael. While he impressed his individual stamp on the movement, his own personality was formed and molded in turn by the Aguda. To understand R. Zisha, one has to understand the Polish Aguda, which had its own characteristic style. Religious Jewry in Germany marched to the banner of "*Torah im Derech Eretz*" as formulated by Rav Samson Raphael Hirsch: strict adherence to *halachah* coupled with a total acclimatization to the language, culture, and lifestyle of Western Europe. By contrast, Poland's Jews dismissed any compartmentalization — pure Torah and tradition had to dominate *all* spheres of life. *Ipso facto,* common Polish behavior

was therefore non-Jewish and to be frowned upon. Agudas Yisrael, as the standard bearer of religious Jews in Poland, sought to stamp a distinctive Torah-oriented imprint on every aspect of communal endeavor, whether it be in business or politics, literature or the Palestine colonies.

R. Alexander Zisha was born in Sochatchov on 11 Av, 1897. His father was a simple *shammas* and his mother supplemented their meager income by trading at fairs. When Zisha was three years old, he knew the whole book of *Bereishis* by heart, and by the time he was nine, his teacher confessed he had no more knowledge to impart and advised his father to enroll him in the local but famous Sochatchov Yeshivah. Fearing envy, his father refused but when he heard that three of the town's wealthy magnates were hiring a choice teacher for their teenage children, Zisha's father asked if Zisha could join them. They were willing to accept the brilliant prodigy for free — or even to pay him! However, Zisha's father insisted on paying his share of the fees, even though this amounted to all his wages. From then on, the family subsisted on the mother's earnings.

Zisha's bar mitzvah *drashah* was a sensation in Sochatchov, with townspeople crowding in at the doors and windows to hear the young prodigy amaze the learned guests with his knowledge and ingenuity. In Sochatchov Yeshivah, his diligence earned the fond regard of the Sochatchover Rebbe, but the family fled to Warsaw at the outbreak of World War I. In Warsaw, the young Zisha continued his learning program and became friendly with the wealthy *lamdan* R. Baruch Gelbart, who offered to support the young student entirely but Zisha was only interested in Torah. Meanwhile, he was tested by the rich Meir Yoel Schwartzstein, who presented him with an expensive watch — a gift he treasured till the end. He also became familiar with Dr. Immanuel Carlebach of Germany who billeted in Warsaw during the occupation and organized lectures in Jewish subjects for the young intelligentsia.

The young Zisha Friedman displayed other talents, too. He was an exemplary *baal korei*; when he led the prayers, his sweet voice pulsated through the congregation. During these War years R. Zisha married. His wife came from a small village near Sochatchov and her father was of simple stock without substantial financial means. Yet her mother was renowned for her outstanding piety and generous to a fault in supporting the needy and *talmidei chachamim* — and this attracted R. Zisha to marry her only daughter.

Joining the Aguda at a young age, R. Zisha naturally gravitated to Zeirei Agudas Yisrael. As a talented speaker, a facile writer, and an excellent organizer, he rose rapidly through the ranks. *Zeirim* were then in their infancy, buzzing with fresh ideas and new recruits. In his capacity as editor of *Digleinu,* R. Zisha attracted many adherents with his polished prose and his innovative thinking. Long after he relinquished his post he was warmly regarded as the father figure of Zeirei Aguda. His speech at the First National Aguda Convention in 1919 enraptured the audience, and he was chosen as secretary of Aguda's central organization, then operating under the name of *Shlome Emune Yisrael*. In 1925 he was promoted to become the General Secretary of the Polish Aguda — a position he held to the last. It was an inspired choice. R. Zisha revitalized the central authority of the organization and instituted regularity. Matters were immediately attended to, letters received a reply, close contact was established with all the branches as well as sister parties abroad. Nothing was too small to merit R. Zisha's meticulous attention, and his bookkeeping was exemplary. None of this deflected him from taking the broad view or transformed him into a party hack. He remained one of the people, with a common touch, yet every action was rooted in *daas Torah*.

R. Zisha shone in yet another public arena when he joined the Warsaw Kehillah Council. Until 1926, the Warsaw Kehillah had traditionally been run solely by the old ruling elite drawn from the famous, the rich, and those from distinguished lineage. No "outsiders" stood a chance. All this changed at the first democratic election in 1926. The Aguda swept the board and formed the largest party with fifteen seats. The list was led by R. Yitzchak Meir Lewin (Aguda president and son-in-law of the Gerrer Rebbe) and a number of rich and powerful tycoons. Despite his growing fame, R. Zisha was sixteenth on the list and so narrowly missed being elected, but he was soon co-opted onto the ruling council.

Officially the Warsaw Kehillah should only have been concerned with internal matters, but it acted in effect as a Jewish mini-parliament with public sittings to discuss international issues. There was intense jockeying for power, since no one party had enough seats to control the Kehillah. Out of the forty-eight seats, the Aguda had fifteen and another two members from the Praga suburb (one held by R. Menachem Ziemba, then an iron merchant, later a Rav in Warsaw). Since R. Itche Meir Lewin took the floor only on special occasions, R. Zisha Friedman was the main speaker for the Aguda bloc. Although he was a young man without wealth or rank, R. Zisha earned the respect of the old ruling class. He was reelected at all subsequent elections and became famous among all circles as one of Poland's foremost speakers.

R. Zisha took public speaking seriously. Not one to rely on his mellifluous voice or agile brain to improvise a dazzling speech on the spur of the moment, he would take time off from his crushing schedule to prepare his address, taking care with both the content and the structure. He had a unique ability to turn a well-worn Chasidic maxim or a well-known passage in the Torah (generally from the weekly *sidra*) into a fresh observation, entirely apt for the occasion. Often his dissertations, with their rhetorical flourishes, were the talk of the town for weeks afterwards.

Much of his time and interest was taken up with education. He was the executive director of "Horev" (comprising the network of the Yesodey Hatorah schools, *Talmud Torahs*, *chadarim* and *yeshivos ketanah),* in charge of *Keren Hatorah* (sponsoring religious education), and an executive member of the Beis Yaakov network and its seminary in Crakow. Furthermore, he established a seminary for religious tutors (in Warsaw at 6 Twarda Street) that raised *melamdim*'s prestige. R. Zisha also had hands-on experience from taking part in the Crakow Beis Yaakov summer sessions out in the country. Likewise, he also wrote a number of primers for teachers and students.

R. Zisha even saw Agudas Yisrael's general activity from a perspective of *chinuch.* When there arose a question of which candidate to put forward as a member of the Sejm (the Polish parliament), he argued that the best candidate would be somebody who looks and dresses as a Rav — with the appropriate clothing and a large skull cap, beard, and side curls — who would have a positive influence on the youth. Indeed, Rav Aaron Lewin of Reischa was chosen to represent the Aguda in the Sejm. R. Zisha was totally involved in all the branches of the Aguda: Zeirei Aguda, Poalei Aguda, B'nos Aguda, and their newspapers.

In fact, he helped set up Poalei Aguda to safeguard the

interests of the religious worker whose rights were not always recognized by some factory owners. Subsequently, Poalei Aguda drifted apart from Agudas Yisrael, yet when they requested *hachshara* to help them prepare for Eretz Yisrael, R. Zisha was most helpful. R. Zisha personally visited Eretz Yisrael in 1934 as part of an Aguda delegation led by R. Itche Meir Lewin and found much to criticize — describing it as "light and darkness operating in confusion" — nonetheless, he felt that there was more light than darkness and encouraged emigration to Eretz Yisrael. R. Zisha's parents emigrated to Jerusalem in their old age and one of his sisters married R. Avraham Mokatowski (better known by his pen name, Eliyahu Ki-Tov). According to R. Avraham Mokatowski, R. Zisha personally wanted to settle in Eretz Yisrael but could not forsake his duties in Poland.

He began his literary activity by editing *Digleinu*, Aguda's first Hebrew periodical, which appeared intermittently from 1919 to 1931; and from 1936 R. Zisha edited the weekly *Darkeinu* — Aguda's official periodical — and also found time to write poetry. Despite these manifold duties, every day R. Zisha spent at least three hours learning Talmud, *halachah* and also *Tanach*. He even managed to help publish volumes of the Sochatchover Rebbe's *sefarim* and also had a booklet of *responsa* between himself and Rav Menachem Ziemba (as well as other *rabbanim*). However, he was most famous for his work on *Chumash* known as *Der Torah Kvall* (now better known as *Meino shel Torah*). In 1939, R. Zisha was about to bring out his own *chiddushim* (novella) to belatedly commemorate his fortieth birthday when the German invasion put an end to his plans.

On November 20, 1939, R. Zisha Friedman was held hostage by the Nazis — together with twenty-one other communal activists — to prevent resistance while establishing a Ghetto (in fact, the Ghetto decree was then postponed). After a week they were freed, and I remember waiting for R. Zisha outside the prison in Danilowiczowska Street. He was freed just before evening and raced home in order to lay *tefillin* before nightfall. Not being allowed *tefillin* in prison had been a great tribulation to him, and he told me he never experienced such joy from *tefillin* as he did on the day he was released from prison.

During the War years, R. Zisha rose to the challenge of the hour and played a leading role in the Ghetto. Soon after the invasion, he established — together with R. Itche Meir Lewin — a large soup kitchen in the Beis Yaakov Hall at 37 Nalewki Street, run by Beis Yaakov teachers. In time, more soup kitchens were set up by the Aguda, where Aguda activists and writers found some employment. These soup kitchens, supported by David Guzik of the Joint and other sources, helped the needy, especially *rabbanim, roshei yeshivah, melamdim,* Torah scholars, and religious activists. As the only religious representative on the Joint, R. Zisha continually demanded with utmost vehemence that the religious Jews should receive better treatment, as they suffered most from the Germans and were unfairly estranged from both the *Judenrat* and Joint.

Later R. Zisha utilized the Joint to set up an elaborate network of religious education, officially masquerading as soup kitchens or kindergartens. When the Nazis began seizing and torturing religious teachers, he managed to "legalize" some of these clandestine institutions under the auspices of TOZ (the Society for the Preservation of Health). In 1941, the ZSS (Jewish Communal Self-Help) began operating, and R. Zisha became one of the directors, representing Agudas Yisrael. Likewise, R. Zisha occupied a central position on the *Ezras Torah*, supporting yeshivos and Talmudic scholars in the Ghetto. When

Judenrat President Adam Czerniakow finally obtained German permission to reopen the schools, R. Zisha Friedman joined his committee representing Horev, and many of the religious schools were officially recognized.

Actually, Czerniakow had frequently invited R. Zisha Friedman to become a *Judenrat* member, but he always refused (even though members were paid a salary of one thousand zloty a month and were relatively free from forced labor and other German persecutions). In February 1942, Czerniakow confessed to R. Zisha that he had decided there was no point to Jewish survival in the Ghetto unless it had some Jewish background and faith. He asked him to help infuse religious input and promised his support. R. Zisha readily agreed to establish the *Judenrat*'s religious committee, and this was the only committee to represent all the various political parties. R. Zisha presided over this committee, and it included David Guzik (Joint), R. Leib Scharanski and Yehudah Yefes (representing Mizrachi), Ackerman and Avraham Mordechai Rogovy (Aguda), R. Shimshon Stockhammer and Rav David Shapira (both members of the *Judenrat*), and myself (representing the *Judenrat*'s Religious Department).

The committee proposed making Saturday the compulsory day of rest. There was much Shabbos desecration in the Ghetto, and for no reason since all Ghetto inhabitants were Jewish. Yet the official day of rest remained Sunday as it had been before the War. Nominally, the *Judenrat* president had the powers and position of a town mayor, and the *Judenrat* immediately issued a decree, with German authority, that all rules and restrictions previously applicable for Sunday now applied to Saturday. This brought about a farcical situation. The people detailed to enforce these new rules were the *Judenrat*'s Jewish police, generally assimilationists and irreligious, and their reports about Shabbos desecrations were written down, there and then, on Shabbos! To prevent this, R. Zisha set up a religious group of "*Shomrei Shabbos*," as it was known, as an adjunct of the tenement block committees. This religious committee also began numerous religious activities, particularly in the spreading of Torah.

In the summer of 1942, when the mass deportations began, the Joint was closed down and R. Zisha was thereby left without any financial support for himself or his activities. The *Judenrat* offered him a position in the archives — where many intellectuals had sought sanctuary — but he again refused, preferring work in a factory or workshop. Eventually, after much pleading and persuasion, he was accepted as a shoemaker in the large workshop of Shultz at 44–46 Nowolipie Street, where Avraham Hendel was the foreman. R. Zisha moved to the apartment of R. Yosef Krill at 59 Nowolipie Street and labored in shoemaking for twelve-hour shifts, either all day or all night.

In that factory many *rabbanim*, Chasidic Rebbes, and scholars also "worked." I once visited there and found him among exalted company: R. Moshe Betzalel (brother of the Gerrer Rebbe), R. David Halberstadt (Rav of Sosnowiec), Rav Avraham Alter (Rav of Pawianitz), Rav Klonimus Shapira (Piasnow Rebbe and author of *Chovos Hatalmidim*). R. Zisha was taking old shoes to pieces, removing the nails — and learning *mishnayos* by heart. Every so often he would steal a glance at a *mishnayos* (*Horev* edition) balanced on his knees below the work table. R. Zisha gave a *mishnayos shiur* at Shultz; when he returned home he would lecture on Talmud in depth for younger students as well as on *Yirmiyahu*. All week, R. Zisha worked hard at the workshop, but Shabbos was a different story. (Officially we were duty bound to toil on Saturdays, too, yet the religious somehow avoided it.) He wore the traditional Chasidic garb for Shabbos and would lead the prayers, revealing himself as a wonderful *baal tefillah* (as a *baal korei* he had always been famous). By becoming a partner in a bakery, he obtained *challos* and also prepared the special Shabbos food. Eventually R. Avraham Hendel invited R. Zisha to eat with him on Shabbos and *Yomim Tovim.*

By that time, R. Zisha was the sole survivor of his family — his parents-in-law, wife, and only daughter, born after eighteen years of marriage — had all been deported. His thirteen-year-old daughter was very intelligent, and R. Zisha showed me a poem of eulogy that he had written on his only child. In it he wrote that he did not know what to pray for — an early homecoming or an easy death, without suffering. I tried to persuade him to leave the workshop and come to the *Judenrat* archives, but he felt safer at the workshops. Between October 1942 and January 1943, the Joint clandestinely started again, and R. Zisha Friedman rejoined to assist religious Jews.

Until April 1943, I was in constant contact with R. Zisha Friedman, who was a member of the Resistance Committee planning the Uprising. Earlier, in March, he had received a Paraguayan passport from R. Chaim Yisrael Eiss in Zurich, Switzerland, but he did not show it to the German authorities and it was too late to save him. For a short time he sought refuge with the family of Hendel before being deported to the labor camp of Trawinki near Lublin, together with Senator Yaakov Trokenheim. From there I still received news until September 1943, and he continued to help and support others in Trawinki. During one of the "selections" he was deported, and all trace of R. Zisha Friedman was lost (the Trawinki Camp itself was exterminated in November, 1943). There had been some attempts to save him but they failed; I tried to alert the Swiss activists with equal lack of success.

RAV MENACHEM ZIEMBA

Throughout the many vicissitudes of the Ghetto, Rav Ziemba's apartment remained a source of light, warmth, and encouragement. He had to move house five times — either because of the contraction of the Ghetto or for his own safety — but always his home was full of people seeking advice or reassurance. They were not disappointed. The wisdom and unshakeable trust of generations was distilled in Rav Menachem's personality; with his genius, he had little difficulty in finding the apt phrase suitable for each petitioner and every occasion. All his sentiments were rooted in Torah sources and reflected the eternal truths. He combined the ice-cold logic and clear vision of the Lithuanian *lamdan* with all the fire and warmth of Polish Chasidim, fusing the *mussar* and perspective of Rebbe Yisrael Salanter with the sharpness of Kotzk *chasidus.* The Nazi terror did not break him; he remained a beacon of light amid the buffeting storm.

Even during those terrible months of July–September 1942, when the deportations accelerated to a frenetic pace, he never ceased his continual Torah study nor stopped producing new Torah insights. During our oppressive plight, he drew his strength and inspiration from the Torah.

I once discovered a thick bundle of his writings (I was familiar with his handwriting). It had a whole section devoted to the subject of *Kiddush Hashem* (sacrificing one's life for Hashem) based mainly on the Rambam, though he quoted other early and later authorities, too. At the beginning it read:

> *What I formulated with Hashem's help during these days of wrath. On the day they took away my beloved wife, who devoted her soul to educate our children in the ways of Torah and Fear of Hashem, thereby allowing them and myself to diligently study the Holy Torah....*

I remember the Sukkos of 1942. Under extreme danger, Rav Menachem broke open the roof of his apartment to construct a primitive *sukkah.* True, it was a tiny *sukkah*, but thousands of people passed through. On *erev* Sukkos I received three *esrogim* from Switzerland. Naturally, I brought them all straight to Rav Menachem Ziemba. (Later I sent one to the workshop of R. Avraham Hendel and the third to R. Berel Gefen at the workshop on 64 Niska Street.) Rav Menachem displayed great delight with his *esrog* and he was joined for the *tefillos* by the two remaining *rabbanim*, Rav Shimshon Stockhammer and Rav Dovid Shapira. Immediately, the news spread, hundreds of Chasidim and *yeshivah bachurim* crawled through attics, tunnels, and cellars to perform the precious mitzvah.

Unfortunately, there were repercussions. In Rav Menachem's apartment block lived a few officers of the Jewish police. They were furious at the gathering of illegals and "*vilder*" ("wild ones" as they termed all those without German numbers or documents — usually young, religious Jews who remained underground to observe *kashrus* and Shabbos without interference). Most of the "masters" of the Jewish police were antisemitic assimilationists, and they arrested Rav Menachem Ziemba, R. Yehudah Leib Orlean, A. G. Friedenson, and N. Warsabiak, among others, and locked them up in the Jewish prison. They were released only after A. G. Ackerman approached the *Judenrat* president personally. (Naturally, this incident inflamed the hatred for the Jewish Police prevailing in the Ghetto.) As a punishment, Rav Ziemba had to leave his apartment in Muranow Street and move to 37 Nalewki Street.

I remember an earlier committee meeting for *Ezras Torah*, on the eighth day of Chanukah, 1942. Besides Rav Ziemba, there was R. Stockhammer, R. Shapira, R. Yosef Konigsberg, Senator Yaakov Trokenheim, R. Y. L. Orlean, Josef Scharanski, A. G. Friedenson, and Ackerman. Rav Menachem spoke on the subject of the solitary flask of oil — if something survives with its purity intact, it can light the whole world. Then the meeting got down to practicalities. During the lull in the deportations, at the beginning of winter, many Jews had arrived in Warsaw from the nearby towns that had recently become "*Judenrein*." These included many *yeshivah bachurim* and a few *rabbanim*. R. Yosef Konigsberg with his customary vigor began organizing *shiurim* for them. These soon developed into full-fledged yeshivos — thanks to Rav Leib Landau (formally of Kolbeil) and Rav Arieh Frumer (formally of Kozieglow), both of them previously *roshei yeshivah* of Lublin. The *Ezras Torah* committee was now set up to supply the yeshivos with food and other necessities. Most Jews responded generously to the appeal to help these yeshivos — and not only religious Jews. All Ghetto Jews recognized the importance of the underground yeshivos. The directors of the

Joint, Gitterman and Guzik, donated money and Abraham Gefner, director of the *Judenrat* Supply Department, offered food at cost price.

Obviously Rav Menachem Ziemba was the guiding spirit behind all these projects. Jews hid in "bunkers" and bolt-holes, in cellars and attics, in cold and fear, and learned Torah in depth and with dedication. He visited the clandestine yeshivos in Nalewki, Nowolipie, and Mila Streets — testing the *yeshivah bachurim* and spurring them to greater achievements. In the Mila Street Yeshivah, they would learn right through the night. Outside panic reigned, no one knew what the unnatural lulls signified, everybody feared what the morrow would bring. The *gedolei Torah*, Rav Menachem Ziemba and his *talmidim*, ignored this bitter reality to soar to the spiritual heights of Torah and *yiras Hashem*.

Until April 1943, I was in constant contact with Rav Menachem Ziemba, and for a short time he was officially a clerk in my Records and Archives Office. By January 1943, when it was obvious that the enemy intended to destroy all Jews — I, together with R. Zisha Friedman and Simcha Rapaport, began pleading with the Swiss activists to provide South American passports. We wrote to R. Chaim Yisrael Eiss, Rabbi Dr. Saul Weingort, and others. (Likewise, from Warsaw and later from Vittel, I personally alerted Dr. Abraham Silberstein in Switzerland on behalf of Dr. Stein and Dr. Schipper.) After a long delay, amid fear and trepidation, those passports finally began to arrive, though very slowly.

When Rav Menachem Ziemba received his passport, he began to consider his options carefully. What, he pondered, would be the fate of his manuscripts? Besides, was it permissible to surrender oneself to the enemy — to enter the Pawiak Prison for onward transfer to a camp for "foreigners"? Yet his main concern remained his precious manuscripts: that his lifetime's work not be wasted. I offered to bury them in the courtyard of the Archives Department (as I had already done for Professor Balaban's manuscript "Bibliography of Polish Jewish History"). Sadly, Rav Menachem Ziemba still hoped and hesitated until it was too late — until the Uprising erupted and Rav Menachem fell prey to the German murderers.

As a consequence, we lost one of the preeminent minds of Polish Jewry. The overwhelming pain still hurts, particularly when we are aware that it would have been possible to rescue many individuals. Unfortunately, our fate was too often entrusted to ineffectual and irresponsible hands who missed many openings. Others acted unilaterally and bungled opportunities, so the lives of great men who could have been saved were squandered.

Even when South American passports were acquired, our lives still hung in the balance, as seen from the sad case of Rabbi Chaim Leibush Berglas (with whom I shared a cell in Pawiak Prison). He was the son-in-law of Rav Shabsi Rapaport, the famous Rav of Pinchow. The Rapaport family were saved from deportation at the last minute when Rav Rapaport's nephew, Rabbi Dr. Saul Weingort, a *rosh yeshivah* in Montreux, Switzerland, sent them Paraguayan passports. As "foreign citizens" they were transferred to Pawiak Prison and — after several weeks — onwards to the detention camp for foreigners in Vittel (in Alsace, France), that consisted of several hotels surrounded by barbed wire. Six thousand prisoners were detained here, mainly from England, USA, and South America, including 173 Jewish holders of Central and South American passports.

Life for these detainees was relatively painless. Food was

supplied by the American Red Cross (free from German tampering), and the Jewish prisoners enjoyed a full religious life with public prayer and *shiurim* — one study group completed Talmud and celebrated with a *siyum*! Also, they were allowed to communicate with the free world by mail, an opportunity they utilized to hint at the mass murder of European Jewry. The Germans were not overly concerned that most of these Jews might not have been foreign citizens. They were content to keep up the pretence in order to exchange them for thousands of German citizens imprisoned in South America as spies, agents, and Nazi propagandists.

After eighteen months' negotiation, it transpired that the South American governments would not recognize these passports, and the Red Cross hastened to inform the German foreign office. All Polish Jewish "foreign" passport holders were rounded up and imprisoned in one Vittel hotel where they were given one month to contact relatives abroad. Desperate pleas to save them and their families were dispatched around the world and eventually, after much effort and lobbying by prominent personages, the US State Department agreed to pressure the South American governments to reconsider. By the time recognition finally came through, it was already too late. These Jews were deported immediately after Pesach 1944 to Drancy Concentration Camp near Paris and on Shavuos to Auschwitz. Rabbi Chaim Leibush Berglas, a brilliant speaker and a right-hand disciple of Rav Meir Shapira, was murdered at the age of twenty-nine together with the Rapaport family.

RAV YITZCHAK MEIR KANAL

Rav Kanal's long life spanned many of the recent vicissitudes beset Polish Jewry. He was born in Warsaw in 1862, the year of the Poles' revolt against the Russian occupation (in which many patriotic Jews fought with the encouragement of Warsaw Rav, R. Dov Berish Meisels). As a young boy he imbibed that heady atmosphere. During 1905, he took a wider interest in world affairs, when many Polish Jews were conscripted and despatched to the front to fight in the Russo-Japanese war. The last years of his life were overshadowed by the German pillage of Poland.

As a young devoted Gerrer Chasid of the Sefas Emes, his elderly mentors were Chasidim of the Kotzker Rebbe and first Gerrer Rebbe (the Chidushei Harim). After serving as Rav of Blashki, a small *kehillah* near Warsaw, he was appointed a member of the Warsaw Rabbinate, the capital of Polish Jewry in 1923. Rav Y. M. Kanal soon showed himself as a man of action, possessing enormous reserves of energy and initiative, generating much excitement in rabbinical affairs; and to Rav Kanal's mindset, there was very little outside the ambit of rabbinical affairs — all mundane matters or economic activity usually acquired a religious angle. Ostensibly the State restrictions on Sunday trading were economic in scope but they had inevitable repercussions on Shabbos observance. Likewise, the anti-*shechitah* campaign in the Polish Sejm (parliament) during the 1930s may have been motivated by spite and antisemitism, but it had a direct bearing on *kashrus.*

By law, each rabbi was responsible for registering births, deaths, and marriages within his respective district as well as dealing with the regular queries in Jewish law and practice. Rav Y. M. Kanal, who lived at 24 Twarda Street, was therefore officially in charge of the Grzybowska district, where all the Kehillah offices, the headquarters of most organizations including the Warsaw Rabbinate, and the international Agudas Harabbanim were situated. Living at the center of Jewish communal life, and possessing an energetic personality, he was rapidly propelled to the forefront of every communal enterprise throughout Poland.

Nominally, Rav Y. M. Kanal was only the vice president of Agudas Harabbanim, but since he resided in the capital whereas the presidency lived in the provinces (R. Mendel Alter officiated in Kalish, as had R. Yechezkel Lipshitz before him, and R. Aaron Lewin was the Rav in Reischa), this effectively left him in charge of day to day affairs. Moreover, Rav Kanal was too energetic a person to be restricted by the rules of protocol. Officially every member of the Warsaw Rabbinate had the right to attend Kehillah meetings only for a month each, on a rota basis, yet Rav Kanal's interest in Kehillah affairs remained constant and extensive, and he achieved significant success in the fields of *kashrus,* Shabbos, and other religious issues.

Because of his boundless love for every individual, he

would turn no one away, and he personally visited the various officials to importune them for help. Indeed, his character was exemplary. He welcomed all positive suggestions and accepted help from any quarter. He had a remarkable ability to heal divisions and repair splits. He did not seek the limelight and was equally happy to delegate or to operate as part of a team. Although a loyal Agudist, he was not governed by narrow party considerations and had warm regard for many in other circles and affiliations. In return, Rav Kanal was popular at home (no mean feat in the pre-War Kehillah of approximately 370,000 citizens) and abroad, in Poland and Lithuania. He remained in close contact with the Gerrer Rebbe and Rav Chaim Ozer Grodzenski of Vilna, and they had the final say in all his decisions.

In the decade-long campaign to safeguard *shechitah* from the machinations of the antisemitic Polish parliament, he was the linchpin; his expertise in *halachah* matching his flair for organization, he pulled together the Jewish senators, parliamentarians, and all the various Jewish institutions and associations. When the Jews finally declared a national strike against the decree, Rav Kanal was among the most actively involved, coordinating the campaign with everyone of influence. After the decree was temporarily suspended and complicated procedures had to be introduced into the processing of kosher meat, it was again Rav Kanal who led in coping with the halachic and practical implications.

His enthusiasm and energy did not flag with old age, though he delegated much of his parochial duties to his grandson by marriage, Rav Gedalia Rubenstien. When the Germans invaded Poland, Warsaw was subjected to heavy aerial bombardment, and the Nazi pilots targeted Jewish areas. Rav

Kanal's apartment went up in flames, killing members of his family, destroying all his possessions, including his extensive library of rabbinical literature. After Warsaw's capture, Rav Kanal fell prey to the typhus epidemic and was bedridden for many weeks. Yet his morale was undaunted, his willingness to help others undiminished. Even before he fully recovered, he was already a source of comfort and encouragement. At that time, when the Germans were still drunk from their lightning victory over the Poles, it was dangerous for any Jew to venture out onto the street. Yet Rav Kanal regularly visited the offices of the Kehillah and other welfare organizations — particularly on behalf of provincial *rabbanim* who had sought refuge in Warsaw. He also supported the yeshivos functioning underground, working hand in glove with Rav Dovid Shapira and Rav Shimshon Stockhammer.

When the deportations began, Rav Kanal had no illusions. He realized the Germans were not taking people away for slave labor — what labor could they expect from a man of his age? He decided that when the Nazis ordered him out of his home he would resist. Whatever the consequences, at least he would receive a Jewish burial. That was precisely what transpired. For refusing to leave his beloved Warsaw, he was summarily shot and was later buried at the Warsaw cemetery. He was eighty at the time but retained the vigor and capability of men half his age.

RAV SHIMSHON STOCKHAMMER

Rav Stockhammer was a man of many talents. He was born in 1899 in Sokal, Galicia where his father, a Belzer Chasid, was a *talmid chacham* and ritual slaughterer. The young Shimshon learned at the local Belzer *kloise* (as the

Galician *shtiebl* was often known) and delivered an astounding *drashah* at his bar mitzvah on the brink of the First World War. Later he visited the Belzer Rebbe a number of times, and at the age of twenty he received rabbinical ordination from prominent rabbis. In 1925, he married into a rabbinical family on the outskirts of Warsaw and drew close to Rav Menachem Ziemba, who was then ostensibly an iron merchant in Praga, the Warsaw suburb. Since R. Shimshon's wife worked in the Warsaw Kehillah, this enabled him to continue his learning schedule undisturbed.

In common with many of Galicia's younger generation, R. Shimshon was a facile writer both in Yiddish and Hebrew and authored numerous articles in Aguda's daily and weekly newspapers. When the *Togblatt* reappeared in 1929, Rav Stockhammer had a regular column every weekend, generally concentrating on *kashrus* or Shabbos observance. His position on the paper was enhanced in 1933 when a controversial article in the *Togblatt* raised the ire of many readers, and R. Stockhammer was delegated to ensure the quality of future issues. Rav Stockhammer's own articles were clear and succinct and fired with all the enthusiasm of his Chasidic soul. He always dealt with the issue at hand, avoiding all personal attacks, and his authoritative writings earned his readers' respect due to his intimate knowledge of rabbinical affairs. In effect, Rav Stockhammer acted as a media

spokesman for rabbinic circles and he was particularly close with the Agudas Harabbanim.

Since 1878, with the passing of Rav Yaakov Gesundheit, Warsaw had not had a Chief Rabbi. Only seven *rabbanim* operated within the Warsaw Rabbinate, ostensibly catering for the largest European *kehillah*, estimated at 370,000 souls. In 1934, two Kehillah leaders, Eliyahu Mazur and Yaakov Trokenheim (both representing Aguda) tried to change this. At first they chose R. Aaron Lewin (Rav of Reischa and Sejm member) as Warsaw's new Chief Rabbi. When that plan ran into technical difficulties they decided to at least enlarge the Rabbinate. After much political bargaining and jockeying between the parties, a number of *rabbanim* were appointed, including Rav Shimshon Stockhammer. Rav Stockhammer took his new appointment seriously, continuing his lifelong interest in *kashrus* and Shabbos observance. His talents as a publicist were given full play, and many Kehillah proclamations and public notices sprang from his fertile pen. Unusually for a Belzer Chasid, he rose to the higher echelons of the Polish Aguda and took an active part in its meetings.

By the outbreak of the War, he was a much respected personality, brimming full with energy and ambitions. When the Germans captured Warsaw in October 1939, Rav Stockhammer was residing in the Praga suburb. Later, after some *Judenrat* members escaped to America and Eretz Yisrael, Rav Stockhammer was co-opted onto the *Judenrat*.

Working together with R. Meshulam Kaminer, R. Isaak-Ber Ackerman, and Rav Dovid Shapira, he displayed hitherto unknown reserves of dedication as one of the few religious voices on the *Judenrat* trying to protect the Orthodox masses. The devout Jews were the hardest hit in the Ghetto. Their distinctive appearance, their lifestyle, and mitzvah observance made them an obvious target for the accursed Germans. Communal organizations also discriminated by employing very few Orthodox Jews among the thousands working for them; the religious did not enjoy the relative safety afforded by *Judenrat* or Joint employment and received little financial support. Since Rav Stockhammer wielded far less influence than the assimilationists who filled the most important posts, he required strenuous effort to help those in need — yet he turned no one away.

On 4 Av 1942, before the deportations began, he was among those temporarily incarcerated in the Pawiak Prison as hostage against any resistance. During the deportations, Rav Stockhammer was profoundly depressed and had no illusions about the deportees' fate. Together with his family, he went into hiding to evade deportation but was captured during Shevat 1943 (his wife and four children had already been murdered by the Germans) and deported to the Poniatowa death camp near Lublin.

From Poniatowa he was transferred to Flosenberg concentration camp in Bavaria, Germany, where he survived for approximately twelve months. Rav Stockhammer was a tremendous source of encouragement to his fellow inmates. He never complained about the backbreaking work nor referred to the destruction of his family. He zealously kept *mitzvos* under unspeakable conditions. During Pesach 1945, he subsisted on water alone for eight days rather than eat *chametz*. Somehow he managed to keep up with the slave labor during Pesach despite his prolonged weakness and previous emaciation. When fellow camp inmates remonstrated that he ought not endanger his life by abstaining from the daily diet of bread, he replied that at least one Jew out of the 2,500 imprisoned in Flosenberg ought to observe Pesach, and he was glad to be that lone Jew!

A month after Pesach, at the approach of the Russian army, the Germans moved their Jewish prisoners westward. The train they were traveling on was frequently bombed by allied aircraft, and Rav Stockhammer was critically wounded by a piece of shrapnel. He never recovered and died on 13 Iyar 1945, three days before liberation.

RAV MENACHEM MENDEL ALTER

One of the foremost leaders of religious Jewry before the War, Rav Alter was a formidable personality — an original genius who never hesitated to speak his mind or act as he saw fit whatever the consequences. As the youngest son of the Sefas Emes and the brother of the current Gerrer Rebbe (R. Avraham Mordechai — the Imrei Emes), he was accustomed to authority, and the mantle of leadership rested easily on his shoulders. Blessed with penetrating insight, a sharp tongue and a sharper brain, he was not one to automatically conform to the general consensus nor follow the common path trodden by others. Born in 1877, as an integral part of the aristocratic family of Gur, he grew up at the center of religious influence and power. He rapidly matured an adult understanding of world affairs and would discuss the problems of the day on an equal footing with venerable

rabbanim and Kotzker Chasidim over three times his age.

He married the Radomsker Rebbe's daughter and they were blessed with a son, but when his young wife died, he married into the rich Prives family of Warsaw. R. Mendel remained in Gur and established a yeshivah, Darkei Noam, where the stress was on diligence rather than studying Chasidic works. In an unusual development, he invited guest *roshei yeshivah* from among the foremost *gedolei Torah* in Poland to deliver *shiurim* for a month at a time. (This yeshivah closed down when R. Mendel left Gur at the onset of the First World War, and as he did not prepare any of his regular *shiurim* for publication — nor any of his voluminous notes from his vast library — everything was lost during the War.)

R. Mendel was concurrently involved in another unusual enterprise — newspapers. There were then Hebrew and Yiddish weeklies and dailies, all fiercely competitive, but united in their antagonism to religion and the devout. Not one to passively accept the status quo, he set up two daily newspapers simultaneously: *Hakol* in Hebrew and *Dos Warsawer Togblatt* in Yiddish (popularly known as "*die kopeke zeitung*" because of its cover price). Since this was a radical departure in Poland, it was difficult to procure competent writers or a ready readership among the religious public. While religious Jews were employed as editors, more often than not the staff writers were irreligious and their work had to be continually checked for content. Despite the large sums raised by R. Mendel from rich admirers, these newspapers soon ran into financial difficulties, and they limped from crisis to crisis until finally folding in 1913. Yet they succeeded in paving the way for the amazing blossoming of Orthodox writing and literature after the First World War.

During the War, R. Mendel, together with the Gerrer Rebbe

and his family, moved temporarily from Gur to Warsaw. R. Mendel then had no plans to devote his vast talents to the rabbinate, and as a scion of the wealthy Prives family, invested his considerable wealth into stocks and shares. Unfortunately, one of his main investments, the Warsaw-Gur railway, was owned by Polish antisemites who conspired to force the price down. To protect him from bankruptcy, Jews and particularly the Gerrer Chasidim, hitherto the main commuters on the railway, retaliated with a boycott until the Poles agreed to repay R. Mendel his original investment. Following R. Mendel's unsuccessful business ventures, in 1921 he was more amenable to accept the position of Chief Rabbi in Pawianitz, near Lodz.

After extensive enquiries in Pawianitz, R. Mendel instituted *takkanos* in *kashrus* and laid down strict rules against waste or luxuries, and also delineated how many guests were allowed for a wedding, engagement, bar mitzvah, or a *bris*. Despite his total involvement in Torah study and *shiurim*, his quick, brilliant mind and warm smile made him popular throughout his *kehillah*, and he was asked to give advice and even blessings. (While not officially a Chasidic Rebbe, he was not averse to accepting *kvitlech* or bestowing *berachos*, as befits the son of the Sefas Emes and brother of the current Gerrer Rebbe.) The fact that R. Mendel was a man of independent means beholden to no one also earned him much respect.

His net was cast wider than Pawianitz. Thousands of Gerrer Chasidim — rich and famous, factory owners and businessmen, Torah scholars and activists — resided in the nearby town of Lodz, the textile capital of Poland and second only in importance to Warsaw itself. Since they all admired R. Mendel and obeyed his summons, this naturally extended R. Mendel's sphere of influence. As a member of the powerful Prives clan, R.

Mendel was also privy to the inner councils of the Warsaw Kehillah.

In 1934, R. Mendel Alter was chosen to succeed Rav Yechezkel Lipshitz as Rav of Kalish. In recognition of Kalish's importance, the previous Rav had been the president of the Polish Agudas Harabbanim and soon R. Mendel himself was chosen as president of the Agudas Harabbanim's *Vaad Hapoel* under the general presidency of Rav Aaron Lewin of Reischa. The Agudas Harabbanim was then one of the foremost organizations in Poland and the only confederation to represent *rabbanim*, uniting the Chasidim under the Gerrer Rebbe and the traditional *misnagdim* under the Chafetz Chaim and Rav Chaim Ozer Grodzenski.

Both in his own right and as brother of the Gerrer Rebbe, Rav Mendel Alter now wielded enormous influence. Despite his robust individual stance inviting much friction, such was his wit and sagacity, his personal charm and charisma, that all antagonism dissipated after meeting R. Mendel face to face. In any event, most other Chasidim had such respect for Gur, the dominant *chasidus* in Poland, that they dropped any private misgivings they might have had. *Rabbanim* from Lithuania were less forgiving. After a number of private disagreements, many of them withdrew from the organization. Nevertheless, in face of constant antisemitic attacks during the 1930s, the Agudas Harabbanim remained the united voice of Orthodox Jewry. In the campaign to safeguard *shechitah,* the Agudas Harabbanim headed the wall to wall coalition of Jewish organizations from the Agudas Yisrael through the many facets of Zionists to the Bund — and Rav Mendel Alter remained at its center.

He was also a member of Agudas Yisrael's *Moetzes Gedolei Hatorah* and attended every *Knessia Gedolah.* Whenever he spoke at Aguda conventions, he was a sensation. Speaking without notes and apparently unprepared, relying on his phenomenal memory and vast knowledge, he would gush forth a torrent of ideas and analysis which kept his audience spellbound. He traveled regularly to the Gerrer Rebbe (his brother), as any humble Chasid, yet he retained close links with many other Chasidim and Rebbes as well as a large network of activists and admirers.

At the outbreak of the War he left Kalish to seek sanctuary in Warsaw. He lived on the fourth story of 11 Pawia Street and spent his days and nights in his small room learning Torah. Every so often he was visited by Gerrer Chasidim seeking encouragement, and R. Meshulam Kaminer, the activist and *Judenrat* representative, who lived in the same tenement, would regularly visit him to discuss the dire situation. Rav Mendel was seized and deported to Treblinka together with most of his extended family (who lived in the same apartment block) on August 7, 1942.

RABBI YEHUDAH LEIB ORLEAN

For such an outstanding pedagogue, R. Yehudah Leib had a deceptively ordinary upbringing. He received no secular schooling, never benefited from a teacher training course, and certainly never set foot inside a university. In fact, he never even studied at a yeshivah. Yet his wide knowledge and subsequent authority over girls' education was to become quite phenomenal.

Born in Warsaw on February 21, 1900 to a typical Chasidic Gerrer family, his father was a wealthy but learned businessman. As a boy he was sent to the best *cheder* available, and later

he learned in the local *beis midrash* as was fairly usual in Poland. Nor was this *shul* at 5 Zamenhof Street the most renowned Gerrer *shtiebl* — most of the sharpest witted Chasidim would study together either at 19 Nalewki Street or 18 Twarda Street. After marriage, he went into business, though he continued to spend a few hours learning at his *shtiebl* and commuted regularly to Gur for *Yomim Tovim.* On the face of it, R. Yehudah Leib Orlean appeared to be a typical young Chasid.

The only remarkable feature was R. Yehudah Leib's resolve to delve behind accepted teachings and discover the sources underpinning Jewish faith and perspective. He devoted much time to the study of *Moreh Nevuchim* (*Guide to the Perplexed*) and knew the Rambam's *Shemonah Perakim* by heart. When Agudas Yisrael was finally established in 1918 at the urging of Dr. Immanuel Carlebach and Dr. Pinchas Kohn, many Polish activists began to absorb the organizational skills of German Jewry. R. Yehudah Leib, however, also mastered the classical German writings of Rav Samson Raphael Hirsch, Dr. Isaac Breuer, R. Yaakov Rosenheim, and Dr. Nathan Birnbaum (of whom he eventually became a close disciple and leading exponent). As R. Yehudah Leib's interest broadened, he began reading up psychology and pedagogy, carefully filtering these secular studies through the screen of Torah knowledge.

Soon he became a regular speaker at the growing network of Aguda branches, sharing with audiences his analytical approach and original ideology. Each lecture was painstakingly prepared, advancing to its conclusion through a series of logical steps, though he allowed leeway for listeners to form their own opinions. Concurrently, he authored a series of polished articles that were as thought provoking in their originality as they were controversial in their resolution. For, belying his quiet exterior, R. Yehudah Leib had become a radical in social affairs.

The Jewish working class were visibly aggrieved with the rich factory owners — many of them from renowned religious lineage. Most of their factories, particularly in Lodz, were legally sold to non-Jewish owners, thus allowing them to stay open throughout Shabbos. Consequently, they usually employed no Jewish workers — despite rampant unemployment — and those that were employed felt unfairly treated. Young Aguda activists publicly castigated the wealthy industrialists for their anti-social and ultimately irreligious behavior towards the Jewish working class. Eventually, they formed a political party — Poalei Agudas Yisrael — with Aguda approval, to represent the religious workers.

Surprisingly, many of the founders were not workers but intellectuals, and R. Yehudah Leib was among their leaders. In 1929 he published a famous pamphlet, *Zum Zatte und Hungrige* ("To the Satisfied and Hungry"), coolly analyzing these social dilemmas and demanding urgent solutions. Later, in 1931, he composed another famous pamphlet, *Der Farshvundene Gan Eden* ("The Lost Garden of Eden"), lambasting excessive luxurious lifestyles and urging self-restraint and moderation more in keeping with the current economic climate. Meanwhile, R. Yehudah Leib had abandoned the business world to enter the realm of education, and he became the director of Beis Yaakov Girls' School at 37 Twarda Street, developing it into an outstanding institution. That brought him to the notice of the Beis Yaakov directorate, and after the void left by the untimely death of Sarah Schenirer, R. Yehudah Leib was chosen in 1935 to head the Beis Yaakov Seminary in Cracow (after a lengthy correspondence between R. Yaakov Rosenheim and the Gerrer Rebbe as to the suitability of a male candidate).

He grew into the role, relinquishing his political activity, his pamphlets and speeches, to throw himself, body and soul, into furthering the cause of girls' religious education. By 1937, the Beis Yaakov network had grown to 250 schools catering to 38,000 pupils, and R. Yehudah Leib ensured that physical growth was more than matched by spiritual development. His lectures were exemplary masterpieces, painstakingly prepared and thoughtfully delivered. Eschewing dazzling flights of fancy and flashy turns of phrase, he displayed due regard for the intelligence and grasp of his female listeners. This respect was reciprocated, and past pupils would consult him at every step of their life or career.

When the War broke out on September 1, 1939, the Seminary was on vacation in the country and it never reopened. R. Yehudah Leib was left without position or employment. He contemplated returning to the business world to support his growing family of six young children, but the Boyaner Rebbe, Rebbe Moshe'nu Friedman, who lived in Cracow and had been closely consulted on Seminary affairs, would not hear of it. "During our precarious situation," insisted the Boyaner Rebbe, "R. Yehudah Leib's talents at the forefront of *chinuch* are indispensable." The Rebbe established a support fund for R. Yehudah Leib and eventually obtained finance from the Joint.

Resuming his lectures on *Tanach* and Judaism, R. Yehudah Leib renewed his many contacts, despatching circulars and personal letters to the Beis Yaakov teachers in the field. Working together with former activists and the young *tzadik* R. Yosef Begun, a clandestine Beis Yaakov network was reestablished under German occupation. Due to the enormous suffering, much of the network was devoted to providing food, supporting soup kitchens, and running children's centers, since R. Yehudah Leib demanded from his disciples a total empathy with the national calamity.

In January 1940, the Germans searched his apartment in Cracow, and though they found no incriminating evidence, they beat him savagely. As soon as he recovered, he left his family to seek sanctuary in Warsaw, where he had many former students and could resume his lectures on *Mishlei, Nach, Mussar,* and Judaism. His pupils (among them Mrs. Gutta Eizensweig, the daughter of Rav Yisrael Alter — later Gerrer Rebbe of Jerusalem) demanded that his *shiurim* illuminate their present situation and deal with the eternal question: why do the pious suffer?

"Mr. Orlean," as they called their beloved teacher, could offer them no easy answers; rather, he harnessed his formidable intellectual prowess to analyze their predicament and attempt, together with his pupils, to arrive at the truth. These profound *shiurim* became so popular with the Beis Yaakov and B'nos Aguda that they had to move the venue out of his apartment at 4 Komitetowa Street to the old school premises on Gesia Street. In general, the German persecution strengthened R. Yehudah Leib's resolve and spurred him to ever greater effort in Torah and prayer. Already at the commencement of the Ghetto, the old Gerrer Rebbe, Rav Avraham Mordechai, remarked admiringly, "From day to day, Yehudah Leib attains more *madreigas....* "

Over the coming years in the Ghetto, he also became very close to Rav Menachem Ziemba.

When the Germans began the mass deportations on *erev* Tisha B'Av 1942, R. Yehudah Leib and his daughter Leah (a Beis Yaakov teacher) were in Warsaw while his wife and his other five children were in the nearby village of Wengrow. He had enrolled in the *Judenrat*, then considered marginally safer, and became one of the "*sefarim* collectors." R. Yehudah Leib saw this work as a holy task, picking up the abandoned *sefarim* lovingly, caressing and perusing them.

By Simchas Torah 1942, out of half a million souls, only a small remnant — approximately 3000 Jews — remained alive in the former capital of Polish Jewry. About fifteen men assembled in Rav Menachem Ziemba's apartment at 37 Nalewki Street to pray and conduct the *hakafos.* They held the *sifrei Torah* and walked solemnly round the table. All of them were broken men, bereft of family and relatives, their hearts overflowing with despondency. R. Yehudah Leib was totally heartbroken on discovering that his wife and five children, whom he had personally educated in Torah and piety, had been brutally murdered. The traditional verses of Simchas Torah, usually sung with such gusto, were instead intoned with sadness.

Suddenly a young twelve-year-old-boy entered the room and picked up a *siddur* to pray. This was most unusual. Hardly any children still survived in the Ghetto; generally they were the first victims of the barbaric Germans. As the congregants stepped heavily around the room, R. Yehudah Leib suddenly sprang from the circle. He grabbed the young boy and, clasping him to the *sefer Torah* in his arms, he began to dance wildly while loudly chanting, "*A yunger Yid mit die heilige Torah* — a young Jew with the Holy Torah!" A shudder went through the small congregation at the strange sight; grown men began to weep quietly. Then they joined in with the improvised *niggun* and formed a dancing circle around R. Yehudah Leib and the boy. R. Yehudah Leib danced with unnatural energy, continually roaring out the words, *"A yunger Yid mit die heilige Torah."* Despite his own profound personal tragedy — his great love for the Torah coupled with a great educator's empathy for an unknown Jewish child found voice in that superhuman dance. That was the final dance on the ultimate Simchas Torah of the last Jews in Warsaw.

In January 1943, R. Yehudah Leib sent a desperate plea to the families of Sternbuch and Eiss in Zurich asking them for salvation, and in February he received a Paraguayan passport. Before Pesach 1943, he and his daughter were incarcerated in the Pawiak Prison as "foreign citizens," and on June 7 he was transferred to the Bergen-Belsen concentration camp which had a special section for foreign citizens with relatively greater privileges. Even here he managed to continue his *shiurim* on *Tanach* and other subjects. He also expressed his regret at not having worked sufficiently for emigration to Eretz Yisrael. For a time, hope remained that holders of these passports would be exchanged for German citizens in Paraguay or would at least be protected until the end of the War. However, Paraguay informed the German authorities of its refusal to recognize these passports, and on Simchas Torah 1943, all these Jews were officially transferred to Birkenau and never heard from again. The great *mechanech* and leader of Beis Yaakov — the last of Polish Jewry's outstanding Torah legacies — was, alas, no more.

RAV ARYEH LEIB LANDAU

Before he became *rosh yeshivah* at Yeshivas Chachmei Lublin, Rav Aryeh Leib had served as the Rav of Kolbeil, a townlet near Warsaw, which allowed him to become extremely close to Warsaw's *rabbanim*. Later he had a crucial role in the underground yeshivos functioning in the Warsaw Ghetto.

Born in 1895 in Izbice, he lived for a number of years after his marriage in Peschischa (both *kehillos* were famous for their respective Chasidic dynasties), where through his own efforts he gained an encyclopedic knowledge in Talmud and *halachah*. Because he was blessed with a sharp, quick mind he simultanously and effortlessly picked up — during the few moments spared from his unremitting toil in Torah — an unusual grasp of history, geography, maths, and science. In 1922, he was chosen as Rav of Kolbeil, a community of only a few hundred families, where he became a much loved figure, with warm words of encouragement for every individual *kehillah* member. Despite his meager wage, he never asked for a raise. (Likewise during the German occupation, he refused all offers of financial support.)

Due to Kolbeil's close proximity to Warsaw, he often traveled there to discuss Torah topics with Rav Menachem Ziemba, Rav Yaakov Meir Biderman, and other *rabbanim*. He possessed a humble, retiring personality and rarely appeared or spoke in public, yet he became an active member and a powerful voice in Agudas Yisrael. R. Alexander Zisha Friedman, the general secretary of the Polish Aguda, became a devoted admirer of his and consulted him on many issues. Thus he became a major — though indirect — influence on Aguda policy, particularly on the newly established network of religious schools for both boys and girls. (Incidentally, Rav Landau had an only daughter whom he taught personally and she eventually became totally conversant in a number of *masechtas*! He excused his conduct by saying he needed a traveling companion with whom he could discuss the new Torah insights that constantly occurred to him.)

After the premature demise of its founder, the charismatic Rav Meir Shapira, the Lublin Yeshivah underwent a financial and moral crisis. Shortly after Rav Aryeh Zvi Frumer of Kozieglow was appointed *rosh yeshivah*, the director, R. Yosef Konigsberg, met R. Aryeh Leib Landau and was enraptured by him. He quickly persuaded him to join Chachmei Lublin, and Rav Landau blossomed into a towering Torah figure. Despite never having personally learnt at any yeshivah nor studied with *roshei yeshivah* — being mainly self-taught — he displayed a phenomenal memory, a logical and easy style of delivery, and developed a close, warm relationship with his disciples. He introduced the Lublin *yeshivah bachurim* to order and method, training them how to think logically and concisely. Although it was difficult to persuade him to speak in public, once he consented to mount the podium he revealed himself as a polished speaker, an original thinker who charmed his audience with beautifully turned phrases and a clear concise message. R. Konigsberg greatly admired him and smoothed his path within Yeshivas Chachmei Lublin.

When the War broke out in 1939, it was *bein hazemanim* (recess) and Rav Aryeh Leib Landau was resting in Kolbeil. During the siege, shortly before the German army entered Warsaw, they exiled many of the male inhabitants from the surrounding towns and villages. It was the onset of winter, with heavy, driving rain, and the roads were nigh impassable from the thick mud. The route out of Kolbeil was extremely difficult, yet the *Wehrmacht* forced them to march at a brutal pace. Those Jews who fell by the wayside were brutally shot by the callous soldiers. At that time, Rav Landau was sick and ailing and would never have managed the difficult trek. Fortunately, one of Kolbeil's residents saved his life by carrying him all the way as carefully as one would a *sefer Torah*.

Eventually, the Jews of Kolbeil were permitted to return, and throughout the early years of occupation, his loyal community spirited Rav Landau out of sight of the German overseer to spare him deportation or forced labor. When the mass deportations began, most of Kolbeil's inhabitants were transported to the death camps. Rav Landau and his daughter managed to hide with the help of a few survivors, but his wife was deported. Later, during Tishrei 1942, the remaining Jews of Kolbeil fled to Warsaw, where Rav Landau stayed with R. Yehudah Leib Orlean while his scholarly daughter hid out in the Aryan sector. Once again, he came into contact with R. Yosef Konigsberg, and they established a clandestine yeshivah that studied day and night in a cellar below Mila Street. A baker provided the group with bread and R. Konigsberg obtained support from the Joint. This yeshivah later moved into one of the bunkers, where it functioned until they were destroyed during the Uprising in Nissan 1943. Rav Aryeh Leib Landau was only forty-eight.

THE RADOMSKER REBBE

Rav Shloma Chanoch Rabinovitch was an unusual Rebbe in many aspects. Even when he was recognized as a prominent Rebbe with thousands of Chasidim, he would still personally travel to many other Rebbes — particularly Rebbe Yisrael Chortkover — as if he were a simple Chasid. When he became Rebbe in 1910, at the young age of twenty-nine, he had already been successful in business — with interests in Berlin, Lodz, Warsaw, and Cracow — so that instead of accepting the customary donations from his Chasidim, he was far more likely to support his Chasidim financially as well as spiritually. Although the Radomsker Rebbe was a formidable Torah scholar blessed with a sharp brain and a retentive memory, coupled with enormous diligence in study and prayer, he shrank from displaying his vast knowledge and eschewed all forms of *pilpul*. Despite his great wealth, he spent very little on himself or his household and devoted most of his riches to a network of thirty-six yeshivos throughout Poland that he had established under the title of "*Keser Torah*." Unlike Lithuania, the formation of yeshivos in Poland, especially by Chasidim, was quite an innovation. The Radomsker Rebbe was not particular that his *roshei yeshivah*, or indeed the *bachurim*, were Radomsker Chasidim; nor did he insist they learn *chasidus*, but he did demand they retain a fear of

heaven and a love of Torah.

Notwithstanding the Radomsker Rebbe's display of robust health, he was in fact quite a sick man who was hospitalized many months a year with diabetes. During Shabbos and *Yomim Tovim*, his *tisch* had to be interrupted before Kiddush so that his physician could administer an insulin injection. He was greatly loved by Chasidim from both Poland and Galicia, and such was his own regard for all other groups and personalities that he steered clear of all politics and argument. The Radomsker Rebbe's humility was legendary, yet carried off in so simple a manner as to render it hardly noticeable.

When the war erupted, the Radomsker Rebbe was in Galicia, resting at the Carpathian Mountains. He returned to Lodz, where his Chasidim urged him to escape on the last few air flights, but he refused, replying simply, "I want to be with all the Jews!" He arrived with his family in Warsaw during Chanukah that year and resided with his wealthy and learned Chasid R. Nosson Pinchas Ehrlich at 30 Nowolipki Street. Throughout the Ghetto's existence, regular *minyanim* took place at his apartment and each Shabbos the Rebbe conducted a *tisch* for *shalosh seudos*. Many Chasidim would gather to hear the Rebbe's *divrei Torah.*

The Radomsker Rebbe's diabetes had deteriorated but he continued his tight schedule of Torah study — mainly by heart because of his failing eyesight. Every so often plans were hatched to spirit the Rebbe out of danger, but the Radomsker Rebbe firmly rejected them all with one standard refrain: "I shall remain with my people!" The Radomsker Rebbe was well aware of the impending catastrophe, yet he remained optimistic that Amalek would eventually be defeated — but he expressed his doubts whether the Jews of Warsaw would survive to see it. Nonetheless, he was firmly resolved to make no attempt to escape.

Despite the danger for religious Jews to appear on the streets, the Radomsker Rebbe continued his unusual custom of visiting other Chasidic Rebbes. He also retained his tradition of generously supporting the needy, though he had been deprived of his vast wealth and was personally subsisting on loans. On that infamous "Black Shabbos" — in the afternoon of 18 Av 1942 — a *Wehrmacht* battalion ran amok in his tenement block, going from apartment to apartment, ruthlessly shooting approximately 150 people. They brutally murdered the Rebbe, his wife, daughter, and son-in-law. The Radomsker Rebbe was buried within the Novominsker *Ohel* at the Warsaw Cemetery.

His son-in-law, R. Moshele, who married the Rebbe's only daughter Raizel, deserves a biography of his own. As his family name, Rabinovitch, implies, he was a cousin of the Radomsker Rebbe. In his home town, Krimilow, he received the standard education at the local *cheder* but his remarkable diligence set him apart from his contemporaries. Nothing interested him outside the study of Torah to which he devoted day and night — literally. He soon became renowned for his wide Torah knowledge, his faultless memory, and penetrating analysis. Famous Torah scholars generally averse to empty compliments nevertheless showered him with praise and acclaim. After his marriage in 1928 at the age of twenty-two, he was entirely free of money worries and could continue to devote himself to Torah — up to twenty hours a day!

When his father-in-law established the Keser Torah Yeshivos, R. Moshele became one of the *roshei yeshivah*, painstakingly examining the yeshivah students and setting their curriculum. Thrice a day he would deliver a *shiur* to the leading hundred and fifty *yeshivah bachurim*, as well as a number of other *shiurim* to the remaining *bachurim*. Despite his retentive memory and wide knowledge, he prepared each *shiur* thoroughly with great responsibility and was greatly loved by his disciples. Unlike contemporary yeshivos, the Keser Torah network under his guidance also studied unusual *masechtas* such as *Zevachim* and *Berachos*, as well as the Jerusalem Talmud.

For personal reasons, he refused to publish any of the outstanding novella he had composed on a number of *masechtas*. However, some of his *chiddushim* transcribed by his students appeared in the yeshivah periodical and made an indelible impression on the Torah scholars of Poland (some of these were later republished in New York by his *talmid* R. Yechezkel Besser). His novellas were unusual yet penetrating, logical, and anything but superficial. Apart from a short period of study with the Tchebiner Rav, he was entirely self-taught. Later, the Tchebiner Rav related that when he met him some years afterwards, he did not recognize him — so far had he progressed in Torah studies.

Despite his father-in-law's enormous wealth, replete with widespread and complicated business dealings, R. Moshele had not the slightest interest in monetary affairs and barely recognized the value of everyday coinage. Even gulping down his meals so as not to waste precious study time, he led a totally saintly existence bound up with heavenly fear, Torah study, and heartfelt prayer.

To free him from forced labor in the Ghetto, he was officially registered as an employee of Mottel Pinkert's Undertakers in Grzybowska Street and wore a Pinkert's work cap as protection. (He used to comment, "Warsaw has become a factory for corpses!") On *erev* Tisha B'Av 1942 he was enrolled in the

Shultz workshop run by Avraham Hendel. Despite the danger, he refused to trim his beard. He was murdered at the same time as his father-in-law, the Radomsker Rebbe, on that fateful Shabbos afternoon of 18 Av, 1942.

REB YAAKOV TROKENHEIM

In countless forums, religious Jewry was ably represented by R. Yaakov Trokenheim. On behalf of Agudas Yisrael, he was a member of the Warsaw Kehillah and its president from 1926. Simultaneously, he was a member of the Warsaw town council for twenty years (from 1919–39), a senator in the Polish parliament from 1935–37, and a member of the Polish Sejm (the lower parliament) from 1937 until Poland fell to the Germans. There was hardly an important Polish arena in which R. Yaakov Trokenheim did not represent Agudas Yisrael.

Surprisingly, R. Yaakov Trokenheim was not a renowned orator nor particularly erudite. Certainly, he possessed as much book learning as the average learned layman, but he was not famed as a scholar. Likewise, in common with most Polish Jews, he was no fount of secular knowledge. Not one to initiate ideas or campaigns of his own, he was scrupulous about carrying out the plans of others. One can sum up his continuing popularity in one word — integrity.

He never claimed to do more than his capability, and though he greeted everybody warmly and listened to their problems in detail, he made no rash promises. Even at election time he did not frame any grand promises and was not fond of empty slogans. He had no false pretensions, fully recognizing his duty to those who voted him in. When he spoke in parliament on Jewish issues, he used the simple everyday language of an ordinary businessman from Nalewki Street, Warsaw. Although he was well aware how publicity brought votes, nonetheless, where he felt the publicity would be counterproductive to those he was helping, he acted as discreetly as possible. He was extremely organized, worked in an objective manner, and did not confine himself to narrow party issues.

R. Yaakov Trokenheim was born in 1888, his father a well-known and prosperous Gerrer Chasid of the Sefas Emes; he later married into the rich Kirshenbaum family of Lublin. With his brother, he inherited a large tenement block at 37 Nalewki Street, housing hundreds of Jewish families as well as four courtyards containing many shops. Following the First World War, in 1919, the Warsaw City Council had democratic elections, and Agudas Yisrael put forward two candidates. Their first was R. Eliyahu Kirshenbaum, who represented the Ashkenazim, so the Chasid R. Yaakov Trokenheim (although he was only thirty-one) was chosen as a counterbalance.

Reflecting his serious nature, R. Yaakov Trokenheim never missed a public sitting of the City Council and always spoke on subjects affecting the Jewish population. He was also involved in private negotiations on behalf of Jewish voters. For instance, Warsaw's City Council planned a new thoroughfare connecting the north and the south which would necessitate knocking down many apartments in the Jewish area, particularly along the Orzech Market which stretched from Senatorska to

Franciszkanska Streets. R. Yaakov Trokenheim spent long hours ensuring the inhabitants of these areas received adequate compensation (yet he resisted all publicity, lest it harm those he was trying to help).

In 1926, R. Yaakov Trokenheim was among the first on the Aguda list for the democratic elections to the Warsaw Kehillah, where he served in various capacities until the War. He thoroughly reorganized the Kehillah's Religious Department, which had been in utter disorder. Since 1922, R. Yaakov Trokenheim had unsuccessfully stood for the Polish parliament a number of times. However, in 1925, the government nominated their own candidates as senators. In a show of independence, it chose nominees not selected by their own parties — including R. Yaakov Trokenheim. At the next elections, in 1937, he was elected as an Aguda member to the Sejm, the Polish parliament. When the anti-*shechitah* campaign was at its peak, R. Yaakov Trokenheim invested much energy into safeguarding *shechitah* and established a *nikkur* institute that was most helpful when a restricted supply of kosher meat was finally permitted. As the only Jewish parliamentarian residing in Warsaw — and concurrently a leader of the Warsaw Kehillah — he was pivotal to the *shechitah* defense, respected by the government and admired for his shining integrity.

When the War broke out in 1939, R. Yaakov Trokenheim fled to one of his sons in Vilna (where he set up a soup kitchen in cooperation with the Joint), while his wife and two daughters remained behind in Warsaw. In obvious peril from Nazi death squads due to his prominent personality, he desperately tried to get a passport to America or a certificate to Eretz Yisrael, despite his reluctance to abandon his family. However, the Russians refused him permission to leave. The Soviet army first overran Vilna on September 19, 1939, yet it was ceded to an "independent" Lithuania until July 15, 1940, when the Russians incorporated all three Baltic States into the Soviet Union. On June 24, 1941, Vilna was captured by the Germans and the mass shootings rapidly began in the nearby Ponary Forest. R. Yaakov Trokenheim (together with his parliamentary colleague, the Agudist R. Leibel Mintzberg) fled to Bialystok where he lodged with the Rav, Dr. Gedalia Rosenman, until November 1941. Despite the danger, he returned to Warsaw together with his son Elazar, and the family was reunited.

At first he hid among friends, but after a number of weeks he realized that the Germans were not searching for him — they viewed all Jews alike, equally suitable for destruction. So he stayed openly with his daughter who ran the Jewish hospital at 1 Leszno Street. In cooperation with R. Zisha Friedman and R. Yosef Konigsberg, he organized soup kitchens for *yeshivah bachurim* and scholars. By being registered as a clerk at the hospital, he managed to evade the early deportations, but in March 1943 he was deported to the Poniatowa Camp near Lublin. R. Chaim Yisrael Eiss sent him a Paraguayan passport from Switzerland but — just as with R. Zisha Friedman, Dr. Yitzchak Schipper, and others who were also in the same camp — this passport was of no avail. In November 1943, he was deported to Majdanek and murdered in the gas chambers.

REB LEIB SCHARANSKI

Reb Leib Scharanski was both a descendant of the Vilna Gaon and of Kotzker Chasidim. Furthermore he personally was a Gerrer Chasid, which led to an inevitable question: The natural party for Gerrer Chasidim was Agudas

Yisrael, so how was it that he rose to the top ranks of Mizrachi, their rivals? To understand that, one has to understand the background of R. Leib Scharanski.

R. Leib was born in 1886 in a little village near Lodz, the textile capital of Poland. His father had emigrated there from Kovno in Lithuania and had become a close Chasid of the Sefas Emes. After marrying into another Gerrer family, R. Leib carried on learning in the Gerrer *shtiebl*, as was usual, for several years before going into business. After some eight years, the First World War broke out, and though he moved to Warsaw in 1914, his business faltered due to the war situation and eventually collapsed.

Warsaw was then home to numerous refugees from the fighting on the Eastern front and R. Leib Scharanski was drawn to help these refugees. His natural organizational abilities brought him to the attention of the Mizrachi leadership in Warsaw, who invited him to join the party. R. Leib had long dreamt of the rebuilding of the Land of Israel. Now, shortly after the Balfour Declaration, he felt it might represent a solution to the thousands of refugees flooding Warsaw. He became a Mizrachi representative at the Warsaw Kehillah, which acted as a mini-parliament for Jewish affairs; its sittings were reported in the Jewish newspapers, who saw it as the public voice of Jewish concerns throughout Poland.

R. Leib was not a man to suffer criticism lightly and always offered a robust defense against anybody criticizing his party or encroaching on its interests. Naturally, being both a Gerrer Chasid and a Mizrachi leader caused him no little awkwardness, but this was partly solved by force of circumstances in 1922, when most parties joined together in one bloc to fight for parliamentary elections (the only party to remain aloof was the *Folkists*). R. Leib Scharanski also represented Mizrachi at many Zionist Congresses from 1921 onwards. Although he was not one of their main speakers at the podium, he was quite important backstage. In Poland, R. Leib Scharanski was influential because Mizrachi had access to the vital certificates permitting emigration to Eretz Yisrael (whereas Aguda, regarded as "anti-Zionist," only had limited access to certificates).

However, his main forum for activity remained the Kehillah. R. Leib was famous as one of the few Chasidim in the Mizrachi party with long beard and sidecurls, and his sharp repartee were famous throughout Warsaw. He became an energetic activist in the Anti-Nazi League established in 1934. During the German occupation, Scharanski was active in setting up soup kitchens in cooperation with the Joint and constantly called for resistance against the Germans. He was present at many meetings planning the resistance and endangered his life attempting to carry out their requests. Likewise, he tried to make contact with the underground Polish Workers Party to organize a general revolt against the Nazis.

Scharanski was also in touch with Mordechai Anielewicz, who ran the underground factory producing hand grenades. Although Anielewicz and his comrades were indifferent to religion, they harbored great respect for Scharanski as a religious Jew, who in the middle of their meetings would move aside to recite the evening prayers. They taught him how to fire a gun, and Anielewicz once told me, "These Religious Jews are very powerful; they are the true zealots, the most fervent for Jewish dignity." R. Leib carried out the most dangerous of their requests, crawling via the underground tunnel from Leszno Street (that was the clandestine contact between the Ghetto and the Aryan part of Warsaw).

He once threw explosives at two uniformed Nazis, and his hand was wounded in the explosion. When the deportations started, signaling the final destruction of Warsaw, he ran from one workplace to another warning Jews that they were actually being taken to death, not forced labor. R. Leib also insisted the rich magnates donate their money and gold to buy weapons from the Poles even at exorbitant sums, as long as some Poles were still prepared to supply arms to the Jews. Finally he was caught by one of the German patrols, and when about to be deported to the death camps, he managed to throw a grenade at them. Regrettably, it missed the target and he died in the explosion. His wife, Devorah, and three daughters were later killed, in Warsaw.

REB MENDEL KAMINER

Reb Mendel Kaminer was an unusual dignitary. A scholar and Chasid with large business interests, all emotion and warmth of heart was internalized so that he appeared totally unemotional. This appearance was further reinforced by R. Mendel Kaminer's public persona — when he decided on a policy, nothing could shake him. Not credulous by nature, he did not base his plans on false hope. He had no time for empty slogans or party propaganda and instead approached each problem and situation as a businessman, going straight to the core of the matter and taking a practical standpoint.

Born in 1861, in Chenchien near Kielce, R. Mendel was a brother-in-law of the Sefas Emes and thus an uncle of the current Gerrer Rebbe R. Avraham Mordechai (the Imrei Emes). He had many business interests and moved to Warsaw before the First World War. Though some of his business interests suffered because of the War, he still remained quite rich from his inheritance.

At the establishment of the Agudas Yisrael, R. Mendel Kaminer was asked to head the central office in Warsaw. He organized many local branches, helped set up many of Aguda's institutions, and was unusually active during elections to the Polish Sejm and Senate. However he was most renowned for his newspaper activity. Ever since the Aguda was founded, it had major problems supporting a party newspaper, Their first central newspaper, *Der Yid*, began in November 1919 as a weekly before becoming a daily, but never really developed properly. Continually suffering from a shortage of cash and plagued by large debts, it had to contend with periodic strikes. Sometimes, publication was halted altogether, and the Aguda was deprived of a public voice.

When *Der Yid* finally collapsed, the Aguda decided to establish a daily newspaper on a completely different basis. Unlike *Der Yid*, which depended on party funding and support, the new publication would be a cooperative in which all the workers and writers would be partners. The new newspaper, which began publication in 1929, was known as *Dos Yiddishe Togblatt*, and R. Mendel Kaminer was its publisher. R. Mendel invested a large amount of his own money and within a fairly short time organized it on a sound economic basis. The paper was successfully run and very soon surpassed the circulation of the *Der Yid*. Its political platform and religious standpoint were identical to Agudas Yisrael but from the financial angle, it was totally independent. This allowed it to develop to a high standard until it became one of the best newspapers in Poland, important to Aguda's development. Certainly it played a major role in Aguda's electoral success to the *kehillos*, city councils, and parliament.

Officially, Kaminer was the publisher and not the editor, yet he still wielded much influence on the general editorial line of the newspaper. He tried to avoid arguments if possible, but once he felt the need to take a certain standpoint, very little could deflect him. He retained much of the toughness of the Kotzker Chasidim and felt scant deference for any institution, group, or activist. Nor did he hesitate to criticize his own party when he felt it justified. R. Mendel Kaminer earned the respect of all the writers and workers employed by the *Togblatt*, even those who belonged to the anti-religious Bund.

When he was approached by private people, he listened quietly without any apparent emotion, yet he always did whatever he could to help. Together with the Gerrer Rebbe, he visited Eretz Yisrael in 1933 and was most impressed. On his return to Poland, he campaigned for more activity on behalf of Eretz Yisrael to encourage religious emigration there.

Due to Warsaw's travail during the prolonged siege, R. Mendel Kaminer fell ill shortly after the Germans captured the capital. He recovered but never regained his full strength, and he died on December 24, 1940. Most of his large family were killed. However, one granddaughter survived in Russia and now lives in Montreal, Canada, while another granddaughter, who taught in Beis Yaakov, is married to R. Yehudah Meir Abramowitz, presently one of the Aguda leaders in Israel.

REB ZEV (WOLF) LIPSKER

Reb Zev Lipsker was one of the most famous and popular writers among Polish Jewry before the War. His satirical columns in *Der Yid* under the name of "*Velvele*" and in the *Dos Yiddishe Togblatt* under the name of "*Lamed Vav*" were read with great enjoyment by thousands of religious readers. Yet R. Zev had a crucial function. The anti-religious writers, who attacked the religious in general and Agudas Yisrael in particular, utilized not logic but barbed criticism to poke fun at anything religious or holy. Writers like R. Zev Lipsker, capable of witty, biting humor, were essential in the battle for hearts and minds. He was always meticulous in avoiding personal attacks — he dealt with the issues and human frailties, not with the human perpetuators themselves. He really came into his own at election time — whether for parliament, city councils, or Kehillahs — and was unrivaled at cutting through the propaganda and bluff to expose the weaknesses in the opponents' arguments. In those situations, his satirical columns in Aguda newspapers were sometimes more important than portentous editorials.

R. Zev did not have an easy life. He was born in Warsaw in 1902 to a poor, Chasidic family. However, they had a respectable lineage as grandchildren of Rav Yechezkel Landau, popularly known as the Nodah Beyehudah. After *cheder*, he learnt at the Gerrer *shtiebl* in Warsaw and absorbed a large knowledge and breadth in both Talmud and Chasidic volumes. As a young man he experimented with poetry and song and soon found his way to the *Digleinu* magazine of Zeirei Aguda under the editorship of R. Alexander Zisha Friedman. He wrote prolifically: poetry, satirical columns, Chasidic tales, and religious ideology. As an author of so many varying articles, he used various different pen names. Later, for his regular columns in the *Der Yid* and *Togblatt*, he still used pseudonyms.

However he had another side to him — a historian. He wrote the biography of his ancestor, the Nodah Beyehudah, in installments in the *Digleinu* during the years 1920–21, and these were signed under his own name. Likewise, he wrote a series of long stories under the name of "S. Leipsiger," as well as the Yiddish anthem *"Nisht Farzweiflen* — Do Not Despair" for the Poalei Aguda. Lipsker was also an activist in the Zeirei Aguda when it was first established and rose to the higher ranks of the movement. He married the granddaughter of R. Mendel Kaminer (a brother-in-law of the Sefas Emes) who was the business administrator of the *Yiddishe Togblatt*. Despite the fame and dynamism of his satirical columns he personally lived quietly and peaceably.

When the War broke out, he lost his employment and suffered poverty and anguish. In 1940, he fell ill with typhus and by the time he recovered, most of the best positions in the *Judenrat* or Joint were taken. He was desperate to find some work at the Kehillah, and religious representatives such as R. Meshulam Kaminer tried to help him, but without success. Nobody could find a place among the ten thousand workers for one of the most famous and successful writers. Most of the new rulers of the *Judenrat* were assimilationists who never even heard of him. They neither read nor understood Yiddish or Hebrew, and they had no respect for writers or journalists — particularly religious Jews. Even in the Joint it was very difficult to find work for a religious Jew. Lipsker therefore, suffered severe hunger.

Only in March 1941 did he manage to get a temporary position in the Ghetto mail service, delivering parcels! Despite his ill health he toiled in this poor position, yet did not earn enough to support himself. He perished in Treblinka during Ellul 1942, together with his family.

REB MICHAEL BER SOKOLOV

Another of the popular pre-War religious journalists, R. Michael Ber Sokolov, was the poetic writer of the *shtetl*. His vivid descriptions, with pen portraits of typical village characters, captured the picturesque atmosphere and had a touch of humor and warmth.

He was born in 1902 in the little village of Kinsk, where the Rav, his maternal grandfather Rav Yoel Yehoshua Weingarten, was famous throughout Poland as a *gaon*. After his bar mitzvah, he learned in the Sochatchov Yeshivah with great diligence. At the age of eighteen he began to publish small stories in the daily Yiddish newspaper "*Dos Yiddishe Vort*," published in Warsaw during 1917–19 by his uncle R. Nahum Leib Weingott.

When the Yeablonaner Rebbe, Rav Yechezkel Taub, instigated his campaign to settle religious Jews in Eretz Yisrael, Michael Ber Sokolov joined his movement and became the Rebbe's secretary. The fourth *aliya*, during 1925–26, included many religious Jews from Poland and Michael Ber Sokolov joined them, shouldering the workload of an common laborer at the *moshav*

Nachlat Yaakov (now known as Kfar Chasidim). Yet he had been extremely content. Unfortunately the Rebbe collapsed under the heavy financial burden and the whole venture crashed, forcing Michael Ber to return to Poland. Eretz Yisrael had made a great impression on his poetic soul and this disaster wounded him deeply. On his return, he passed through Paris and Germany, where his outlook was broadened. In Palestine he had written stories of life in Eretz Yisrael for the Hebrew weekly *Kol Yisrael*, and when he returned to Warsaw in 1927 he wrote similar stories for *Der Yid, Darkeinu* (in Hebrew), the *Orthodoxishe Yugend Blette*, and *Beis Yaakov Journal*.

In 1929, the cooperative newspaper *Dos Yiddishe Togblatt* was created in Warsaw, and Sokolov was one of its founding members, on its editorial board. In addition, every *erev* Shabbos he published a story or vignette, generally of the *shtetl*, that attracted a large readership. The villages then were in much intellectual ferment — most of the youth being drawn towards the Aguda, Zionists, or Bund. Many were nostalgic for an earlier age when life was hard but simple; and this was the sentiment captured in Michael Ber Sokolov's stories and descriptions. Unlike other writers and colleagues, Michael Ber was not interested in public speaking or political activism, he remained solely and purely a writer.

During the occupation, Michael Ber worked in a soup kitchen supported by the Joint and the *Judenrat*, and in Ellul 1942 he was deported to Treblinka, together with all his family. Little of his writings remain since he never compiled them into book form. However, some of his stories were republished in 1955 by R. Moshe Prager in New York.

DR. MORDECHAI ROSNER

When religious Jewry organized themselves under the banner of Aguda, Dr. Mordechai Rosner was in much demand as one of the few religious Jews in Poland with university diplomas and doctorates. Even after being drawn into the political arena, Dr. Rosner remained characteristically studious, constantly amassing knowledge throughout his short life. He had the remarkable ability to sit among the hubbub and debate, quietly engrossed in his own work. With most issues, whether secular or religious (he had the whole Talmud at his fingertips), he generally tried to avoid any argument.

Dr. Rosner was born in 1899 in Podvolocisk in eastern Galicia (on the border between Austria and Russia before the First World War). His father, a Torah scholar and a Viznitzer Chasid, originated from Bukovina while his mother was a member of the wealthy Breitman family, which made him a nephew of Rav Meir Shapira. In 1914, during the First World War, his family sought refuge in Tarnopol where he drew close to his uncle, Rav Meir Shapira, likewise a refugee. Under Rav Meir Shapira's tutelage the young Mordechai became a diligent scholar, acquiring a thorough knowledge throughout Talmud.

In 1922 Rav Shapira, then the Rav of Sanok in central Galicia, was chosen as Aguda representative to the Polish Sejm.

Aguda now had eight representatives in parliament so it needed a secretary with an intellectual background, proficient in Polish. The obvious choice was R. Meir Shapira's nephew, Dr. Mordechai Rosner, and it fell to him to prepare proposals for parliament and memorandums for the government.

Likewise he wrote many of the speeches of Aguda leaders. Unofficially, the parliament secretarial office had become the central powerhouse of Aguda, now that many of Aguda's parliamentary representatives were also its leaders. Few people were aware of Dr. Rosner's existence, because most of his work was backstage combined with his natural reticence. Shortly afterwards he became involved in the daily *Der Yid* and other Aguda newspapers in Yiddish and Hebrew. His articles were meticulous yet succint, displaying an intimate knowledge of many subjects. Intellectually he was drawn to the Poalei Aguda Worker's Movement, but he received his employment from the central Aguda.

After he received all his doctorates in 1929, he accepted the position of lecturer at the Religious Teachers Seminary (in Gesia Street, Warsaw) where teachers were trained to work within the government school system. However, as a totally devout man with an impeccable intellectual background, he remained indispensable to religious Jewry. When R. Meshulam Kaminer, Aguda's Warsaw Kehillah representative, successfully established a religious school in Praga (the Warsaw suburb) he chose Dr. Mordechai Rosner as director — confident he would obtain government recognition. Yet, at the same time, he was a member of the editorial staff in the daily *Dos Yiddishe Togblatt* — Dr. Rosner required three assignments, since he supported his wife, who suffered from ill health. Only a man of his diligence could hold down these three separate positions and fulfill each to everyone's full satisfaction.

His primary duty at the *Togblatt* was to read the European newspapers, mainly those in German, and translate them into Yiddish. Yet he did not see this merely as a technical formality and would analyze and adapt these articles until they contained much of his own personal input. He was responsible for translating the great German thinkers — Dr. Yitzchak Breuer, Rabbi Dr. Pinchas Kohn, R. Yaakov Rosenheim, and Dr. Nathan Birnbaum — into Yiddish. (Dr. Nathan Birnbaum personally wrote some of his articles in Yiddish, but many others were translated and adapted by Dr. Rosner.) Even after a full day's exertion he did not rest. Dr. Rosner also adapted, in a private capacity, other works into Yiddish for a Warsaw publishing house. For instance, he translated the classical philosophical work, the Rambam's *Guide to the Perplexed* with an anthology of commentaries, which appeared in fortnightly installments during 1936. Due to Dr. Rosner's easy and simple style, this philosophical work gained a surprising number of adherents among the non-intellectuals.

Dr. Rosner was an early victim when the Germans captured Warsaw, and he was incarcerated in the Pawiak Prison with a number of other Jews for two months until his miraculous release. By the time he was freed, there was no work available for him. The Seminary, school, and newspapers had all been closed down, and he was left without any means of support. R. Meshulam Kaminer battled mightily for him but only secured him a position at the *Judenrat* after a lengthy struggle. Unfortunately, there was still no actual work for him so R. Meshulam drafted Dr. Rosner to edit and correct his new Yiddish translation and anthology on *Tehillim* and *Chumash*. R. Meshulam composed it overnight and brought it into the *Judenrat* each morning, where it was typed out by various clerks, before Dr. Rosner edited the transcripts and added his own ideas.

Until April 1942, he worked in the Kehillah Record and Archives Office. After the schools were permitted to reopen, he reassumed the directorship of the Religious School in Warsaw. During the deportations, Dr. Rosner hid in the Kehillah building together with his family, his wife and only son of fifteen years. On 17 August, 1942, he was seized and deported to Treblinka, and his wife and son followed him about three weeks later.